Contemporary Southern Identity

CONTEMPORARY SOUTHERN IDENTITY

Community through Controversy

Rebecca Bridges Watts

University Press of Mississippi / Jackson

www.upress.state.ms.us

The University Press of Mississippi is a member of the
Association of American University Presses.

Copyright © 2008 by Rebecca Bridges Watts
All rights reserved
Manufactured in the United States of America

First printing 2008

∞

Library of Congress Cataloging-in-Publication Data

Watts, Rebecca Bridges, 1973–
Contemporary southern identity : community through
controversy / Rebecca Bridges Watts.
p. cm.
Includes bibliographical references and index.
ISBN: 978-1-61703-708-5

Civilization—20th century. 2. Group identity—Southern States.
I. Title.
F216.2.W39 2008
975.3′041—dc22

2007015876

British Library Cataloging-in-Publication Data available

And he has committed to us the message of reconciliation . . . as though God were making his appeal through us.
—2 Corinthians 5:19–20

For the sons and daughters of former slaves.
For the sons and daughters of former slave owners.
Threads that connect us. Words that free us.
—Angel Quintero and Sherman Evans, African American entrepreneurs, founders of NuSouth Apparel, which juxtaposes the pattern of the Confederate battle flag with the colors of black liberation

Contents

Acknowledgments ix
Introduction: Looking Toward a New Rhetoric of Southern Identity 3

1
Uniforms, Walls, and Doors: Social Mystery and Gender Integration at the Virginia Military Institute 18

2
When Richmond Gained Perspective by Incongruity: Old South Tradition and New South Change in the Confederate Capital 49

3
Stories of the War: The Confederate Flag in South Carolina 87

4
Senator Trent Lott: Southern Sinner, Scapegoat, and Sacrifice 117

Conclusion: Dialectical Rhetoric as the New Rhetoric of Southern Identity 154

Notes 165
References 179
Index 195

Acknowledgments

MANY PEOPLE have helped to make this book possible. First, I acknowledge my family, through whom my own Southern identity was formed on visits to my parents' hometowns, Cuthbert, Georgia, and Smiths Grove, Kentucky. I also thank my parents for supporting my education over the years and helping to care for my daughter as I revised the manuscript for publication.

As I have worked on this project, I have received much support from my husband, Tyler, and daughter, Olivia, especially as I revised the manuscript for publication. I appreciate their patience with me going into the office on the weekends and staying up all hours and their entertaining themselves during a summer vacation in Lexington while I did archival research.

Friends have also provided me with the support and encouragement I needed to see this book through to completion. Lisa Blackwell has provided the understanding only a fellow author could. Kevin Kerr has shared my interest in Southern studies. Karen Beckett, Penny Gowen, and Melody Meyer have also been supportive. Laura Lancaster provided the inspiration and example for me to go to graduate school. Christi Moss has been a friend and a co-laborer in the study of Southern rhetoric.

In addition, I have been blessed with generous, astute, and wise professors. The most influential has been Jim Aune, who worked with me on this project in its earlier form as my doctoral dissertation in the Department of Communication at Texas A & M University. I also thank Charley Conrad, Leroy Dorsey, and Jan Swearingen for serving on my dissertation committee and offering good advice for turning my dissertation into the book that it is today. Marty Medhurst was helpful in the early stages of writing the Confederate flag chapter. Vanessa Beasley's example provided encouragement throughout my time at Texas A & M. I also learned much from Kurt Ritter about rhetoric in the public sphere. At Clemson University, Martin Jacobi and Beth Daniell introduced me to the study of rhetoric; I am especially thankful to Martin Jacobi for his introduction to the ideas of Kenneth Burke and Richard Weaver, which heavily influenced this project. Finally, the solid foundation in writing, research, and critical thinking that I received as an undergraduate at Stetson University, especially as a student in the Department of English and the Honors Program, has made all my further studies possible. I hope I can provide as solid a foundation to the students I am now teaching at my alma mater. I am also appreciative of the Department of Communication Studies and Theatre Arts and the College of Arts and Sciences for allowing me the opportunity to return home to Stetson as a teacher and researcher.

I am appreciative of the Virginia Military Institute Archives for allowing me access to back issues of the VMI student newspaper, *The Cadet*. I also would like to thank John Clarke of the *Richmond Times-Dispatch* and Bryan Collars of the South Carolina Department of Archives and History for their help in securing permissions for some of the photographs included in this book.

Finally, I appreciate the detailed and honest yet kind feedback from the anonymous reviewer, who helped me discover my manuscript's potential. I especially thank Craig Gill of the University Press of Mississippi for expressing an interest in this project and helping me see it through to completion, and Ellen Goldlust-Gingrich for her careful copy editing.

Contemporary Southern Identity

Introduction: Looking Toward a New Rhetoric of Southern Identity

Part of Southern culture is the recognition that there are some things worth fighting for.
—Jim Thompson, editorial page director, *Athens (Georgia) Banner-Herald*, in a 2005 *Christian Science Monitor* article headlined, "Battle Over the Past Rages in the Evolving South"

Tradition . . . or Discrimination? VMI Plan for Women Goes to Court.
—*Norfolk Virginian-Pilot*, February 8, 1994

Ashe Statue a Monument to Controversy
—*Richmond Times-Dispatch*, December 17, 1995

Irreconcilable? Past Crashes into Present; Flap over Lee Mural Underscores City's Daily Life in Shadow of Civil War
—*Richmond Times-Dispatch*, June 6, 1999

Those with Close Ties to Confederacy Have Differing View on the Flag
—*Greenville News*, January 16, 2000

Burned by Remark, Lott Apologizes
—*Gulfport-Biloxi Sun Herald*, December 10, 2002

THE ABUNDANCE of debates cited in news headlines such as these can be seen not only as evidence of the South's battle over the past but also as evidence of a South in dialogue with itself (and often with others). The presence of these frequent, widespread debates throughout the South highlights the diversity of voices that are now permitted to be expressed in the shared, continuing conversation of what it means to be a Southerner at the beginning of the twenty-first century. The participants in these debates may disagree with one another about what Southern identity should be, but they all seem to agree—by the fact of their participation—that such debates are a crucial "part of [a] Southern culture" that "recogni[zes] that there are some things worth fighting for."[1] And perhaps Southerners find nothing more worth fighting for than Southern identity itself.

But who are Southerners? In common parlance, *Southerners* often refers to white Southerners—specifically, those white Southerners who proudly identify themselves as such. In *White Southerners*, Lewis M. Killian argues that white Southerners constitute a "minority group" whose members hail largely from "a southeastern region corresponding roughly to the Old South"—that is, the former states of the Confederacy plus select border states. Killian defines the white Southerner as either "a white person who has been born and raised at least until young adulthood in the South and who thinks of himself as a southerner or . . . a white person who, no matter where he was born and raised, lives in the South and identifies himself as a southerner." Specifically, Killian argues that white Southerners constitute "a sociological minority group in the over-all context of American society" as reflected in both "the attitudes and actions of others in the larger society" and their perception of themselves as "the object of prejudice and discrimination."[2]

John Shelton Reed took the project of figuring out who Southerners are and what they are all about directly to the people. Through years of public-opinion polling, Reed has established himself as an expert—if not *the* expert—on Southern identity quantified. To Reed, whether a person sees himself or herself as Southern and whether others see someone as being Southern are more relevant to determining Southern identity than where someone was born or lives. Among those who self-identify as Southerners, "the most common reason given . . . is affection for other Southerners, a feeling of closeness to them and their ways—in other words, a sense of identification with the regional group." How self-identifying Southerners see themselves in contrast with non-Southerners (and vice versa) is another way of understanding Southern identity; by this measure, Southerners are "slower, more traditional, and more polite and friendly than other Americans." But as friendly as Southerners may be seen by themselves and others, Reed also finds that a "sense of grievance on the South's behalf . . . is part of what it means to be a Southerner." This "grievance-based identity," hypothesizes Reed, may mean that (1) if Southerners cease to have region-related grievances, their sense of "regional identification may be eroded" and (2) anyone who adopts or shares in the South's grievances may be considered a Southerner for that reason in itself, regardless of other factors such as place of residence. None of these elements of Southern identity is necessarily linked to race; all of these characteristics allow for people of any race, including whites, African Americans, and others to self-identify as Southerners and to be so identified by others.[3]

However, considering the frequent association of Confederate history and symbols with Southern identity, Reed notes, "it would seem almost necessarily to be racially exclusive (although the number of black athletes and cheerleaders who play and cheer for teams called the 'Rebels' is startling). It strikes me as remarkable that Southern blacks are willing to tolerate their white neighbors' nostalgia on that score, and it seems altogether too much to expect them to subscribe to it." But although some observers may find it unimaginable that some African Americans identify themselves as Southerners in light all of the Confederate baggage, the fact is that there are indeed many African American Southerners—both in their own eyes and in the eyes of African Americans elsewhere. In his polling, Reed finds "not only that black Americans now regard Southern blacks as Southerners but that they are less ambivalent about this identification than they were just a few years ago." In David Potter's theory that the persistence of a folk culture makes the South distinctive, he observes that black Southerners may even experience this Southern folk culture to a greater degree than whites. This could be read as saying that African American Southerners are not only Southern but are even *more Southern* than white Southerners. However, Reed and his colleagues "suspect that 'Southerner' still primarily means white Southerner for most of the region's dominant racial group, although many Southern whites would, on second thought, probably allow that Southern blacks are indeed Southerners, too." While common parlance may imply whiteness when speaking and thinking of Southerners, we do not have to accept the limitations of such common usage in determining who may call themselves Southern. As David Smiley finds in his "Quest for the Central Theme in Southern History," "Those of whatever persuasion or tradition who believe themselves Southern are indeed Southern."[4]

Similarly, while W. J. Cash recognizes in *The Mind of the South* that there are indeed "many Souths," that valuable cultural and geographical diversity exists within the region, he nonetheless argues "that there is also one South," characterized by "a fairly definite mental pattern, associated with a fairly definite social pattern—a complex of established relationships." This distinctive "mind of the South" is characterized by a tendency on the part of white Southerners to conserve the region's past social hierarchy or "complex of established relationships." Southern conservative rhetorician Richard Weaver also recognizes the importance of an "established" order to these tradition-bound white Southerners, arguing that "distinctions of many kinds will have to be restored" if the contemporary world is to recapture the sense of order that Weaver believes was one of the admirable traits of the Old South. But while Weaver wants the South and the nation to return to some of the more clear-cut social divisions of the past, as a rhetorician he recognizes that "considerations of strategy and tactics forbid the use of symbols of lost causes. There cannot be a return to the Middle Ages or the Old South under slogans identified with them. The principles must be studied and used, but in such presentation that mankind will feel the march is forward. And so it will be, to all effects."[5]

Weaver likely would be disappointed in contemporary Southern conservatives, for they have largely ignored his rhetorical counsel. Many of those who have most vocally declared themselves Southerners at the turn of the twenty-first century have made it their mission to defend Lost Cause symbols and institutions—and with such vigor that they seem to be fighting the Civil War all over again. In so doing, these past-oriented Southerners risk repeating a mistake C. Vann Woodward saw Southerners committing in the 1950s and 1960s, when Southern identity and pride were "identified with a last ditch defense of segregation," which he predicted would make young Southerners consider "rejecting their entire regional identification, even the name 'Southern.'"[6]

Recent debates as to the place of Old South and Confederate symbols and institutions in the South of the new millennium provide evidence of a changing order. Perhaps, as John Hurley, president of the Washington-based Confederate Memorial Association, stated in 2005, "The culture of the South is an expanding thing rather than a xenophobic and dwindling thing."[7] But a changing South is no less a distinctive, continuing South. A distinctive Southern culture based on a sense of order has existed and continues to exist amid the larger American culture. If some form of "Southernism" is to continue as a distinctive mind-set and way of life in the twenty-first century, Southerners will need to learn to strike a balance between their past, with its ruling order of division, and the present, with its ruling order of identification. If Southerners can find unity in their division and distinctiveness in their identification, they may even be able to serve as a model for the increasingly divided and diverse United States. The debates portrayed in the mass media as evidence of the "unfinished Civil War" can instead be interpreted as evidence of a South that has progressed to the point of having a common, continuous dialogue as to what its diverse denizens (and concerned others) want it to be.

Any consideration of Southern identity, including this discussion of its contemporary rhetoric, must begin with the question of whether a South distinctive from yet part of the rest of the United States has ever really existed and, if so, whether such a distinctive South still exists today. Some scholars would answer these two questions in the negative, arguing, in Cash's words, that the South "is all a figment of the imagination, that the South really exists only as a geographical region of the United States." Cash responds, that "nobody, however, has ever taken [such claims] seriously. And rightly." Those who place themselves in the interdisciplinary field of Southern studies obviously share the basic assumption that the South indeed exists as a distinctive cultural entity. But even for Southern scholars such as Potter, the South has been "an enigma . . . a kind of sphinx on the American land" that may even "hold a secret, an answer to the riddle of American life." Scholars of Southern history, literature, and culture have, over the years, developed a number of theories that seek to answer the riddle, to explain why the South is distinctive in the American nation. Smiley even argues that "in the history of Southern history . . . the central theme has been the quest for the central theme." However, as James Cobb concludes, such historians' and others' "obsessive insistence" on establishing the fact of and reason for the South's distinctiveness "may actually prevent southern historians from fully understanding why the South is like it is (or like it was) and southerners themselves from knowing who they really are and, perhaps, even from becoming everything they could really be." Nonetheless, some of the theories generated by Southern historians in their "obsessive" quest for a "central theme" are especially helpful in advancing my contention that a source of Southern distinctiveness has been Southerners' concern, throughout their history, with order.[8]

Some historians, such as Ulrich B. Phillips, attribute Southern distinctiveness to its omnipresent race consciousness. Others, such as the "Twelve Southerners" who penned *I'll Take My Stand*, argue that what made the South not only distinctive but also superior was its agrarian lifestyle and economy, which contrasts favorably with the urban, industrial lifestyle and economy of other regions. Though each of the twelve focused on different aspects of Southern culture, all agreed in their support for "a Southern way of life against what may be called the American or prevailing way . . . Agrarian *versus* Industrial." Both Phillips's and the Twelve Southerners' theories of Southern distinctiveness are rooted in the "peculiar institution" of plantation slavery, which is what initially made the South distinctive in terms of its racial makeup and relations as well as in its patterns of agricultural development.[9]

However, Potter points out that Phillips's theory, while accurate in some respects, is flawed in its failure to take a stand against the South's racism. Likewise, Potter finds the agrarians' view problematic in its vision of "a subsistence economy, agricultural diversification, a wide distribution of small landholdings, a large class of independent husbandmen, and an unstratified society," none of which "has ever been dominant in the South." For Potter, Phillips's and the agrarians' theories are oversimplified in that they rely too much on just one element (race or agriculture) of the Southern culture to explain its distinctiveness. Potter's own answer to the enigma that is Southern distinctiveness is that it derives from "the culture of the folk [that] survived in the South long after it succumbed to the onslaught of urban-industrial culture elsewhere." This view of a distinctive Southern folk culture synthesizes the issues of race and agrarianism, as Potter argues that in such a folk culture, "the relation between the land and the people remained more direct and more primal in the South than in other parts of the country" and that this may have been true even more so for blacks than whites.[10]

Just as slavery is central to race and agriculture in Southern identity, so too does it lie at the root of another central element of the Southern identity: the loss of the Civil War and the Confederacy's bid to secede from the Union. First Weaver and then Woodward propounded the thesis that the Southern experience has been distinctive from the American experience because of the region's firsthand knowledge of tragedy and loss, initially through the Civil War and subsequently through Reconstruction. As Weaver observes, "There is something in [the South's] heritage, half lost, half derided, betrayed by its own sons, which continues to fascinate the world. . . . It is this refuge of sentiments and values, of spirituality, of belief in the word, of reverence for symbolism, whose existence haunts the nation.'" This acquaintance with loss, derision, and betrayal resulted in Southern distinctiveness through "the Southerner's discipline in tragedy."[11]

In a similar vein, Woodward contrasts five aspects of American and Southern history to prove his contention that the South's experience has differed from that of mainstream America in large part because of slavery and the war lost to protect states' right to uphold human bondage. Whereas America has experienced "economic abundance," the South has been better acquainted with "scarcity and want." While America boasts a tradition of "success and invincibility," the South has tasted the cup of "frustration, failure, and defeat." Though America has embraced a belief in "innocence," "moral superiority," and "human perfectibility," the South has had to deal with a "tortured conscience," a "preoccupation . . . with guilt, with the reality of evil," and "tragedy." Alexis de Tocqueville observes that while Americans are "born free," many in the South were born into slavery. Finally, Woodward echoes author Thornton Wilder's contention that Americans are by nature "abstract" and "disconnected," in contrast to the centrality of place in Southern culture, especially in the literature of such Southern authors as Eudora Welty and William Faulkner. Overall, Woodward argues that the South's distinctive experience of loss and tragedy is "a dimension of historical experience that America very much needs, a heritage that is far more closely in line with the common lot of mankind than the national legends of opulence and success and innocence."[12]

Likewise, Carl Degler argues that the continuity of certain aspects of Southern culture—including race consciousness (à la Phillips) and agriculture (à la the Twelve Southerners)—from colonial times through the present has made the people of the South distinctive: "The South's distinctiveness presents a problem to those who would talk about national character, for Southerners indubitably live in America; but equally indubitably, they are not like other Americans. They are more conservative, more nationalistic, more self-identified, more defensive, and more romantic than other Americans. . . . Southerners are less rich, less urban, less diverse demographically and religiously, and more likely to be black than the rest of Americans." According to Degler, the "individualism and lack of social discipline" that caused the South to lose the Civil War "surely can be traced in large degree to the agricultural nature of the antebellum South, with its enduring frontier, its widespread violence, its lack of urbanization. All of these can be traced back to slavery." This defeat, in turn, further "enhanced the distinctiveness of the South. . . . No other Americans have experienced directly an army of occupation." In the years following Reconstruction, the "fundamental difference between the sections in regard to race was the institutionalization of white supremacy in the South through legal segregation and disenfranchisement."[13] Degler thus integrates the elements of race, agriculture, and the Lost Cause of the Confederacy within his particular view of Southern distinctiveness.

While Degler's theory emphasizes continuity, Louis D. Rubin Jr. stresses change. But like Degler, Rubin also sees in Southern history the quality of continuity, but it is a continuity that is distinctive in its ability to weather change. Rubin hypothesizes that the South is distinctive because it has retained its identity through the many changes of time. The South, Rubin observed in 1980, "has changed a great deal—it is always changing, and in recent decades the change has been especially dramatic. But there is little conclusive evidence that it is changing into something that is less markedly southern than in the past." Instead, Rubin argued, the "South has long had a habit of incorporating seemingly disruptive change within itself, and continuing to be the South. . . . Each juncture in the region's history . . . has been proclaimed as signaling the end of the line, so far as the preservation of regional identity and distinctiveness are concerned. Yet an identifiable and visible South remain."[14] The ability to endure not in spite of but because of the countless changes in its social order has given the South the very distinctive identity that is the subject of the four debates considered in this book.

Based on those four topics as well as on the work of previous scholars of the South, I have formulated a new theory about what has created and maintains a distinctive Southern identity. I seek both to account for the persistence of a distinctive Southern identity and to offer a potential new direction for the continuation of a distinctive Southern identity. I believe that the unifying theme thus far in the quest for Southern identity is a concern with order. As Weaver writes, "Civilization is measured by its power to create and enforce distinctions. . . . To the extent that the South has preserved social structure and avoided the creation of the masses, it has maintained the only kind of world in which values can long survive."[15] Through these debates regarding the propriety of continuing to venerate Old South symbols, leaders, and institutions in the changed rhetorical situation of the contemporary or New South, the common thread of order—in particular, the order of division—runs through the issues of slavery, secession, states' rights, and segregation.

During the many years in which slavery, secession, states' rights, and segregation were the rule, the South was distinctive because its leaders—those endowed with the power to determine how the region would be ordered—chose to structure Southern life by keeping its people divided. First through slavery and then through segregation, Southern leaders sought order by creating and maintaining divisions among the South's people—principally according to race but also according to gender and socioeconomic status and often through some combination of these factors. And through their quest for states' rights through secession and other means, Southern leaders sought order by creating and maintaining divisions between the states—principally between the South and the other regions of the United States. By thus keeping Southerners divided both from one another and from the rest of the nation, those who led the South created and maintained a distinctive regional identity from the earliest days of the republic through to the middle of the twentieth century.

At the time of the Constitutional Convention, tensions already existed between the slaveholding and nonslaveholding states. These factions differed in their view as to whether slaves should be counted toward a state's population for the purposes of legislative apportionment. The slaveholding states—ironically, considering that slaves were in other matters considered nonpersons—wanted slaves to count toward their states' populations, while the nonslaveholding states did not. The resulting compromise allowed each slave to be counted as three-fifths of a person toward a state's population for the purposes of determining how many people that state could send to the House of Representatives. Another aspect of the compromise between the two camps as well as between large and small states dictated that the number of senators would be the same for every state, while the number of representatives would be determined by population.

While this early conflict over how to count slaves in the population was ameliorated through such compromises, by the early 1800s new tensions flared between the northern (more industrial) states and the Southern (more agricultural) states. Southern political leaders such as John C. Calhoun believed that the North was taking advantage of the South through the imposition of unfair tariffs, which affected Southern businessmen more than their northern counterparts. In 1828, Calhoun, writing anonymously, proposed via the *South Carolina Exposition and Protest* a system of compromise, known as the concurrent majority or nullification, that would have allowed a state dissatisfied with a particular piece of legislation the option of nullifying it. That is, a state would have been able to opt out of particular laws that it found against its interests as a state. Calhoun believed that this system would allow for majority rule but provide greater protections of minority rights. However appealing this proposal may have been in Calhoun's abstract, philosophical mind, not even his fellow Southerners accepted the idea in practice, so relations between the slaveholding states of the South and the nonslaveholding states of the rest of the nation continued to deteriorate.

Tensions were further exacerbated by the question of whether slavery should be expanded into the new territories. The Senate debate among the Great Triumvirate—Calhoun, Daniel Webster, and Henry Clay—led to the Compromise of 1850.[16] Championed by Clay, this compromise admitted the newly acquired California as a free state; stopped the slave trade in the District of Columbia; divided the rest of the newly acquired Mexican land into the territories of

New Mexico and Utah without declaring them slave or free; and enacted a new, stricter fugitive slave law. However, the agreement would not last. The Southern states continued to grow dissatisfied. With the secession of South Carolina and President Abraham Lincoln's determination that the Union remain intact, the Civil War ensued.

Though the Union won the war and the Confederate states were forced to return to (or remain in) the Union, many Southerners developed a spirit of having fought honorably for their Lost Cause as they struggled under the rigors of Reconstruction. When white Southerners became free of the yoke of federally enforced Reconstruction, they did not take long to re-cement the spirit of white supremacy through Jim Crow (race-based segregation) laws despite the freedoms seemingly promised to former slaves and their descendants by the Emancipation Proclamation and Reconstruction. With the hardships brought by an economic downturn in the 1890s, the "already fragile relationship between blacks and whites became much more intense. . . . The dearth of jobs, the mounting debts and declining returns from farming, and the dwindling of money for the essentials of life fueled elemental fears" about "competition for jobs, housing, and public services." These financial fears in turn fueled whites' fears of a more "phobic, irrational quality," such as the intense, pervasive fear of white women being raped by black men (the oft-stated reason for the lynching of many black men). In response to these rational and irrational fears, Southern whites set up as many barriers as possible between themselves and blacks. By 1895, this "racial caste system," a "system of de jure and de facto subordination of blacks in the South," was solidly in place. Unwritten rules required Southern blacks to "use only the back door at the home of a white and [to] address a white by title and last name while whites almost always used the first name or nickname of a black." Written codes required that "blacks were segregated or excluded altogether from virtually all public places," especially the polling place on Election Day.[17]

With the rise of the civil rights movement after World War II, this order of division came into question in the South and elsewhere. White Southerners stubbornly sought to maintain this order through the efforts of political leaders such as George Wallace and Strom Thurmond and through the grassroots efforts of the White Citizens' Councils and the Ku Klux Klan. But the combination of efforts by civil rights leaders such as Martin Luther King Jr. and organizations such as the Southern Christian Leadership Conference with Supreme Court rulings such as *Brown v. Board of Education* and federal legislation such as the Civil Rights Acts of 1964 and 1965 meant that a new order was coming to the fore in the South and throughout the United States—the order of unification or identification. By federally mandating that people of different races could no longer be kept separate in public institutions such as schools, both aspects of the South's previous identity-maintaining order of division were struck down by the courts: No longer could the South's people be divided among themselves according to race (at least not legally), and no longer could the South call on its sacred states' rights to maintain its division from the rest of the nation. Not surprisingly, white Southerners resisted accepting such sweeping changes: decades would pass before a majority of Southern hearts and minds accepted the integration mandated by the courts. In the interim, those self-identifying themselves as Southerners sought to maintain their preferred order of division.

While judges and legislators could mandate a change in the ordering of institutions, Southerners sought to maintain their identity of division on an emotional or spiritual level through symbols, especially symbols of the Lost Cause of the Confederacy. The religion or myth of the Lost Cause is the belief that although the Confederate States of America lost the Civil War and thus its bid to secede, the South still won in the sense that Southerners believed that they (or their forebears) had fought on behalf of what was right and consequently could maintain their sense of honor. The idea of the Lost Cause, as Gaines Foster describes, "acknowledges the defeat of the Confederacy" while suggesting that the "South had fought less for independence than for philosophical principles that might yet triumph." The Lost Cause is viewed as having helped "southerners assimilate defeat" and as having unified "southern society."[18] Thus, when the civil rights movement swept across America, especially across the South, those white Southerners who were averse to the changes advocated by the movement resurrected Lost Cause symbols, such as the Confederate battle flag, to rally others to the defense of segregation as the Southern way of life. Calling on such symbols provided a way of conveying that although Southerners were losing their battle against integration, they remained in the revered tradition of the Lost Cause—losing but maintaining their belief in what they felt was the superior order. By the turn of the twenty-first century, legalized integration had been well established, and the voices of various identity groups, including many previously silenced through the order of division, had become more influential. At this time, though unification or identification was the legally established order, division remained the ruling symbolic or spiritual order among many "unreconstructed" white Southerners.

In his famous definition of man, Kenneth Burke observes that we are "goaded by the spirit of hierarchy (or moved by the sense of order)/and rotten with perfection." This statement certainly is true of the group of men and women under study here. White Southerners in particular seem "moved by the sense of order," which includes "the incentives of organization and status." They often have been driven to pursue their particular brand of order—division—to such lengths that they make the seemingly innocuous idea of order "rotten with perfection." Burke describes in more detail how order can become rotten: "Despite any cult of good manners and humility, to the extent that a social structure becomes differentiated, with privileges to some that are denied to others, there are the conditions for a kind of 'built in' pride." Burke classifies the differentiated privileges of such a rotten order as the "secular analogues of 'original sin.'" Disguised by the veneer of Southern gentility and civility (as apt an example as any of a "cult of good manners and humility"), the white South's desire to maintain its strictly enforced social hierarchy devolved into its staunch defense of segregation's system of giving "privileges to some that are denied to others." And so the men and women of the South have wrestled with their sins—sins that have sprung from their yielding to the temptation to take their distinctive order of division too far, past any possibility of perfection and into the realm of rottenness and pride. As Burke elaborates in his explication of entelechy (the principle of perfection), within the "drive to make one's life 'perfect'" lies the potential "that such efforts at perfection might cause the unconscious striver great suffering."[19] And so it has been with the people of the South.

For Burke, there are two basic types of order: identification and division. At first thought, these two orders seem quite oppositional: identification entails the joining or reconciling of people and their interests, while division involves keeping people and their interests separated or segregated. However, Burke believes that "identification implies division," arguing that "identification is affirmed with earnestness precisely because there is division. Identification is compensatory to division. If men were not apart from one another, there would be no need for the rhetorician to proclaim their unity. If men were wholly and truly of one substance, absolute communication would be of man's very essence." Without division, there would be no aspiration to attain identification or consubstantiality. Further, Burke also allows for the possibility of simultaneous identification and division, as in the following scenario: "A is not identical with his colleague, B. But insofar as their interests are joined, A is identified with B. Or he may identify himself with B even when their interests are not joined, if he assumes that they are, or is persuaded to believe so. . . . [T]wo persons may be identified in terms of some principle they share in common, an 'identification' that does not deny their distinctness." In other words, just because two entities are identified or consubstantial in one respect does not require that they lose their other distinctiveness or differentiation in other respects. Two entities may determine that their interests are joined in one or more respects but nonetheless remain two distinct entities.[20]

Another avenue in which Burke discussed order is in terms of pieties, which codify society's "sense of what properly goes with what." Designating which ideas or people belong together and which apart is bound up with Burke's overarching ideas about identification and division. In his explication of the concept of perspective by incongruity, Burke advocates that "we deliberately cultivate the use of contradictory concepts." Doing so results in a "new perspective [that] realigns something so profoundly ethical as our categories of allegiance" in such a way that "members of the same race or nation who had formerly thought of themselves as allies become enemies, and members of different races or nations who had formerly thought of themselves as enemies become allies." In this spirit, Burke believes (or hopes) that the "segregational, or dissociative state cannot endure—and must make way for an associative, or congregational state." By bringing side by side people or ideas typically considered discordant, the "symbol-using" and "symbol-misusing" humans of Burke's definition have *the potential to overcome* their propensities to be "separated from his natural condition by instruments of his own making," to be "goaded by the spirit of hierarchy," and to be "rotten with perfection."[21] In this idea we can begin to see hope for a South that may in time overcome its propensity for keeping itself divided and thus rotten by the hand of its own outdated idea of divided perfection. Through debates such as those analyzed here, the people of the South have sought and can continue to seek identification through discussions that juxtapose the differing views of themselves and their region that have thus far kept the South perpetually "goaded by the spirit of hierarchy" into being "rotten with perfection."

From a rhetorical perspective informed by Burke's ideas, I will examine four debates in or about the South that occurred between 1989 and 2002: (1) the admission of women to the Virginia Military Institute (VMI) and the Citadel; (2) the integration of displays of public art in Richmond, Virginia, to feature Confederates and African Americans side by side; (3) the removal of the Confederate battle flag from public spaces such as the South Carolina Capitol; and the public outcry that forced Mississippi Senator Trent Lott, who seemed to speak out in support of the South's segregated past in comments praising Strom Thurmond, from his position as a legislative leader. At issue in each of these debates is whether the South's ruling order should remain one of division or should be supplanted by identification. Judging from the outcomes of these four debates, the order of division seems to be waning just as the order of identification seems to be waxing in influence over the turn-of-the-millennium South.

My rhetorical analysis of these debates begins with "Uniforms, Walls, and Doors: Social Mystery and Gender Integration at the Virginia Military Institute," which focuses on the 1989–96 debate regarding whether women should be admitted to the all-male yet state-funded VMI. At around the same time, a parallel debate concerned the admission of women to South Carolina's Citadel. I focus on the VMI debate, which more clearly involved principles than did the Citadel debate, which was more ad hominem, focused on the efforts of a particular young woman, Shannon Faulkner, to gain admission to that school. At VMI, identification was and is inculcated among "institute men" or "citizen-soldiers" through a highly structured class system of discipline and governance. However, VMI's all-male tradition created a wall of division, separating those within VMI's system of social mystery (men) from those outside of it (women) on three levels: gendered social mystery, martial social mystery, and Southern social mystery. In June 1996, the Supreme Court required VMI to admit women to its fortress-like campus steeped in Southern martial tradition. By 2000, a female cadet held a leadership position, and in 2001 VMI marked the first graduation of female "institute men."

Chapter 2, "When Richmond Gained Perspective by Incongruity: Old South Tradition and New South Change in the Confederate Capitol," analyzes two closely related debates over public art in the former Confederate capital. The 1995–96 debate focused on the propriety of permanently placing a statue of Richmond native Arthur Ashe—tennis champion, social activist, and author—on the city's famed Monument Avenue, which had previously featured only the likenesses of Confederate luminaries. Two strands of debate ran through this controversy: the propriety of placing a statue of a contemporary, non-Confederate figure on Monument Avenue, and the propriety of placing a statue of smaller scale and more contemporary design amid the older, "grander" existing statues. Identification eventually came from the division—Ashe was included on the avenue. In 1999, debate centered on the propriety of featuring a likeness of Confederate general Robert E. Lee in a collection of canvas banners to be displayed on the city's floodwall as part of Richmond's riverfront redevelopment project. While the floodwall murals ostensibly sought to unify previously divided elements of the city through the common bond of Richmond's shared history, the issue of the propriety of including Lee's image caused division. In the end, identification in the form of compromise prevailed, when a civilian-attired image of Lee was displayed as part of a larger collection of images from the city's past. In both of these debates, the issue concerned Richmonders' differing senses "of what properly goes with what." The bringing together of symbols and images previously considered incongruous gave Richmonders the opportunity to gain a new perspective on themselves and their city. Whether they actually acquired this new perspective remains to be seen, considering that yet another debate over public art in Richmond—this one over a statue of Abraham and Tad Lincoln—erupted shortly thereafter. These events may well illustrate the idea of the common, *continuous* debate that may eventually bring the two sides closer together on some level through their conflict.

Chapter 3, "Stories of the War: The Confederate Flag in South Carolina," focuses on the 1996–2000 debate regarding the propriety of continuing to display the Confederate battle flag atop the South Carolina Capitol and within its legislative chambers. This controversy is representative of similar debates throughout the South in recent years, notably in Mississippi and Georgia, two states that faced the issue of whether to retain state flags that prominently feature the Southern cross. I analyze the various narratives used by South Carolina's flag proponents, middle-grounders, and opponents as they told stories to explain why the South seceded and the war was fought, why the flag was initially hoisted atop the Capitol in 1962, and why the flag remains an issue today. The Confederate flag has been used to identify contemporary "unreconstructed"

Southerners with their Lost Cause forebears, but that same flag also divides them from their African American contemporaries. On July 1, 2000, the Confederate battle flag was removed from the South Carolina Capitol to a Confederate memorial on the Statehouse grounds, a compromise that some observers found less than satisfactory: the Rebel flag, which many people find evocative of the old order of division, flew at street level at a major Columbia intersection, Main and Gervais. While some participants and observers consider the debate resolved, the National Association for the Advancement of Colored People (NAACP) has continued its tourism boycott in hopes of removing the flag from the Capitol grounds altogether and into a place such as the nearby Confederate Relic Room. The narratives about how and why the flag was removed from the Capitol will be added to the collections of stories opponents in the larger debate over Southern identity use to defend their respective causes of identification and division.

Finally, chapter 4, "Senator Trent Lott: Southern Sinner, Scapegoat, and Sacrifice," examines the December 2002 debate regarding the propriety of Mississippi Senator Trent Lott's praise of South Carolina Senator Strom Thurmond on the occasion of his one hundredth birthday. Lott's evocation of Thurmond's racist past caused Lott to be identified with the old order of division in an age in which the legally established and (crucial to Lott's fate) politically correct order is that of identification. Lott's identification with the Thurmond of division caused Lott, the Senate majority leader–elect, to be cast aside (at least for a while) in the wake of this controversy as little more than an artifact of the old Southern order—though he retained his Senate seat after the controversy subsided and in November 2006 even returned to a leadership position.

After considering each of these debates, the vision of a new rhetoric of Southern identity will be more clear. One possible resolution to the continuing debate over Southern identity is to continue the gradual shift from the old order of division to a new order of identification. Such a shift would entail Southerners of differing perspectives and backgrounds emphasizing their common concerns as Southerners while continuing to recognize the value of each other's differences. Such simultaneous consubstantiality and differentiation is possible, for as Burke notes, "two persons may be identified in terms of some principle they share in common, an 'identification' that does not deny their distinctness."[22] This gradual shift in the South toward an identification that embraces distinctness or diversity is occurring through continued public debates such as the ones examined here.

As Chaim Perelman notes, "It very often happens that discussion with someone else is simply a means we use to see things more clearly ourselves." Burke also speaks to the benefits of dialectic. Throughout his writings, Burke advocates judging objects and ideas through multiple lenses to provide a clearer, more comprehensive view. In contrast to the fear that looking at an issue through multiple terministic screens may lead to relativism, Burke argues that "it is by the approach through a variety of perspectives that we establish a character's reality. If we are in doubt as to what an object is, for instance, we deliberately try to consider it in as many different terms as its nature permits." In fact, because of its "use of mutually related or interacting perspectives," Burke calls dialectic the "perspective of perspectives." Writing on "the relation between rhetoric and dialectic," Burke states, "Bring several rhetoricians together, let their speeches contribute to the maturing of one another by the give and take of question and answer, and you have the dialectic of a Platonic dialogue. But ideally the dialogue seeks to attain a higher order of truth, as the speakers, in competing with one another, cooperate towards an end transcending their individual positions. Here is the paradigm of the dialectical process for 'reconciling opposites' in a 'higher synthesis.'"[23]

The participants in this dialectical process about Southern identity competed with one another, promoting their divergent views on the various issues while simultaneously being joined together as Southerners in the experience of participating in a shared discussion of what it means to be Southern, of what symbols, institutions, and leaders would represent Southerners as Southerners. Through the competition of ideas inherent in these debates, the South and its people can be seen as being refined by a purifying fire of dialectical rhetoric that "guides us in the *process* of coming to agreement."[24] The result is a South that transcends the various positions of its debaters to become a more reconciled synthesis of Southern identity than that which preexisted each debate.

As will become apparent as we consider these four debates about Southern identity, the ultimate purpose of these debates, though perhaps not even consciously realized (let alone admitted) by some of the participants, appears to have been more dialectic than eristic, more working toward eventual identification than toward continued division. As Gregory Clark argues, "A rhetoric of democratic practice enables people to *accept each other as they bridge the gap that separates them in order to collaborate in defining the common ground upon which they can continue to build their sense of collectivity.*"[26] As this volume reveals, those on all sides share a common concern with debating the symbols, institutions, and leaders that together represent Southern identity. Recognizing the value of these shared discussions of the Southern experience, which include Southerners representing many differing vantage points, is a first step toward identifying Southerners with one another while respecting the richness of the distinctions that continue to exist among them.

1

Uniforms, Walls, and Doors: Social Mystery and Gender Integration at the Virginia Military Institute

IF EVER A Southern institution embodied the region's fixation with order, it is the Virginia Military Institute (VMI). The institute's highly regimented system of discipline, based on a strict system of classes and rules, has since its inception in 1839 served to instill a sense of order in its cadets. VMI's particular set of traditions, rituals, and rules—its system of social mystery—has served both to identify those within VMI and to set apart or divide VMI from those outside it. Within VMI, cadets wear the same uniform worn by generations of cadets before them; they go through the same harsh "Rat Line" of discipline during their first year; they participate in the same time-honored traditions, such as the New Market Ceremony each May; and they swear to uphold the same gentleman's code that prohibits lying, cheating, and stealing. And while a strict class system on one level divides VMI cadets according to year entered, it also identifies cadets with one another, as those in their first year know that the upperclassmen providing discipline to the Rat Line at one time were the Rats being disciplined. As a result, all cadets identify with one another as Brother Rats.

But just as VMI's system of social mystery identifies those within it with one another, it also divides them from all those who remain outside of the system. Until 1968, VMI did not admit African Americans. In 1989, women still remained outside of VMI's system of social mystery, not permitted even to apply for admission. After a long series of court cases begun that year, the question of whether women could be admitted to VMI reached the U.S. Supreme Court in 1996. The debate that ensued, both in the Court itself and in the court of public opinion, revolved around whether VMI should remain divided from half of its state's population—women—by not affording them the opportunity to pursue an education there.

That VMI still remained closed to women near the end of the twentieth century reflected its identity as a Southern institution. Southern conservative Richard Weaver argues that the order of division between the sexes should be maintained:

Distinctions of many kinds will have to be restored, and I would mention especially one whose loss has added immeasurably to the malaise of our civilization—the fruitful distinction between the sexes, with the recognition of respective spheres of influence. The re-establishment of woman as the cohesive force of the family, the end of the era of "long-haired men and short-haired women," should bring a renewal of well-being to the whole of society. On this point Southerners of the old school were adamant, and even today, with our power of discrimination at its lowest point in history, there arises a feeling that the roles of the sexes must again be made explicit.[1]

If women entered VMI as well as its South Carolina sister school, the Citadel (also the subject of a gender integration debate in the mid-1990s), Weaver and his ideological progeny foresaw the further deterioration of the division of the sexes into distinct "spheres of influence." If women as well as men could be VMI cadets—short hair and all—the South's traditional order of division would be imperiled. But from the perspective of those lobbying for women's admission to these schools, women's entrance would further the ascendance of identification as the ruling order in the South and the rest of the nation. The central issue in this case was whether it was better to keep people divided by limiting the pool of those eligible for admission into VMI or to open the possibility of a wider group of people who could identify with one another within VMI. Both sides valued VMI's distinctive system of social mystery and the benefits to be had by entering it. But they found themselves divided over the question of whether that system of social mystery could continue to exist and remain valuable if women were allowed to put on the VMI uniform, enter its barracks, and attempt to survive the rigors of the Rat Line.

Supporters of VMI's all-male tradition believed that ending the single-sex educational opportunity the school offered would result eventually in the end of single-sex education altogether, even at private colleges. Those on this side of the debate argued that the distinction between public and private colleges and universities is faulty because it is merely one of degree—public schools tend to receive about 60 percent of their budget from public support and 40 percent from private support, while private schools tend to receive approximately 60 percent from private support and 40 percent from public support. In this view, making VMI coeducational would take away from the diversity of educational opportunities offered by public institutions of higher education in Virginia. Moreover, opponents of the change contended, many students came to VMI precisely because it was all male and thus provided an opportunity not only for male bonding and male-to-male mentoring but also for a more focused learning environment in which male students were not distracted by or trying to impress women. In addition, those who favored a continuation of the current policy posited that

VMI's system of psychological and physical discipline, especially the very difficult first-year experience of the Rat Line, would become less rigorous if women were admitted and believed that much of the value and uniqueness of the VMI education stemmed from this harsh, adversarial approach to instilling discipline. If even minor adjustments were made, they contended, the whole system would suffer. Overall, defenders of an all-male VMI argued that the particular combination of traditions and practices at VMI produced positive results, as evidenced in the success of its graduates; to change the VMI formula might result in less positive outcomes. To VMI's defenders, opponents of the school's all-male tradition in truth opposed the whole institution, seeking not only the admission of women admitted but also changes to VMI's entire system of traditions.[2]

On the other side of the debate, supporters of women's admission asserted that because VMI is a publicly funded institution, the State of Virginia was obligated under the Equal Protection Clause of the Fourteenth Amendment to offer an equal educational opportunity to women. Proponents of this view noted that while VMI had admitted students from twelve other countries, Virginia's women could not attend. Those who would open VMI to women did not equate ending single-sex education at this particular school with the end of single-sex education across the board and asserted that citizen-soldiers, the production of which is the goal of VMI's educational program, are not defined by anatomy or gender. Because the federal service academies and the military itself already admitted women, they must also be capable of handling the VMI experience. The supposedly equal educational opportunity provided women by the proposed new Virginia Women's Institute for Leadership (VWIL) did not begin to compare in rigor, approach, or reputation to that of VMI. They also argued that admitting women would not mean the end of VMI, noting that the school had not only survived but thrived in the wake of other changes to its student body and tradition, including racial integration and the admission of out-of-state and international students. Admission of female students would improve the relevance of a VMI education to the "real world." In sum, advocates of a gender-integrated institute held that it excluded women for no other reason than to maintain its status as an exclusive, aristocratic fraternal organization, in itself proof that VMI was simply living in the past.[3]

I will analyze the arguments and means of persuasion used by both sides of the controversy from a rhetorical perspective informed by Kenneth Burke's conception of social mystery. Rather than emphasizing the arguments put forth in the courts, I will focus primarily on the various arguments put forth in the public forum via press releases and media outlets because the ways in which "the public" negotiates such controversies lie at the heart of participation in our democratic American society and therefore deserve scholarly attention. It is appropriate to look at these communications in terms of Burke's conception of social mystery, his idea that "*mystery* is equated with *class distinctions*"—with class in this case determined by gender, involvement in militaristic activity, and regional identity.[4] Looking at texts generated by "the people" is also germane in that, as members of the various classes involved in the dispute—men and women, military and nonmilitary, Southerners and non-Southerners—they have a direct stake in the negotiation of class distinctions inherent in the system of social mystery that is VMI.

In *Rhetoric of Motives*, Burke enters into his discussion of social mystery through reference to Thomas Carlyle's ideas about symbols of social mystery, with clothes being Carlyle's chief example.[5] This idea of clothes signifying authority was seen in the VMI controversy, as the central image of VMI is of rows of cadets marching in their vintage gray uniforms. Likewise, the images used by the VMI press office and in turn the media to signify the successful integration of women into VMI were images of young women in those same uniforms. What the women who sought to attend VMI wanted—and what the activists who worked on their behalf wanted for them—was the image of them in uniform, an image that signified they had broken down the barrier that had kept women outside VMI's system of social mystery. Also symbolic of the mystery of VMI are its fortress-like barracks. An important element of the motivating vision for getting women into VMI was the metaphor of "opening its doors to women." To obtain knowledge of the previously all-male mystery of VMI, women needed to get inside the barracks. Once there, the women would be inside the walls of VMI's mysteries rather than standing outside, powerless, trying to look in but only able to imagine what was going on inside.

Burke points his readers to a passage in which Carlyle "sees through the 'clothes' of class distinction to the naked universal man beneath, but restores with one hand the very hierarchic reverence he would take away with the other." Some observers characterize Justice Ruth Bader Ginsburg, who delivered the majority opinion of the Supreme Court, as doing just this, arguing both that "the notion that admission of women would downgrade VMI's stature, destroy the adversative system and, with it, even the school, is a judgment hardly proved" and that "admitting women to VMI would undoubtedly require alterations necessary to afford members of each sex privacy from the other sex in living arrangements, and to adjust aspects of the physical training programs."[6] Especially notable in the context of Carlyle's clothes theme was the installation of shades on barracks room windows so that both male and female cadets would have privacy while dressing and undressing—a fact that underscores precisely the gender differences that the court otherwise denies significance.

Prior to the Supreme Court's decision, these differences were symbolized by men's admission to VMI and thus wearing its uniform while women were not admitted and thus were allowed to wear only civilian clothes, which more easily distinguished them as women. Only when both men and women were allowed to wear the VMI uniform were they, in the eyes of the court, stripped of the gender differences signified previously by their differences in clothing. In other words, the same clothing signifies the same power; different clothing signifies different power.

This reflection on what today could be summed up in the cliché "the clothes make the man" allows us to make sense of the VMI case as a controversy sparked by social mystery. Indeed, the uniforms worn by VMI cadets are an element of the social mystery of the institution, the system of signifiers that differentiates between those who are part of its ranks of social power and those who are not.[7]

VMI, located in Lexington, Virginia, was founded in 1839. Stonewall Jackson served as a physics professor prior to the Civil War, and its cadets fought in the Battle of New Market and its campus was destroyed during that conflict. U.S. general and diplomat George Marshall was a graduate. VMI's mission statement reveals how the school characterizes itself:

> The Virginia Military Institute . . . is a state college supported by the Commonwealth of Virginia, for the purpose of offering higher education in the fields of the liberal arts, sciences, and engineering. In addition to being a college it is and will remain a military institute with its entire undergraduate student body organized as a military unit. In the words of one of its founders, Col. J. T. L. Preston, "The military feature" is "essential to its discipline" although "not primary in the Institute's scheme of education." The basic purpose, then, of the Institute is to provide academic study of the highest possible quality conducted in, and facilitated by, a rigorous system of military discipline.[8]

Although the "rigorous system of military discipline" is but one aspect of the VMI experience, it is the one that most distinguishes a VMI education from one to be had at a typical college or even at another military academy. It is said that when cadets enter the institute and are put through the Rat Line, everyone is made equal, no matter who they are in the world outside the institute. Students progress through the class system and into positions of leadership through their efforts as individuals and as class members helping one another. This system includes "three elements that cadets and alumni consider most striking": "the honor system, the rat line, and an outgrowth of it, the class system." At the heart of the honor system is, of course, the honor code, which states that each cadet will "conduct himself according to the code of a gentleman, who does not LIE, CHEAT, or STEAL." The code is enforced by reporting violators to an elected Honor Court of fellow cadets.[9]

The Rat Line is the system by which freshman cadets, or Rats, learn "personal habits and traits that will serve [them] well throughout [their] cadetship and afterwards." These "habits and traits" include "soldierly bearing, responsibility, self-control, respect for authority, neatness, orderliness, and consideration for others." They learn these principles through such tactics as "running . . . for an hour or more in military formation, in fatigue uniforms, carrying rifles—

Rat Kim Herbert from Herndon, Virginia, flanked by two of her Brother Rats from B Company, sounds off on August 20, 1997, as a member of the Cadre leans over her shoulder. Courtesy *Richmond Times-Dispatch*.

double time," doing chores for their mentors, or "dykes," and attending "sweat parties" in which cadets are awakened in the middle of the night and herded en masse into a dark, steam-filled shower room. Relationships built within the Rat system are considered sacred and are a chief benefit of the VMI experience; fellow class members are called Brother Rats, and each Rat is assigned an older dyke to emulate. Finally, the VMI class system provides leadership and organization for the military aspect of VMI life. According to VMI historian Henry Wise, "much greater stress is placed on class organization than at other colleges. Each class is a tightly knit organization; its members are . . . jealous of their class privileges. As seniority increases, responsibility and authority over the lower classes increase."[10]

In 1989, an anonymous young woman from Northern Virginia resolved to be a VMI cadet, perhaps inspired by Stonewall Jackson's words etched over the entrance to VMI's barracks: "You may be whatever you resolve to be." But in her case, a simple resolution was not enough. She was notified that her admission application would not be considered, and she filed a legal complaint. The result was a series of court decisions regarding whether it was legal for VMI, a state-supported institution of higher education, to deny admission based solely on gender to a segment of the state's population. In 1991, a U.S. district court ruled in favor of VMI, saying that it was not in violation of the Constitution and that it served an important state function. However, the U.S. Department of Justice appealed the ruling, and in October 1992 the Fourth Circuit Court returned the case to the district court and gave VMI four options: admit women, go private, create an equivalent program for women, or find some other solution. VMI chose the third option; close to a year later, plans were announced for the creation of the VWIL at nearby Mary Baldwin College (a private women's college). The VWIL would not offer students an all-female version of VMI's very harsh, adversarial training program but would instead give them leadership training based on more nurturing, positive reinforcement. At around the same time, Shannon Faulkner filed a 1993 suit against the Citadel, a publicly funded military college in South Carolina. Citadel officials did not realize that Faulkner was female and admitted her to the school. When they learned of her gender, however, they rescinded the offer of admission, and *Faulkner v. Jones* began to make its way through the courts.[11]

In May 1994, a U.S. district court ruled that the VWIL was an acceptable alternative to VMI. The Justice Department, disagreed, however, and appealed. In January 1995, a panel of three judges from the Fourth Circuit ruled two to one in favor of VMI. In August 1995, the first women entered the VWIL program. They traveled to VMI for their ROTC classes.

The Justice Department again appealed, and the case went to the U.S. Supreme Court, which heard arguments in January 1996. On June 26, 1996, the Supreme Court ruled seven to one that the VWIL program did not provide an equal educational opportunity for women. The decision was written by Justice Ginsburg, and only Justice Antonin Scalia dissented. (Justice Clarence Thomas recused himself from the case because his son, Jamal, was a member of the VMI Class of 1996.) VMI's board of visitors then had to decide whether the institute should remain public (and therefore admit women) or become private (and retain its all-male tradition). Going private was within the realm of possibility because VMI's exceedingly strong alumni support had given the school an $185 million endowment (the largest per capita endowment of any public college and an amount that grew during the court battle). At the time, the State of Virginia provided VMI with $10 million per year, a third of its operating budget (and, interestingly, the same amount the school spent on its legal defense). VMI ultimately chose to remain public. But even then the conflict was not over.

Once the board of visitors decided to admit women, decisions had to be made as to what accommodations, if any, should be made for them. In 1997, VMI administrators determined the expectations (such as physical fitness requirements, treatment on the Rat Line, and standards for haircuts, uniforms, and makeup) for female cadets as well as adjustments to be made to the campus before their arrival that fall (such as the installation of privacy shades in the barracks and the

Upperclassmen Megan Smith (left) and Mia Utz bring gear to their barracks on August 14, 1998. Courtesy *Richmond Times-Dispatch*.

conversion or construction of additional women's restrooms on campus). In August 1997, the first female cadets entered VMI, including thirty freshmen as well as transfer students and exchange cadets from already coed military colleges such as Norwich University and Texas A & M University. (These exchange students were intended to help ease VMI's and the female Rats' transition.) In May 1998, the first reported case of fraternization between male and female cadets resulted in the male senior being expelled and in the female exchange cadet leaving the institute. With the fall 1998 football season came the first female VMI cheerleaders; previously, women from nearby colleges had rounded out the Keydets' cheerleading squad. In May 1999, the first transfer cadets graduated from VMI, and the first class of cadets to go through the four-year VWIL program graduated from Mary Baldwin. At the same time, a top-ranking male cadet was expelled for using his position on the Honor Court to sexually harass female cadets.

After two years at VMI, some of the female cadets who had entered in the fall of 1997 were gaining membership in the Cadre, those cadets responsible for the training and discipline of first-year students on the Rat Line. In April 2000, Erin Claunch was named one of the Corps of Cadets' two battalion commanders for the 2000–2001 academic year, thereby becoming the first female cadet to hold a senior leadership position.[12] Then, in February 2001, came the first reported case of a pregnant cadet. Inspired by her situation, VMI's board

Thirty women started as Rats at VMI in 1997; on April 24, 2001, thirteen remained enrolled (left to right): Kelly K. Sullivan, Melissa S. Williams, Maria M. Vasile, Alexis Abrams, Tamina M. Mars, Jennifer N. Boensch, Kimberly H. Herbert, Erin N. Claunch, Kendra L. Russell, Megan K. Smith, Tennille Chisholm, Angela L. Winters, and Rachel Love. Courtesy *Richmond Times-Dispatch*.

of visitors passed a resolution on May 12, 2001, stating the institute's "family policy" would from then on bar cadets not only from marrying (already formally banned but was tolerated under the table) but also from becoming parents. Future pregnant students (and, in theory, male cadets who were expectant fathers) would have no option but to leave the institute for violating the policy. Also in May 2001, thirteen of the original thirty "Sister Rats" graduated from Virginia Military Institute. They had reached a major milestone. But what had happened to the school's social mystery?

When women were not allowed into VMI, social mystery was at work on three distinct yet intertwined levels: (1) the mystery of Southern aristocracy, signified by saluting the campus's prominent statue of Stonewall Jackson and inherent in the good-ol'-boy network whose privileges and connections lead to power; (2) the mystery of military rituals signified by the wearing of not just any uniform but the distinctive VMI uniform; and (3) the mystery of secret male-bonding rituals signified by the tall stone walls of the barracks in which they were thought to take place. These three social mysteries of combined to form a mys-

A statue of former professor and Confederate General Stonewall Jackson outside the VMI barracks. Photograph by Tyler Watts.

tery perceived by those outside of it as so powerful that it had to be opened up for all the world to see, thereby equalizing the social knowledge and power of those previously barred from the rituals leading to such knowledge and power. I will analyze texts from those advocating and opposing the institute's gender integration in light of Burke's (and Carlyle's) concept of social mystery. The presence of social mystery—of social knowledge and privilege held by one group and not by another—lay at the root of the conflict about whether to admit women into VMI and all the social mystery contained in its walls, its traditions, and its network of institute men.

Southerners found the idea of allowing women students at VMI especially troubling because it violated the traditional view of Southern women as physically and emotionally delicate and meant to be educated solely for their role of supporting men in the domestic realm. In traditional Southern culture, each sex has a proper role and proper place in the scheme of things—men and women are divided into their separate realms of public and private life yet unified through the rituals of courtship and the bonds of married family life. For a Southern man, the ideal is to be a gentleman, which requires him to live as "the chivalrous warrior of Christ, the knight who loves God and country, honors and protects pure womanhood, practices courtesy and magnanimity of spirit and prefers self-respect to ill-gotten wealth." Southern military institutions such as VMI had as their goal the training of the aristocratic class of Southern gentlemen. As Rod Andrew astutely describes, "A policy of aggressive military preparedness may have provided partial justification for Southern military schools before the war. But afterward the Southern military tradition existed mainly in the realm of legend, myth, and cultural notions of what it meant to be an honorable man." In this light, it is not surprising that in his dissenting opinion, Justice Scalia praised the "Code for a Gentleman" included in VMI's Rat Bible, which includes the proper manner in which these Southern gentlemen-in-training should relate to ladies. From Scalia's perspective, "In an odd sort of way, it is precisely VMI's attachment to such old-fashioned concepts as manly 'honor' that has made it, and the system it represents, the target of those who today succeed in abolishing public single-sex education. . . . I do not know whether the men of VMI lived by this code; perhaps not. But it is powerfully impressive that a public institution of higher education still in existence sought to have them do so. I do not think any of us, women included, will be better off for its destruction." Specific tenets of VMI's code of gentlemanly conduct require that the gentleman "not speak more than casually about his girl friend," "not go to a lady's house if he is affected by alcohol," and never discuss "the merits or demerits of a lady." According to Brad Edmonds, "In essence, being a Southern Gentleman exemplifies being the best we can be. In this abstract sense, men and women everywhere should emulate the model of the Southern Gentleman." However, while Edmonds allows that women too can "open doors" and "carry heavy things," men ultimately take on more of these particular sorts of gentlemanly duties because "men should make use of their physical gifts by being helpful." Overall, to be a proper Southern gentleman requires that men use their physical strength, their military training, and their innate sense of honor to be, as the Rat Bible's "Code for a Gentleman" states, "the descendant of the knight, the crusader . . . the defender of the defenseless and the champion of justice." Chief among the "defenseless" to be defended by Southern gentlemen trained at VMI are Southern ladies. Amy Thompson McCandless finds that "the southern tradition of treating women as ladies [can] conflict with the military goal of treating women as soldiers." But if Southern women were to attend VMI, how could they be both defender and defended, ladies and soldiers? For those opposed to admitting women to VMI, the answer was that Southern women could not be both, lest the whole traditional Southern worldview and way of life—and the opponents' place in that world—be rendered meaningless and obsolete.[13]

For a Southern woman, the ideal is to live first as a Southern belle and then as a Southern lady. As Anne Goodwyn Jones describes, "The belle is a privileged white girl at the glamorous and exciting period between being a daughter and becoming a wife. She is the fragile, dewy, just-opened bloom of the Southern female: flirtatious but sexually innocent, bright but not deep, beautiful as a statue or painting or porcelain but, like each, risky to touch." After she marries—and it is assumed that she should and will marry—she is a Southern lady with "a different job: satisfying her husband, raising his children, meeting the demands of the family's social position, and sustaining the ideals of the South. Her strength in manners and morals is contingent, however, upon her submission to their sources—God, the patriarchal church, her husband—and upon her staying out of public life, where she might interfere in their formulation. But in the domestic realm she can achieve great if sometimes grotesque power." Thus arises the stereotypical vision of the Southern woman: the coquettish, beautiful, seemingly fragile girl who becomes the strong yet seemingly submissive wife and mother, the "steel magnolia," strong yet beautiful in her femininity. And yet, as Maryln Schwartz declares in the *Southern Belle Primer*, "The belle is a breed that has endured for generation after generation. That's what she's best at—enduring and surviving.... So forget all those stories about a Southern belle being a fragile flower that wilts at the first sign of adversity. A favorite saying in the South is a true belle is a bulldozer—she's just disguised as a powder puff."[14]

Some Southerners, especially the Brother Rats and institute men of VMI, had difficulty envisioning a young Southern woman who could not only enter the Rat Line but survive and become one of them. In this view, young Southern women were meant for Virginia women's colleges, such as Hollins and Sweet Briar, where as budding young belles they would date VMI cadets and be groomed and educated for their future lives as the kind of Southern ladies who married VMI men. From this traditional Southern perspective, young women certainly were not meant to become VMI cadets. As McCandless's interviews of cadets at the Citadel after the admission of women there show,

> The combination of southern and military stereotypes made for a potent combination. "This is definitely a testosterone breeding ground," one [Citadel] cadet noted. The type of man who chose a military school often held very traditional views of gender identities, roles, and relations. The "macho" attitudes of the men made it difficult for them to relate to women. "They get here, and they got females, and some of them are by definition 'more manly than them.' Not only are they intimidated by the fact that females can be stronger and tougher than them, but the fact that they can still be female." For many men, this was frightening. "They're not mature enough to handle the fact that they're not going to be the knight in shining armor, that sometimes they might be the ones getting rescued, and she might, the typical female here, be the one saving them. And it scares them."[14]

Here we see the Southern, martial, and gendered social mysteries at work together, intertwining and overlapping in all of the complexity that is the American South. At VMI and the Citadel and throughout Southern culture, it was difficult—if not impossible—to imagine a military college that included women as students. Many defenders of an all-male VMI concurred with John D. Cocke IV, opinion and editorial editor of VMI's student newspaper, the *VMI Cadet*, when he pronounced, "If you have not realized it by now, the Virginia Military Institute will end as we have all come to know it, August 18, 1997," when women would enter the hallowed barracks.[15] If VMI and the Citadel were to include women in their ranks, could these Southern military institutes continue to exist? After all, such schools were the last of their kind, veritable training grounds where college boys were shaped into gentlemen who would defend the honor of belles and ladies.

A long-standing and intimate connection exists between military education and the training of the Southern gentleman. As Andrew notes in his study of Southern military schools after the Civil War, "A policy of aggressive military preparedness may have provided partial justification for Southern military schools before the war. But afterward the Southern military tradition existed mainly in the realm of legend, myth, and cultural notions of what it meant to be an honorable man." The goal of military education came to be seen not so much in terms of tactical strategy but "in more abstract, mythical terms—honor, patriotism, duty, respect for the law, sacrifice, and even piety." And so it is with today's VMI—only about 18 percent of its graduates enter military service. Many of the rest use their VMI connections to help them achieve success as business professionals and civic leaders. But the VMI experience has until recently prepared cadets for another role, that of Southern gentlemen.

Nevertheless, the central event in VMI's history (aside from the gender-integration controversy) occurred in 1864, when 247 cadets were called to the defense of the Confederate States of America at the Battle of New Market, where "their exploits became legendary." As Andrew succinctly summarizes, "After advancing under fire with casualties to the center of the Confederate line, the cadets came under particularly heavy Union fire. An enemy artillery blast knocked the VMI commandant, Colonel Scott Ship, unconscious. The cadets regrouped and charged, scattering the enemy in their front and awing both Confederate and Union veterans. When it was over, the cadet force of 247 had suffered 57 casualties, 10 of whom were wounded mortally."[16] The battle is commemorated in the annual New Market Ceremony, held each May 15 on the VMI campus. But the sacred sacrifice of those ten cadets on the field of battle has had more lasting effects on VMI than this annual observance. The New Market legend has resulted in cadets' reverence for that one shining moment in the lost war in which a battle was won by a group of young men working together in the united spirit of the corps and the South.

For critics outside the South or for those who do not identify themselves as Southerners, VMI's preeminent place in Southern culture served to further mystify the institute. Other Americans have long regarded Southerners as overly concerned with setting themselves up as a class apart—in their insistence on maintaining an economy based on classifying some people as slave and some people as free, in their desire to secede from the Union, and in their stubborn maintenance of social and economic boundaries between blacks and whites well into the twentieth century. Based on these usual (yet understandable) stereotypes of Southerners as advocates of division, VMI is by virtue of its Southernness also associated with social and economic class stratification, a desire to be set apart from others.

Many accounts of VMI's twentieth-century court battles referred to the institute's role in the Civil War. In response to a negative 1990 opinion column about VMI, alumnus Pedro Alvarez of the Class of 1979 reminded his ideological foe that "VMI survived an attack by Union forces during the Civil War and continues to produce honorably leaders for Virginia and America. Your misplaced words are relatively weak when compare[d] to the Union cannonballs that struck VMI and can still be seen in some barracks rooms. VMI will survive your attack well." But critics as well as VMI backers employed such Civil War imagery. A July 11, 1996, press release issued by the American Civil Liberties Union in reaction to the Supreme Court ruling linked VMI's current court battle with the secessionist battles of the state's past: "R. Kent Willis, the executive director of the American Civil Liberties Union of Virginia, said that lengthy resistance to federal court orders had a long history in Virginia. 'Among traditional Virginians,' Mr. Willis told the *[New York] Times*, 'there's this secessionist notion that if they dig their trenches deep enough, the Feds will go away.'"[17] Often implied is a parallel between the small victory of the New Market cadets within the larger battle of the Lost Cause and VMI's efforts to defend its all-male tradition within the larger battle for conserving tradition in an era characterized by great social change.

As evidenced in D. Grier Stephenson's observation in *USA Today* that "this was not the first time the school had faced long odds. . . . [C]adets from VMI had helped to defeat seasoned Union troops at New Market, Va.," the New Market parallel also could be used to justify VMI's quixotic legal crusade on behalf of its all-male tradition, as Geoffrey Norman did in introducing his *American Spectator* article, "Crashing VMI's Line." Norman retold the New Market story as an allegory for the contemporary battle for an all-male VMI. Describing the 1996 New Market Ceremony, Norman observes that the cadets, wearing "white pants, gray coatees with crossed dykes, and shakos . . . marched in perfect alignment, looking like the nineteenth century on review." This description leads into an account of the battle that the ceremony commemorates:

> The battle of New Market was a Confederate victory, and the charge of the VMI cadets had turned the tide. The action did not change history. Union troops, after all, came back up the Valley not long after the battle of New

Market while, in other theaters, Sherman and Grant were squeezing the life from the Confederacy. The battle of New Market had virtually no influence on the outcome of the war, other than to add to its lamentable casualty rolls and long lists of legends. The effect on the Virginia Military Institute, however, was incalculable. Nothing like that had ever occurred—schoolboys marching into battle, as a unit, and actually defeating an enemy. So, for VMI, the battle became a kind of sacred and somewhat mysterious event, and its spirit first helped rebuild the school (it was shelled and burned by Federal troops a few weeks after New Market) and then infused it with a kind of unique ardor that still exists.[18]

This parallel implies that the contemporary battle of VMI, despite its small victories, would in the end be fought on behalf of another Lost Cause based on social stratification, though this time around the social mystery being negotiated revolved on gender rather than race. Latent in Norman's version of the New Market legend and its effects on the VMI spirit is a statement about the efforts of a small Virginia school that enthusiastically responded when dared to take on the Supreme Court. The "sacred and somewhat mysterious" Battle of New Market explained much about VMI's willingness to defend its unique way of life— its "peculiar institution" (to borrow a phrase typically used describe slavery in the Old South) of all-male education—against the onslaught of the more dominant, change-oriented American culture.

Both of VMI's infamous battles may be understood as fights on behalf of "peculiar institutions" of class distinction. One was a battle for states' rights— in particular, their right to determine for themselves the legality of slaveholding, which entailed giving one race of people the power to buy and sell another. The other was a battle for a state's right to determine what kind of education it should offer its citizens—in particular, whether it was legal to give just one of the sexes access to social power and privilege through a publicly funded single-sex education.

While VMI's Civil War exploits are central to its identity as a school rooted deeply in Southern tradition, there is more to VMI's Southern identity than the enduring legend of the New Market cadets and the enduring legacy of the gentlemen who have gone before. Chief among VMI's unique traits, unable to be replicated through an education at VWIL or any of the federal military academies, is its especially strong network of alumni connections. But the connections deemed most valuable to cadets past, present, and future are those that benefit them as individuals within a network of fellow, supportive institute men who help advance one another's fortunes professionally, socially, and politically. As former state senator Emilie R. Miller, a Democrat from Fairfax who sponsored legislation to open VMI to women, argued, "They have a power structure in Virginia, and they don't want women to enter into that good ol' boys network of power." The National Organization of Women (NOW), in a January 1996 press release, quoted a judge from the *Faulkner v. Jones* case as stating that VMI and the Citadel "have everything to do with wealth, power, and the ability of those who have it to decide who will have it later. The daughters of Virginia and South Carolina have every right to insist that their tax dollars no longer be spent to support what amount to fraternal organizations whose initiates emerge as full-fledged members of an all-male aristocracy."[19]

While supportive alumni networks certainly exist at schools beyond the Mason-Dixon Line, those in favor of opening VMI to women used language that emphasized the Southernness of VMI's particular alumni network. In a July 1991 issue of *Time*, reporter Emily Mitchell notes that most of VMI's graduates "move smoothly into the Old Dominion's most powerful business and political ranks. Barring women from the school effectively curtails their access to that old-boy network." Likewise, City University of New York sociologist and gender-power relations expert Cynthia Fuchs Epstein points out that VMI and the Citadel "give their sons handsome educations . . . and a lifetime 'old-boy' network of contacts."[20] Both Mitchell and Epstein used the phrase *old-boy network* to recall the Southernness—as in good ol' boys—of this particular system of social hierarchy. Common to all of these critics' characterizations of VMI is the image of a secret society, membership in which allows one to gain the social knowledge—via shared experiences and thus unparalleled interpersonal connections—requisite to climbing the ladder of social success in all aspects of life as a Southern gentleman. Inherent in these views is an essential awareness of the class disparity between those who have and those who have not—of those who by their initiation into the ranks of the social mystery that is VMI have unparalleled access to the halls of power and those who attribute their lack of such access to their previous exclusion from the ranks of VMI.

And just as strongly as some observers attribute to VMI's rituals and traditions the capacity to keep authority in the hands of a select few, others attribute to that same system an equalizing influence. VMI commandant Josiah Bunting III asserts, "In our system all who enroll are reduced at once to a culture of utter equality: race, birth, money, prior attainment mean nothing. All new cadets are thrown exclusively upon their own resources of determination, guts, and wit." But this view is not held only by those located within the realm of VMI's social mystery. Jeffrey Rosen of the *New Republic* observes that the "most striking feature" of both VMI and the Citadel "is their success at educating poor black students. The Citadel has the highest retention rate for minority students of any public college in South Carolina: 52 percent of black students graduate within four years. Moreover, white students come from modest backgrounds (and only 18 percent go on to military careers), which makes it all the harder to claim that VMI and the Citadel are powerful agents of the patriarchy." Similarly, Wilfred McClay points out that "one of the notable virtues of VMI and the Citadel . . . is their extraordinary success with black students, who thrive in circumstances where the 'adversative' method levels the playing field, reduces consciousness of racial difference, and breaks down traditional barriers to interracial friendship and comradeship."[21] For these writers, the VMI experience is not about social mystification but instead about the possibilities an adversative system of military training offers for social demystification through the experience shared by cadets from a variety of social and economic backgrounds. Such observations about the benefits for racial minorities as well as the "typical" white military-school boys flies in the face of stereotypes of the racial oppressiveness of all things Southern. No matter a cadet's background or experience before entering VMI, by the time a class has endured four years there, all cadets will stand the equal footing of institute men—and, now, institute women.

Despite the "Code of Gentlemanly Conduct," cadets at the all-male VMI were at times very brash and even coarse in their deportment, a phenomenon sometimes magnified by the stress of the gender-integration debate and of being under the media microscope. In April 1989, when the initial lawsuit was filed, VMI's public relations director, Tom Joynes, published a "Message to the Corps" in the student newspaper (juxtaposed next to an opinion column titled "Shedets???") in which he reminded cadets that "the sidewalk in front of barracks is a public thoroughfare, and its pedestrian traffic includes, among others, many women and children." As a result, he pleaded, cadets should "stop the shouting, and particularly the profanity which is often associated with it. Surely gentlemen can converse without bellowing or cursing." The timing of Joynes's message and the beginning of the gender-integration debate and its attendant media attention could not have been coincidental. Similarly, in May 1997, when MTV's Tabitha Soren visited the post, "the unsuspecting reporter was greeted by hoots and hollers from the horde of cadets gathered on the stoop." In response, the editors of the *Cadet* published a warning to their readers: "For the last time this year, we state that VMI is under constant biased media scrutiny; any deviation from gentlemanly conduct may result in negative press and undue castigation." These student editors realized that all cadets' reputations were on the line and that continued immature, thoughtless behavior could result in the loss of VMI's reputation as a school for Southern gentlemen.[22]

Gregory Chaisson, the father of a VMI cadet, wrote a letter to the editor regarding "respect for womanhood." On one hand he told cadets that "no one need lecture you regarding the duties toward women of either an officer-gentleman or a citizen-gentleman, VMI exists to prepare you for that. Thanks to your parents and to your VMI training, you have a mature understanding of the need in our society for respect for womanhood." On the other hand, he argued, the condom machine in the basement of the barracks was a "symbol which does not belong" among VMI's other proud traditions. He closed by challenging VMI cadets to remove it.[23]

In a February 1997 opinion column, cadet Mike Kelleher argued that men in general, including VMI men, should point their fingers at themselves when it came to blaming someone for taking away their all-male school. In trying to figure out "why a woman would want to come to VMI," Kelleher theorized that women, tired of being oppressed by men's disrespect (as evidenced by their use of pornography and their desertion of women who then became single mothers) had decided to rise up and challenge a system that they, as women, saw as oppressive. Kelleher concluded by charging his fellow cadets to "take your finger and point it at yourself because we have done just as much to hurt our role as males, through disrespect and irresponsibility, as any women's liberation movement ever could."[24]

In yet another paradox, the issue of bringing women into the VMI fold made the school's men look more closely at themselves and their manhood. Under scrutiny from the courts, women's rights activists, and the media, VMI began to scrutinize itself. Are we really living as gentlemen? Are we protecting and honoring women as we say we should? The preceding comments indicate that although some VMI men fell short in this regard, others still cared enough about the code of the Southern gentleman to call on themselves and others to reexamine the meaning of being institute men.

The mysteries inherent in the military tradition that shapes Rats into institute men were also the subject of debate. The military dynamic of VMI shapes the way its cadets sleep, eat, study, and relate to others. Both sides in the debate regarding gender integration argued for the inherent value of these militaristic rituals. After the Supreme Court ruled that women must be admitted if VMI was to remain a publicly funded institution, the focus of the debate shifted to how best to "assimilate" (to use VMI's word) women into the VMI military experience.

In a May 1993 *Fortune* column, Daniel Seligman questioned whether women were being deprived of anything by being denied admission into the ranks of VMI: "Does anybody really believe that college-age women suffer deprivation in not having an opportunity to get hazed remorselessly on the 'rat line,' where first-year VMI students are systematically treated like dirt (and called rats, proclaimed to be the lowest animal on the earth)? Or that young ladies would possibly wish to deal with the school's boot-camp regimen, featuring total lack of privacy, near-permanent mental stress, and minute regulation of behavior?" Seligman basically argues that women do not want to be initiated into the kind of social mysteries VMI offers, so the debate is without merit and thus easily dismissed with a couple of humorous rhetorical questions. If women indeed desire initiation into VMI's rituals and traditions, the precise social mysteries into which such women want initiation will, as a consequence of women's presence, no longer exist. Many proponents of keeping VMI all-male used this argument, which is best articulated by Stephenson: "The very thing prospective female students sought would be altered, diminished, or perhaps destroyed by their presence." McClay, a history professor at the University of Tennessee-Chattanooga who is associated with the conservative-libertarian Intercollegiate Studies Institute, echoes this belief when he states, "it is unthinkable that the 'rat line' could survive as a common, base-line experience at a coeducational VMI, if only because it is hard to imagine well-mannered VMI men routinely dishing out such treatment to women."[25] In other words, the nature of the social mystery would be unavoidably altered by the admission of women, thereby making true initiation of women into the system of social knowledge and power that was VMI an impossibility. This argument apparently sought to discourage women from seeking initiation into the VMI rituals and traditions with the hope that doing so would keep intact VMI's system of social mystery. If everyone can access the knowledge of a social mystery, it is no longer a social mystery and no longer an avenue for gaining privileged social knowledge and power.

Offering a somewhat different argument, Elizabeth Fox-Genovese and Leon Podles justified maintaining an all-male VMI by contending that "boys need an initiation into masculinity" because "without the decision to be a man at the cost of his pleasure or even of his life, a boy will never grow up. He will only get older. All societies have some system of paideia, of education to initiate boys into the mysteries of life and death, of what it is to be a man in a world in which struggle and mortality are inevitable."[26] They argued that initiation into a system of social mystery such as VMI is necessary for the development of young men into ethical, unselfish men. Rather than characterizing women as weak and unable to survive the rigorous VMI experience, Genovese and Podles asserted that college-age women have already learned the principles of self-sacrifice and self-discipline that lie at the heart of the VMI education. Rather than implying that women should not be initiated into social mystery, they characterized women as already possessing the social knowledge that is inculcated through VMI's rituals.

In articulating the majority opinion of the Supreme Court in the case of *United States v. Virginia,* Justice Ginsburg stated that "the notion that admission of women would downgrade VMI's stature, destroy the adversative system and, with it, even the school, is a judgment hardly proved" and that "VWIL affords women no opportunity to experience the rigorous military training for which VMI is famed." But she also argued that "admitting women to VMI would undoubtedly require alterations necessary to afford members of each sex privacy from the other sex in living arrangements, and to adjust aspects of the physical training programs." McClay points out that "despite disdain for gender stereotypes, Ginsburg ends up employing them herself . . . the complete absence of privacy, the uniformity of standards, all the way down to the shaved head of every 'rat,' are central features of VMI life."[27] He contends that Ginsburg wants women to be admitted into the system of VMI tradition because they deserve equal access to the social knowledge and power it confers but that she also admits essential differences between men and women in her demand that accommodations be made to protect women's privacy, thereby replacing one set of mysteries with another.

At the September 21, 1996, press conference announcing the board of visitors' decision to admit women rather than go private, Bunting reassured alumni and cadets that VMI's rigorous standards would be upheld for the good of all involved, including the women who would be integrating VMI: "I believe fully qualified women would themselves feel demeaned by any relaxation in the standards the VMI system imposes on young men." In the same spirit, Bunting stated in a December 1996 *Newsweek* column, "To change any of these standards or expectations—physical, military, or intellectual—to accommodate the enrollment of women at VMI is to compromise exactly what those who apply—male and female—are seeking. The practice of gender-norming, in which different standards are set up for women and men, is most iniquitous of all. There is no gender-norming in the world of affairs into which we send our graduates."[28] Many other observers echoed the idea that if the women admitted to VMI were truly to be included in its system of social mystery, it must not change for them. Like all other cadets, he argued, female cadets would be expected to be transformed by the system into something better, something they were not when they entered the school: citizen-soldiers. After the Supreme Court's decision, VMI traditionalists took the stance that rather than reinforcing the walls of social stratification, VMI instead breaks down the barriers of social mystery that divide cadets before they enter the institute. Cadets may enter VMI in a state of social classification and mystification, but they leave it joined with one another in a state of demystification and unification, though they are set apart as a class—as VMI graduates, institute men, and citizen-soldiers—from the rest of the world.

When women were finally initiated into VMI's system of martial social mystery through their participation in the Rat Line, upper-class cadets wondered whether the system would retain its harsh standards. James E. Duncan, editorial page coeditor for the *Cadet*, writing less than a month after the first women entered VMI, argued, "With the administration breathing down our backs constantly, we have not been able to give these Rats what they came here for.... Ruth Bader Ginsburg wrote that there are a select few women who are able to take that which VMI has to offer. Permit us to give this to them—not a kinder, gentler version of that which they signed up for.... I have talked to numerous Rats, male and female, and they have told me that this year has been easier than they anticipated." In the same issue of the *Cadet*, the writer of an anonymous letter to the editor "was appalled" at hearing Colonel James Joyner announce publicly that the current rat class was "three to four weeks ahead of most previous classes ... in terms of military and physical training." The writer chastised

Joyner and the VMI administration for playing to the media and at the same time fueling most Rats' "arrogant, don't-give-a-damn attitude and [allowing] them to think, falsely, that the low standards they have held thus far are good enough, that they are better than the upper classes." Both of these cadets believed that the VMI administration, seeking to protect the school from media and Justice Department criticism, had prevented upperclassmen from carrying out their duties of thoroughly disciplining their Rat charges and thereby adequately inducting them into the VMI military tradition.[29]

After women had been present at VMI for a few years, those who had kept a critical eye on their treatment lauded the successful integration of women into the mysteries of the system. On April 10, 2000, *U.S. News and World Report* declared,

> Cadets . . . sleep on thin mattresses on wooden racks, but the spartan surroundings, lack of privacy, and physical and psychological hazing of first-year students have a purpose: to create total equality, discipline, and lifelong bonding. It was this vaunted "VMI experience" that school officials anticipated women would shatter—and they deeply resented being forced to change by outsiders. . . . But the new cadets . . . complied. . . . Even the assumption that women would interfere with the bonding process turned out to be somewhat exaggerated. A cadet, it seems, is a cadet. "They're our brother rats," says [Derek] Bogdon. . . . "They went through the same thing that we did."[30]

Such positive accounts validated earlier contentions by women's advocates such as Karen Johnson, who recounted her own experiences in the military as well as the experiences of women who served in Operation Desert Storm as part of an argument that women were indeed capable of carrying out the physical rituals requisite to initiation into VMI's system of social mystery. When the Supreme Court began hearing the VMI case in January 1996, Johnson pointed out, "I stand before you as one citizen-soldier who dedicated 20 years of my life to serve my country in the United States Air Force. I stand before you as one of the over 1.2 million veterans who are women. I was on active duty during the Persian Gulf War when 33,000 sister soldiers put their lives on the line the desert. Those women were U.S. Soldiers experiencing the same hardships as their male counterparts and they performed their jobs admirably."[31] Johnson contended that she and many other women had been initiated into the system of social mystery embodied in the U.S. military and had completed its most rigorous initiation rite: service during time of war. She argued by analogy that if women were capable and legally a part of the nation's military, they should also be admitted into a school known for its education of military leaders.

Likewise, Jeffrey Rosen, writing in February 1996, argued that the women at VWIL did not seem satisfied with its "kinder, gentler" leadership training. The VWIL cadets, he noted, were "naturally drawn to the hierarchy that their professors rejected [and] have voted to wear uniforms all day on Monday and are debating whether or not to adopt a permanent rank system along the VMI model."[32] Women, assumed by "nature" to want something very different from the VMI experience, in fact sought out such military rituals as uniform and rank. Not only, as Johnson argued, were women capable of participation in military rituals, but, as Rosen asserted, some young women very much wanted to be initiated into such rituals and specifically those of VMI.

For many VMI cadets and alumni, one of the hallmarks of the harsh VMI experience is living in its barracks. Indeed, the Rat Bible, 1992–93 edition, preaches, "It is in the barracks that all cadets learn and live equally in an environment deliberately totally lacking in privacy." While cadets concede that "the lifestyle of any military environment should be spartan and contain few luxuries," they complain that "at VMI, however, 'spartan' is used as an adjective when 'cheap' would be a much better description." Cadets in 1993 complained that they "live[d] like dogs." The VMI barracks lacked fans and telephones, while students at other military schools had "computer access in their rooms, practical recreation centers, and barracks that aren't falling apart." But the lack of amenities is not the only difficult aspect of barracks life. Prior to 1997, cadets' rooms lacked window shades and door locks. Rosen examined a thought-provoking parallel between Jeremy Bentham's *Panopticon* and the complete lack of privacy in the VMI barracks. The VMI barracks form a quad with a guard tower in the center. Before the admission of women, all barracks activities were visible from the tower through the unobstructed windows in each barracks room door. According to Rosen, such a system (in the words of Michel Foucault) "induce[d] in the inmate a state of conscious and permanent visibility that assures the automatic functioning of power."[33]

Opponents of women's admission to VMI saw the potential changes to the barracks—the addition of window shades and door locks as well as of private bathroom stalls and showers—as in themselves meaning an end to VMI as they knew and loved it. R. C. Coupland, VMI Class of 1950, wrote to the editor of the *VMI Cadet*, "Women who might attend VMI would not receive a VMI education, simply because the Barracks life at VMI plays such an immense role in the hourly and daily education and development of VMI's men. . . . The overwhelmingly important fact is that women cannot be integrated into VMI's intimate, spartan, 24 hour a day Barracks life, void of any privacy. . . . The alternative is to construct walls, isolating women from the male Barracks life and system, or construct separate Barracks for women." Another alumnus, George Graham, Class of 1979, wrote a 1996 letter to the editor that was published as the board of visitors was deciding whether to make VMI a private institution: "I remember barracks life as being a place of extremes, just like human nature. I saw instances of beastial [sic] behavior. I saw instances of heroic, chivalrous behavior. . . . Certain behavior cannot be repressed without unraveling the entire patchwork of

Barracks life. The amplitudes of these extremes would be reduced. . . . VMI would evolve into an ordinary school. . . . VMI becomes Virginia Tech." Even a 1962 alumnus, Josef D. Prall, who wrote to the *Cadet* editor in 1997 "to congratulate the Corps on the assimilation of the female cadets," qualified his support for women at VMI by adding, "It's just the extra privacy factor for all that bothers me." Despite VMI graduates' misgivings, the shades seem to have been warmly received by cadets, who within the first month of a gender-integrated VMI published a "Top Ten" list of "Reasons Why Shades on the Windows Are Great." No. 3 was, "WELL . . . YOU KNOW," and No. 1 was "Have you seen the exchange students!!!"[34]

The admission of women thus significantly decreased the omnipresence of the all-seeing authority. The system of mystified social authority thus became less effective. However, in the face of the court-ordered integration of women into all aspects of the VMI system, opponents of women's admission shifted their rhetorical strategy to argue that the particular combination of rituals and requirements that constituted VMI's military tradition could not and should not change.

But what exactly made men and women so different that the presence of women would so dramatically change VMI that it would, in the eyes of some observers, cease to exist? The answer often came down to matters of anatomy and physiology. Men have penises, while women have vaginas and uteruses. Men usually require less privacy while using the toilet or the shower than do women, based in part on anatomical differences and in part on social customs. Men are less noticed as cheerleaders than are women due to women's cheerleading uniforms, which reveal their more curvaceous busts and legs. And, perhaps most significantly, men can impregnate someone without their paternity "showing," while women, based on the biological fact that their bodies carry pregnancies, cannot long hide their maternity. All of these issues came up as gender integration advocates and opponents debated whether to open VMI's doors to these gender differences.

Advocates of a gender-integrated VMI perceived the social mystery of VMI as rooted, at its most basic level, in differences of anatomy. The language of Johnson, NOW's national secretary, vividly explained that women had been kept out of VMI's rituals and traditions because those in power wanted to prevent people with different sex organs from sharing in that power. In a January 17, 1996, press release, she stated, "We are here in support of the notion that citizen-soldiers come with and without penises. We are here to ask the Supreme Court to do the right thing and end the phallocracy, the rule by the phallus, that is practiced at VMI." In the spirit of Carlyle, Johnson believed that beneath the gendered clothing of our culture, those of different classes—in this case, men and women—will be revealed as being the same, all specimens of the "naked universal man" (though Johnson likely would substitute *person* or *being* for *man*). Johnson continued, "VMI fears that persons without penises would destroy unit cohesion and esprit de corps, lower the prestige, change the methods [of] educating the citizen soldier and, of course, break with tradition." In this, Johnson made the lowest common denominator of VMI's single-sex policy the factor of sexual anatomy rather than any other, more complex reasons VMI used to explain its own policies. By explaining VMI's exclusion of women in terms of those who have penises and those who do not, Johnson creates on VMI's behalf a system of social stratification so ludicrous that those inclined toward the arguments of NOW would feel, as Johnson did, outrage at being excluded from initiation into a system of privilege solely on the basis of their anatomy. The only alternative VMI offered to those lacking the essential male sexual organs, posited representatives of NOW, was second rate: "Virginia residents who meet requirements for admission to VMI but who are without a penis may now attend the Virginia Women's Institute for Leadership . . . a pale shadow of the VMI program."[35] Johnson implied that the VMI "phallocracy" saw women and their sexual organs as worthy of no more than a second-rate, quasi-military program.

One unusual argument advanced on behalf of opening the doors to the secrets of VMI was advanced in a letter to the editor published in the October 11, 1996, *VMI Cadet*. The author, Jane R. Taylor, characterized herself as "a long time admirer of VMI and a believer that the college should be for men only." But her positive view of VMI had recently been tainted by "the vehement remarks, the reported threats to potential female applicants, [and] the slightly sadistic outbursts that the male cadets will show no mercy to females." In light of this disappointing behavior, Taylor formulated a theory regarding VMI men's vociferous protests of women's admission: "Much as I try, it is difficult to chase away from my thoughts that you young men must be engaging in unnatural practices. Practices you feel will either be exposed or curtailed once women are among your ranks. I sincerely hope these unsavory thoughts are without basis, however, I would like you to have the benefit of the impressions you are imparting to the general public." This theory combines elements of both the idea of a VMI phallocracy and the view of VMI as an exclusive, secret society whose unknown practices had to be protected by keeping its doors closed.[36]

The notion of revealing to women what had previously been hidden from them goes beyond revealing bias based on sexual anatomy. Supporters of a coeducational VMI often used the metaphor of opening or unlocking closed doors. Margaret Carlson opened a column about VMI by asking, "Do you ever get the feeling that the men in the world might not care if the door closed and there were no women in the room?" Such metaphors communicate the image of a secret world, an all-boys' clubhouse with a "No Girls Allowed" sign. In this vein, NOW's Johnson pointed out that similar institutions have demystified themselves by eschewing their "boys-only" status: "Two decades after our military academies at West Point, Annapolis, and Colorado Springs opened their doors to women, VMI still shuts its doors to women." In a subsequent press release, issued on June 26, 1996, the day of the Supreme Court ruling, NOW executive vice president Kim Gandy used similar language praising the court's opinion: "VMI will have to open the doors of opportunity to the daughters of Virginia, as well as to the sons.... And taxpayers will no longer sponsor a system that locks those daughters out of a lifetime of networking." Similarly, *U.S. News and World Report* declared on July 8, 1996, "In the end, it was an anonymous Virginia woman who tore down the barriers keeping women out of the Citadel and the Virginia Military Institute.... [L]ast week, the walls came tumbling down, ending over a century of male exclusivity." But an element of paradox sometimes lurked in the pro-gender-integration rhetoric. Writing before the Supreme Court decision, Carlson suggested that "VMI and the Citadel might want to start building those women's bathrooms now."[37] Carlson lamented having doors of opportunity closed to women but simultaneously advocated the building not only of another door but also of whole rooms that have as their object the separation of men and women. Nonetheless, despite these contradictions, advocates of gender integration at VMI repeatedly used the images of impenetrable walls, barriers, doors, and locks as metaphors for the policy of allowing men only initiation into the system of social mystery.

Just as Carlson suggested in her column, VMI built women's restrooms. In the spring of 1997, VMI held a number of "assimilation orientations" for cadets and published a series of "assimilation reports" in the campus newspaper. In one such forum, Colonel Mike Bissell, chair of the executive committee for assimilation, responded to an "issue of concern raised by cadets" that "the women's shower and toilet facilities and the fact that they may differ slightly from the present men's facilities." At this point, VMI administrators such as Bissell were acting as integration advocates, persuading cadets and alumni of the necessity of installing doors on toilet stalls and creating separate shower stalls to open VMI up to women, as the Supreme Court had ordered. Bissell helped justify the women's toilet stall doors by assuring men that they, too, would soon have doors on all of their toilet stalls. As for the showers, Bissell noted, "In addition to the building code and structural requirements for the women's showers, there are health reasons.... As I hope most of you know, women's and men's bodies are in fact different. Women need to have a degree of privacy and the opportunity to clean themselves particularly during menstrual periods (which addresses concerns involving blood borne pathogens). The inability to have this opportunity may well lead to problems with urinary tract infections.... I ask you to appreciate this difference in the sanitation requirements for men and women when it comes to health issues." For all of the metaphoric appeals to open the doors, the reality was that opening the doors of admission required the construction of new doors to protect privacy and health of both women and men. In the wake of the Supreme Court decision, VMI administrators transitioned from gender-integration opponents to gender-integration advocates, making the case to their constituents for the necessity of privacy at an institution that had traditionally valued the "equalizing" effect of the lack of privacy.[38]

Proponents of a coeducational VMI saw not only doors and walls but also conventions of physical appearance such as haircuts and clothing (a means of social mystification that would not surprise Carlyle or Burke) as socially stratifying men and women. An April 2000 report in *U.S. News and World Report* concluded with thoughts on boxer shorts as evidence that VMI had indeed changed in response to women's presence: "No one questions that some routines at VMI have changed. Guys are less likely to lounge in their boxer shorts. Use of obscene words for female genitalia has decreased. Women's hair sometimes creeps from uniform caps. . . . But so far, the loss of the freedom to be profane and parade in boxers has not been the death knell of VMI's time-honored traditions." A postdecision article in *Black Issues in Higher Education* focused almost solely on the physical appearance of the women in VMI's ranks:

> Women cadets . . . will get close-cropped haircuts and can't wear makeup. They'll sleep in unlocked barracks. . . . If male and female cadets are in a room together, "the lights will be on, shades will be up, and each cadet will be properly clothed," the report [filed in U.S. District Court] said. . . . VMI's report included computerized pictures of a woman sporting the "clean cut" haircut and the slightly longer hairstyle that will be allowed six weeks after women arrive. Previously, new cadets . . . have had to maintain the short cuts for most of the first year. "The hair is going to be really short to start with, for the male and the female cadets," VMI spokesman Mike Strickler said. "Then we're going to let it grow some. It's part of the cadet equalization process." The school will ban jewelry and cosmetics for the first semester.

This emphasis on clothing and hair provides evidence of how material things work to signify sameness or difference in social classification. In the first passage, male cadets' change in leisurewear signified their accommodation of female cadets in the context of the VMI system as a whole, though this example is somewhat contradictory in its implication that male cadets were prompted to cover up what had been more exposed. In the latter passage, women were portrayed as being initiated into knowledge of VMI's social mystery as they took on the appearance of VMI authority by putting on the institute-mandated uniform and haircut. They were made equal to men, in this characterization, in their willingness to take on the same appearance. This idea, however, seems at odds with many feminists' contention that women's roles (as with aging models and actresses and even with corporate women) should not be determined by their physical appearance. Yet in this case, roles of authority often are communicated through material or physical self-presentation. This is consistent with the experiences of Erin Claunch, who rose to the highest rank, battalion commander, in the VMI Corps of Cadets. Claunch "just wanted to blend in and be a good cadet" and did not "mind rules like the one that forbids women from wearing makeup or earrings during parades."[39]

Generally speaking, however, cheerleaders are not about blending in; by definition, they literally stand out from the crowd. In the fall of 1998, the start of women's second year at VMI, female cheerleaders made their debut at football games. They stood out even more than cheerleaders usually do. VMI's cheerleading squad had previously comprised male cadets augmented by female cheerleaders from other nearby colleges. The 1998 squad was controversial not merely because it included females but because it included nine Rats (two male and seven female), who generally were not allowed the privilege of cheering. Most jarring of all, however, was the sight of female Rats wearing the short, flouncy skirts typical of a college cheerleaders yet with closely shaved heads.

In October, cadets passed around a petition protesting the presence of the female Rats on the squad. The situation escalated at the Parents' Weekend football game a couple of days later when some cadets in the stands threw peanuts at the cheerleaders and shouted, "You suck!" Cheerleading sponsor Ned Riester, a VMI alum, said, "I was not embarrassed about the girls with the haircuts. The embarrassing thing was that we would have people in the corps that would do this." The female cheerleaders refused to give in to the petition and the heckling: as squad leader Randy Eads put it, "They're showing a lot of determination and will power to come out here. . . . I have more respect for these cheerleaders than just about anyone in the corps." But the situation points again to the double-edged expectations of women cadets at VMI; as women they are supposed to not be too tough or "butch," but as cadets they are not supposed to show their feminine side or participate in typically female pursuits such as cheerleading. Gussie Lord, one of the two sophomore squad members, argued, "Just because we go here doesn't mean we're not feminine, that we're not women." As *Roanoke Times* reporter Matt Chittum observed, "This is all an unlikely problem. Who would have thought that a young woman could have simultaneous urges to attend a stronghold of masculinity like VMI and to bounce in a tight sweater and wiggle some pompoms? . . . Femininity aside, these women don't limit themselves to the usual 'Block that kick!' kind of cheers. During Saturday's game against archrival The Citadel, the VMI squad smiled gleefully and shook their pompoms in time with cadets who bellowed 'We want blood!'" It was, perhaps, an unexpected dilemma. Wrote Washington columnist Marianne Means, "This is an odd twist on the gender wars. Some of us thought that equal rights were supposed to free women from having to be cheerleaders on the sidelines while men got to be the players on the central field. It is something of a role reversal that men are now jealous that their female classmates are among the cheerleaders." Seeing female cadets with buzz cuts and short skirts was an exercise in perspective by incongruity for those VMI cadets who protested and heckled them. As

Jason Clough, a cadet from Melbourne, Florida, opined, "They shouldn't be down there. . . . They don't look like cheerleaders. They look like men in skirts." These seven women embodied both toughened VMI cadets, marked as Rats by their buzzed-off hair, and participants in that most girly-girlish of pursuits, the pom-pom squad. The men who chose to attend VMI—men who had grown up respecting the traditionally delineated gender roles of Southern culture—found this sight particularly jarring to their sensibilities.[40]

In February 2001, just a few months before the first women were set to graduate after four full years at VMI, word got out that one cadet was pregnant. In planning for the admission of women, VMI officials had anticipated this possibility but had chosen not to create a specific pregnancy policy. Instead, administrators had decided to use the existing policy for dealing with medical conditions. Thus, when this pregnant cadet became known, she faced a few options typical for a cadet with a medical condition: (1) she could stay in the barracks and deal with her condition there until the end of the semester, (2) she could be moved to the post hospital and temporarily live there until her "condition" had passed, or (3) she could leave VMI temporarily to deal with her condition, retaining the option to return in the future. The cadet in question chose the first option, and as the semester wore on, cadets saw a pregnant woman living in the famously spartan barracks. In May 2001, VMI's board of visitors instituted a "family policy" barring cadets from marrying (a limitation already in place but not strictly enforced) or becoming parents: "A VMI cadet who chooses to marry, or to undertake the duties of a parent (including causing a pregnancy or becoming pregnant by voluntary act), by that choice, chooses to forego his or her commitment to the Corps of Cadets and his or her VMI education. Such a cadet will be expected to resign from VMI."[41]

Three and a half years after women had entered VMI, the presence of a pregnant cadet brought back to the surface with great vividness all of the concerns with the physiological and anatomical differences between women and men that had been voiced so loudly prior to gender integration. As advocates of both coeducation at VMI and women's rights repeatedly pointed out, pregnancy requires both a woman and a man. Thus, after the new family policy was instituted, women's rights activists called attention to the fact that while a woman cannot hide her pregnancy for long, a man can hide indefinitely his role as a prospective father. As Willis, the executive director of the Virginia ACLU, argued in a letter to the board of visitors, "This is not a policy that treats men and women the same. . . . A woman cadet could not possibly hide a pregnancy more than a few months. A man who causes a pregnancy, on the other hand, may never be detected. . . . It is hard to believe the people who thought up this rule were not aware of this gross discrepancy." Similarly, a *Roanoke Times* editorial observed, "Nor does the college succeed in cloaking the regulation in an aura of equality by extending its expulsion rule to any male cadet who impregnates a woman. A pregnant cadet is a visible target; a male cadet who has fathered a child is anonymous unless he or someone else discloses his involvement. It takes little imagination to guess which sex would bear the brunt of the policy." Jocelyn Samuels of the National Women's Law Center took the argument a step further, arguing in a letter to Bunting, VMI's superintendent, that "substantial evidence [shows] that VMI adopted its policy precisely as a means to exclude pregnant female cadets."[42]

For an institution that had, by most accounts, done a respectable job of assimilating females into the Corps of Cadets, the pregnancy issue constituted a setback. Women's rights advocates portrayed VMI as deliberately making life more difficult for female cadets faced with a pregnancy than for male cadets in the same situation despite official pronouncements to the contrary. VMI administrators justified the new family policy by pointing out that "the duties of a Cadet are incompatible with marriage and parenthood.... VMI has had a long-standing policy that marriage was inconsistent with the duties and responsibilities of a Cadet, and it was VMI's expectation that this implied parenthood as well. It has become clear, however, that the inconsistency of parenthood, in addition to marriage, needs to be spelled out." In an interview with a reporter from the *Richmond Times-Dispatch*, Bunting stated, "The cadetship of [VMI] would seem to make demands that are incompatible with those kinds of things.... We're trying to develop a policy which is equitable and fair, but within the particular constraints of a military institute—in which all are obliged to live in a single barracks."[43] But the fact remained that in instituting this new family policy, VMI was reifying long-held societal notions regarding blame for unexpected out-of-wedlock pregnancies.

Perhaps more than any other aspect of the VMI gender integration debate, the controversy over pregnant cadets most clearly illustrates the idea of gendered social mystery. Unseen, secret sexual encounters result in pregnancies that may easily be seen. But since a father-to-be does not physically carry the child, his paternity may remain a secret, while a mother-to-be is usually visibly marked as pregnant by sometime in the second trimester, if not before. The "mystery" of pregnancy is that while society can easily see the mother-to-be, the father-to-be must reveal himself if society is to see him as the father.

One indicator of the stark changes in attitudes toward women among VMI cadets between the beginning of the debate in 1989 and the admission of women in 1997 appears in the pages of the *Cadet*. A survey of the issues of the paper from the 1989–90 academic year, when the gender-integration debate began, shows women portrayed as objects of social and sexual pursuit. The *VMI Cadet* published numerous reports of mixers with "girls" from nearby women's colleges such as Sweet Briar, Mary Baldwin, the Southern Women's Seminary, and Randolph-Macon Women's College. One cadet's stream-of-consciousness thoughts about his quest for the right woman appeared under the headline,

"Gurls, Gurls, Gurls." Parodies depict women as focused on marriage (on finding the perfect man—"smart, kind, and ... in a good fraternity"—"to buy [their] Volvo station wagon") and more concerned with fashion and domestic pursuits than more academic ones ("taking the history of furniture ... will really help me when I become an interior designer"). Another parody imagines an all-female military college that would bring together women from five nearby women's colleges in which "we could stage cat fights between the girls, in which one merit would be given per clump of hair pulled." The paper also published a number of sexist cartoons: one portrayed a voluptuous, scantily clad woman in an advertisement for members of the "Old Corps" to subscribe to the paper to "Keep Abreast with the VMI Cadet," while others showed a coed VMI with the traditional sweat parties becoming aerobics workouts, feminine women being transformed into butch G.I. Janes, and interactions between male and female cadets fraught with ambiguity as to whether they could constitute harassment or fraternization. The sports section ran a story about a University of Arizona woman who wanted to play on that school's rugby team under the headline, "Macho Woman Takes the Rugby Pitch!"[44]

In contrast, issues of the *Cadet* from the 1997–98 academic year, the first year in which women were admitted, portray women as cadets and colleagues. In contrast to the unflattering article about the University of Arizona rugby player, the *Cadet* published a balanced, front-page October 1997 piece cowritten by a male cadet and a female exchange cadet, "Female Cadet to Tackle VMI Rugby Team." While the article led with the pronouncement that "The inevitable controversy between women and athletics has arrived," the writers later seemed to squelch this controversy with the reassurance that "despite what most people are thinking, she is not trying to make a statement. [Natasha] Miller is simply continuing a sport she enjoyed at Norwich University before she came to VMI." Miller is portrayed as a skilled player welcomed enthusiastically by her coach and fellow players. In addition, a series of first-person "From a Rat's Perspective" columns were published that fall, first anonymously and then under the byline of a female Rat, Jen Jolin. These columns seem to have had two purposes, giving female Rats such as Jolin a voice and demystifying their experience for the rest of the institute. Jolin noted the double-edged sword of gender stereotyping: "Visitor[s] to the Institute expect to see larger-than-life, 'Hua,' G.I. Janes. Nope, none of them here. I hate to break it the civilian world, but that's fiction. You'll find a female like that at VMI as soon as you find Forrest Gump in the Armed Forces. . . . On the other hand, there are those who expect us to be fragile little girls with bows in our hair, who skip down the stoop instead of strain. That's not happening either. The most frequently asked question of me is 'Are they being nice to you?' Hello! I didn't join a sorority when I signed the matriculation book." A week later, however, Jolin seemed troubled by the frequent "gender errors" she encountered as a cadet with short hair in military attire. Both civilians and brother Rats mistook her for a man, including one instance where an older woman barred her from the women's bathroom at a restaurant. In light of such incidents, Jolin argued that while she was "proud of VMI for not giving in by letting us keep our hair," she believed that the "women of VMI should be viewed as cadets, not scary butch-girls." Overall, the 1997-98 issues of the *VMI Cadet* seem much more professional and respectful in their portrayal of women in the midst of their integration into VMI than had been the case eight years earlier.[45]

The controversy over the admission of women to VMI can best be explained by Burke's contention that there is "the presence of a mystifying condition in social inequality."[46] Some women, perceiving themselves not on equal footing with men in terms of educational and professional opportunities, saw in the mysterious rituals and traditions of VMI the trappings of social knowledge and power—privileges these women felt that they were prevented from accessing based solely on gender stratification. But those who sought to defend VMI's system of social mystery saw in its rituals and traditions a way of bridging the divisions that, outside of VMI, would keep them socially stratified. However, for all their differences on the subject of whether women should be admitted to VMI, both sides in this conflict valued the VMI experience and its capacity to identify people who had been previously divided, with gender integrationists touting the identification of men and women and all-male traditionalists touting identification among men of varying racial, ethnic, and socioeconomic backgrounds. This contentious issue of bringing together people previously considered incongruous and thus kept separate under the old ruling order of division was not limited to the debate over gender integrating VMI, however. In 1995-96 (concurrent with the VMI debate) and again in 1999, a debate raged in Virginia's capital, Richmond, regarding the propriety of bringing together artistic representations of people previously considered incongruous and thus segregated, whites and blacks—and not just any whites and blacks, but white Confederates and black civil rights activists.

2

When Richmond Gained Perspective by Incongruity: Old South Tradition and New South Change in the Confederate Capital

> [O]ne of the unique aspects of my life is the juxtaposition of disparate events and people.
> —Arthur Ashe, *Portrait in Motion*

THE GOTHIC WALLS of the VMI barracks were not the only site of conflict between division and identification in the Virginia of the late 1990s. Virginia's capital, Richmond, also was riddled with not one but two such controversies during this period. Whereas VMI's conflict focused mainly on the shift from the segregation to the integration of the sexes, Richmond's controversies stemmed mainly from the shift from the segregation to the integration of the races. Richmonders debated the appropriateness of bringing together symbols of the Old South's order of division, in the form of depictions of Confederate leaders, with symbols of the New South's order of identification, in the form of representations of civil rights leaders. While the presence of these debates may, at first glance, seem indicative of the deep racial divide still present in the city's public and private lives, the juxtaposition of these previously incongruous symbols ultimately provided a venue in which Richmonders could identify with one another in their shared concern and reverence for the history of their city and their region.

Richmond is a place where the past looms large in the present, a city remembered even today as the capital of the former Confederate States of America. As an expert on Richmond's culture comments, "Richmond is known as a city obsessed with its past." One of the places in which the past most asserts its influence in present-day Richmond is Monument Avenue, which features statues of Confederate generals Robert E. Lee, J. E. B. Stuart, and Thomas J. "Stonewall" Jackson; Confederate President Jefferson Davis; Confederate oceanographer Matthew Fontaine Maury; and, joining them there in 1996, tennis champion, author, and social activist Arthur Ashe Jr. Monument Avenue "serves as a shrine" to the city's obsession with the past, infusing Richmond "with a mythology and demonstrat[ing] how history and perceptions of the past change, and how new meanings are created."[1] However, as fixated as Richmond is on its past, it is trying to revitalize itself by capitalizing on that history, as are many other cities. In 1999, therefore, as part of its Canal Walk redevelopment project, which sought to reenergize the city's economic and cultural climate, the Richmond Historic Riverfront Foundation (RHRF) installed on the city's floodwall a set of thirteen murals commemorating scenes from Richmond's history, including one featuring Lee. These juxtapositions of past and present—Monument Avenue and its Confederate statues with a contemporary African American and his likeness, and Lee and other historical images with the city's gleaming new redevelopment project—created or brought to the surface tension among Richmond-area residents who held seemingly incongruous perspectives on the city's past, especially the history of its involvement in the Civil War and its subsequent race relations.

The juxtaposition of these disparate images gave Richmonders the opportunity to gain what Kenneth Burke calls "perspective by incongruity." Some residents found it incongruous that a statue of a twentieth-century African American athlete, author, and activist would be placed on the same ground of tradition as that occupied by monuments to Confederate luminaries. And by the same token, other citizens found incongruous a mural featuring the likeness of a nineteenth-century slavery-defending Confederate general on ground being hailed as the latest symbol of the city's progress, the Canal Walk redevelopment area. When such terms, images, or symbols normally considered at odds with one another are placed side by side, dissonance results. And as the presence of the debates over the Ashe and Lee public art indicates, such dissonance manifests itself on a collective level as community conflict. In both of these controversies, an icon of the Southern tradition of division was juxtaposed with an icon of the Southern shift toward identification: Ashe, a symbol of change, was placed in the context of Monument Avenue, a symbol of tradition. Likewise, Lee, a symbol of tradition, was placed in the context of the Canal Walk, a symbol of change. Furthermore, the presence of these mirror-image debates within just a few years of one another in the same city can be seen as yet another level of juxtaposition in turn-of-the-century Richmond.

I will examine these two controversies through the lens of perspective by incongruity. These public debates and their resulting compromises offer evidence that previously "mutually exclusive" entities can indeed be "methodically merged" through their juxtaposition. The change of perspective that results from such juxtaposition, also known as the comic frame, ideally "should enable people *to be observers of themselves, while acting*. Its ultimate would not be *passiveness*, but *maximum consciousness*. One would 'transcend' himself by noting his own foibles."[2] Juxtaposing these previously segregated symbols of Southern tradition and change, of division and identification, allowed Richmonders to see these symbols and in some cases themselves in a new way, a perspective that allowed them to see through surface differences to a level of shared essences.

Burke elaborates the concept of "perspective by incongruity" in *Permanence and Change*, which "was written in the early days of the Great Depression, at a time when there was a general feeling that our traditional ways were headed for a tremendous change, maybe even a permanent collapse. It is such a book as authors in those days sometimes put together, to keep themselves from falling apart." Just as Burke was writing in a time of great upheaval, when the existing order seemed to be giving way to a new one, so too is the South of the late twentieth and early twenty-first centuries undergoing a similar shift in identity and values. Thus it is appropriate to look at Richmond's debates between tradition and change through the perspective of incongruity, a perspective that became clear to Burke just as he, like late-twentieth-century Richmond, was "finding himself divided."[3]

The most straightforward way of understanding perspective by incongruity is to think of it as the clashing together of two entities—words, images, objects, institutions, or ideas—that previously had not been brought together. Just as the physical forces of centrifugal motion and centripetal motion may move simultaneously in opposite directions, away from and toward a center, yet together cause their common system to move, so too may social forces be understood as concurrently working against and with one another. In the Richmond debates, some forces advocated tradition (upholding Confederate symbols), while others opposed it (questioning the sanctity of those Confederate symbols).[4]

Perspective by incongruity can also be thought of in terms of violating established pieties that codify society's "sense of what properly goes with what." For example, one would violate the piety, or sense of propriety, of a word by using it in a context other than that in which it is normally used. Applying this way of thinking about perspective by incongruity to the Richmond debates, we see that some citizens objected to placing the Ashe statue on Monument Avenue because they felt that a statue of a twentieth-century African American athlete would not "go with" the other monuments, all of which depict nineteenth-century Confederate leaders. One objector likened putting a statue of Ashe on Monument Avenue to placing a statue of Babe Ruth adjacent to the Lincoln Memorial.[5] Others stated that their opposition to the Ashe statue on Monument Avenue stemmed from the juxtaposition of such disparate styles of sculpture, claiming that it would not be aesthetically pleasing to have a contemporary-style statue by a self-selected local artist in the presence of more traditional sculptures that were the product of international design competitions. Still others argued that to place Ashe's statue on Monument Avenue would give credence to the characterization of the Confederate leaders as heroes, that Ashe was too good a man to be placed among the defenders of slavery. Similarly, in the Lee mural controversy, some Richmonders believed that the likeness of Lee should not be juxtaposed with the likenesses of what were to them more honorable images from the city's past; others thought that the image of Lee, a symbol of the

Old South, did not fit in with the Canal Walk redevelopment, a symbol of Richmond's place in the New South.

In each of these instances, new and old, change and tradition, progress and status quo can be perceived only in relation to one another. Burke observes that Nietzsche's "subject-matter was specifically that of reorientation (transvaluation of *all* values)—yet in facing the *problematical new* he spontaneously felt as a poet that he could glorify such a concern only by utilizing the *unquestioned old*."[6] To create new pieties, old pieties must first be recognized; only then can they be violated. Thus, the desire to place a statue of Ashe on Monument Avenue meant that those wanting to do so acknowledged the established sense of what belonged there.

In seeking to understand perspective by incongruity, it is also important to consider the element of purpose behind juxtaposing seemingly incongruous entities. For example, in the planned incongruity achieved by juxtaposing Ashe with the Confederates on Monument Avenue, these men who seemingly had nothing in common beyond their shared connection to Richmond were revealed to share essences such as honor, vision, and commitment to their respective causes. The purposeful juxtaposition of a descendant of slaves with defenders of slavery served to unite them all, in some eyes, under the banner "Virginia heroes," revealing not only their differences but also, perhaps unexpectedly, their common attributes. Looking again to the Richmond debates, we observe perhaps unexpected alignments of friends and foes. In the Ashe statue debate, for example, both those who had utmost respect for Ashe and those who had extreme respect for the Confederates opposed placing the statue on Monument Avenue; though their motivations differed enormously, they shared a common goal. In the Lee mural controversy, two African American city council members, whom many members of the African American community had expected to support the removal of Lee's image, supported reintroducing Lee into the collection of murals, neutrally acknowledging that Lee was part of Richmond's history. Perhaps a more vivid and unexpected example of such realigned allegiances came in the person of L. Douglas Wilder, who served as Virginia's governor (and the first African American elected governor in the United States) from 1990 to 1994 and in 2005 was elected mayor of his native Richmond. At the Canal Walk dedication ceremonies, Wilder, who had strongly supported the addition of the Ashe statue to Monument Avenue, stood to salute the Confederate flags displayed by some of those protesting the Lee mural's removal. And African American civil rights lawyer Oliver Hill, who worked to desegregate Virginia's schools, expressed his hope that "in a spirit of reconciliation and forgiveness," opponents of Lee the general would embrace the achievements of Lee the educator. To overcome the entrenched Southern pieties regarding which symbols belong together and which people belong together, turn-of-the-century Richmonders needed to recognize that "planned incongruity should be deliberately cultivated for the purpose of experimentally wrenching apart all those molecular combinations of adjective and noun, substantive and verb, which still remain with us."[7]

Just as the debates regarding the Ashe statue and the Lee mural center on the tension inherent in juxtaposing the seemingly incongruous, so too is the recounting of Richmond's history marked by incongruity among the various accounts of its race relations. Depending on which version one reads, one may get the impression that Richmond was more or less progressive than other Virginia localities when it came to the integration of its schools, neighborhoods, and other public institutions. In *Richmond: The Story of a City*, first published in 1976 and revised and republished in 1990, former Richmond newspaper editor Virginius Dabney articulates his sanguine perspective on the city's racial integration and reconciliation. In contrast, Robert A. Pratt, in his 1992 study, *The Color of Their Skin: Education and Race in Richmond, Virginia, 1954–89*, offers a significantly less satisfied account of the nature and pace of Richmond's racial desegregation efforts.

From Dabney's perspective, the fact that Richmond kept its schools open in the wake of *Brown v. Board of Education* while other schools in Virginia closed in "massive resistance" to court-mandated integration signifies that the city was more progressive than other localities: "In contrast to schools [elsewhere in Virginia], Richmond's schools were kept open. They were integrated gradually at first and then more rapidly." But from Pratt's vantage point, the same phenomenon was "passive resistance": "As Virginia's massive resistance lay dying, Richmond's *passive* resistance was just being conceived. . . . [T]he public schools in Richmond remained open throughout the state's massive resistance campaign—open, but segregated. . . . Richmond's officials . . . while equally committed to maintaining segregated schools, were considerably less conspicuous in the pursuit of their objectives."[8] These two accounts provide disparate versions of the same events. In Dabney's view, school integration in Richmond was slow but sure, but from Pratt's perspective, Richmond officials were deliberate in their slowness, delaying progress as a way of protesting the mandated changes.

Integration was not just an issue affecting school systems, however. If integration of the races was to be complete, then equal opportunities would need to exist to all in aspects of life—from seating on buses and in restaurants to use of public water fountains and restrooms and opportunities for employment and recreation. From Dabney's more satisfied outlook, the "great majority of whites were not happy over the rapid advance of the blacks into areas formerly closed to them, but they realized that a new day was coming and they did not believe in defying the courts. Integration went steadily forward, so much that the liberal Washington *Post* published an article in 1962 . . . bearing the headline 'Richmond Quietly Leads Way in Race Relations.'" From Pratt's more questioning perspective, however, the situation was less rosy: "Whites feared that if blacks could demonstrate that they could excel in any field of endeavor if given opportunities equal to those whites received, then they would prove once and for all that their exclusion from white society was based, not on their innate racial inferiority, but on whites' ingrained racial prejudice."[9]

These two authors' views of Richmond as it moved into the late twentieth century are equally divergent. With the organization "in the early 1980s . . . of Richmond Renaissance," Dabney observes, a "definite effort was made to alleviate interracial feeling in the city and to bring the two groups together." "Richmonders," concludes Dabney, "are engaged no longer in fighting the Civil War again." In contrast, Pratt argues that little progress occurred in Richmond's racial integration in the decades after *Brown v. Board of Education*: "One finds that the scenario has changed very little: Richmond's public schools, as of [1992], are 88 percent black. . . . It is perhaps cruelly ironic that steps designed to bring the races closer together succeeded only in driving them further apart" by instigating "white flight" to the suburbs.[10] Juxtaposing these two quite incongruous readings of Richmond's history of racial integration affords enhanced insights into the state of race relations there. These two incongruous historical accounts parallel the equally incongruous accounts of the Civil War and contemporary race relations that are at issue in the debates considered here.

In the summer of 1992, Richmond sculptor Paul DiPasquale was asked to take a group of children, including his own, to an appearance by Ashe at a tennis clinic. DiPasquale was inspired by the way the accomplished and renowned Ashe interacted so humbly and meaningfully with the young people. DiPasquale recalled being so impressed that he "couldn't believe this guy was walking on the Earth." Later that year, DiPasquale contacted Ashe about the possibility of creating a likeness of him to be displayed in Richmond. Ashe agreed to have DiPasquale create a sculpture with the caveat that it be displayed in the context of the proposed Hard Road to Glory Hall of Fame, inspired by Ashe's series of books tracing the history of African Americans in sport. According to DiPasquale, Ashe also stipulated that he be portrayed with children, wearing a sweat suit with untied tennis shoes (as was his practice when not on the court), and emphasizing books over tennis. The two planned to meet in early 1993 to continue their discussions of the project. Ashe promised to send DiPasquale some recent photographs because Ashe wanted the sculptor to show him as he was at that time in his life. However, on February 6, 1993, Ashe succumbed to AIDS (contracted years earlier through a blood transfusion while undergoing heart bypass surgery). Just days later, Jeanne Moutoussamy-Ashe sent DiPasquale the photographs her late husband had planned to send. Inspired by these photographs and by Ashe's memorial service, DiPasquale rendered the first sketch of what would become his sculpted tribute.[11]

An artist's vision, however, is not enough to see a piece of public art through

Old South Tradition and New South Change in Richmond   55

Sculptor Paul DiPasquale's sculpture of Arthur Ashe at the intersection of Monument Avenue and Roseneath Road. Photograph by the author.

to completion. Also necessary are funding for the labor and materials as well as a public space for its display. While DiPasquale used some of his own money to get the project under way, he knew he would need more, so he approached possible financial backers. In December 1993, Virginia Heroes, a foundation established in conjunction with Ashe to provide mentors to Virginia youth, made a commitment to raise funds for the sculpture. To spearhead the fund-raising efforts, the organization signed on Thomas Chewning, a longtime friend of Ashe's and fellow tennis player who was now chief financial officer of Dominion Resources, a Richmond-based energy corporation. The sculpture was to be donated to the City of Richmond in the hope that it would one day stand on the grounds of the proposed Hard Road to Glory Hall of Fame. But because the Hall of Fame remained years away from construction (and as of 2007 did not yet exist), a "temporary" display location was needed. Thus, Virginia Heroes, the planning commission, and the Urban Design Committee began site searches. In the end, the three most discussed possibilities were Byrd Park, to whose tennis courts Ashe had been denied access during the segregated days of his youth; downtown Richmond, where space was available for a park either at the site of two abandoned department stores or at the historic armory; and Monument Avenue.[12]

The Arthur Ashe statue and its upscale neighborhood. Photograph by the author.

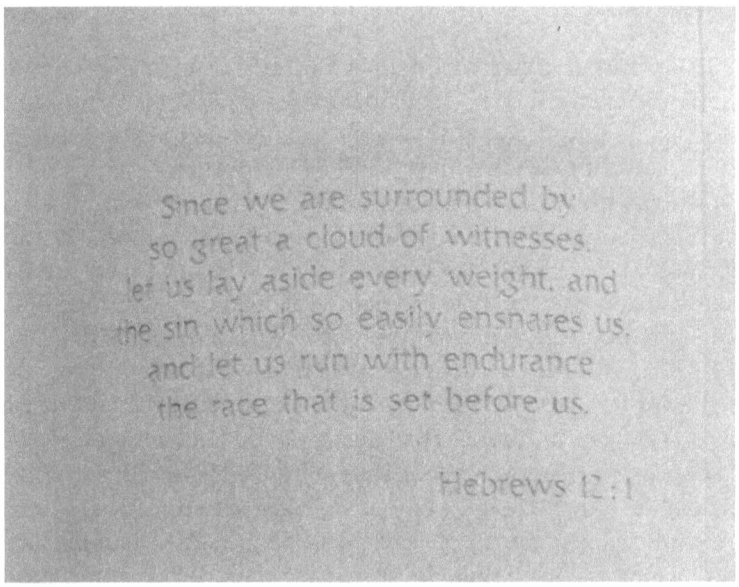

The inscription on the pedestal of the Arthur Ashe statue. Photograph by the author.

Early on, Wilder announced his support for the Monument Avenue site, stating in December 1994 that placing the statue there would send "a transcending message." State Senator Benjamin Lambert, an African American Democrat from Richmond and a member of the Virginia Heroes site selection committee, also backed the Monument Avenue location, arguing that "it makes the right statement."[13] Wilder and Lambert are representative of the group of people who supported placing Ashe's statue on Monument Avenue precisely because it would juxtapose aspects of Richmond's history heretofore kept divided—its Confederate history and its African American heritage. In short, supporters of displaying the Ashe statue on Monument Avenue wanted it there as a step toward identifying or bringing together two strands of Richmond's identity that had long been viewed as incongruous or divided. If statues of such seemingly disparate entities as Arthur Ashe and the leaders of the Confederacy could stand together on Monument Avenue, went the thinking, perhaps Richmonders of the present and future, regardless of race and other aspects of their identity, could also learn to stand together.

However, other African American community leaders, including Mayor Leonidas Young (also pastor of Fourth Street Baptist Church) and editor Ray Boone of the *Richmond Free Press*, an African American weekly, believed, at least initially, that Monument Avenue was not good enough for Ashe. In Boone's words, Ashe "deserves better": placing his statue on Monument Avenue "would be giving credence to the false proposition that these were heroes."[14] Young and Boone represent the people who see Monument Avenue not as a place of honor but rather as a place of dishonor because of its purpose as a shrine to the Confederacy, to people who fought to keep African Americans enslaved. In a sense, this argument promotes a continued division of Richmond on the basis of race. However, the difference in this case is that African Americans were now choosing to keep themselves separate rather than being forced into separateness by slavery, Jim Crow laws, and other such institutions of division. Just as white Richmonders had an opportunity to choose their heroes (Confederates) and where to honor them (Monument Avenue), so too could contemporary African Americans choose their hero (Ashe) and where to honor him (someplace *other* than Monument Avenue). Thus, African American leaders such as Young and Boone were seeking for their community the right to have the same experience as white Richmonders of previous decades by creating a distinctive community identity and legacy—on their own terms, in their own space. By seeking to keep Ashe separate from the Confederates of Monument Avenue, these leaders were in a sense choosing to keep Richmond's African American heritage, identity, and community separate from the Confederate-oriented heritage, identity, and community espoused by many white Richmonders, past and present. But as has often been the case with historically subjugated groups, a claim to separateness or division can be a step toward creating intracommunity strength. In other words,

The Jefferson Davis Monument on Monument Avenue. Photograph by the author.

The Stonewall Jackson Monument on Monument Avenue. Photograph by the author.

The Robert E. Lee Monument on Monument Avenue. Photograph by the author.

by keeping the Ashe statue off Monument Avenue, African American leaders sought to unite or identify their community around a new symbol in a new context. Placing Ashe in the context of the Confederates on Monument Avenue was not necessary to give Ashe or themselves legitimacy, honor, or respect. Rather, by keeping their community hero symbol separate, they could choose the terms of their identity rather than being defined in reference to hero symbols and a place chosen by others—specifically, white Richmonders of the city's past.

Still others disapproved of the Ashe statue being placed on Monument Avenue because they considered it an affront to what R. Lee Collins, president of the Heritage Preservation Association, called the "hallowed ground" of Monument Avenue. Collins and others, including members of the Sons of Confederate Veterans (SCV), argued that the city should find another location for the Ashe statue to "pay the proper tribute to a great athlete without violating the historic sensibilities of Richmond's Confederate-American population." Placing Ashe on Monument Avenue generated controversy in large part because doing so would place Confederates, whom many African Americans and others perceive to have been defenders of slavery, side by side with Ashe, an African American defender of human rights. This juxtaposition disturbed the sensibilities of many Richmonders who revered the Confederates as well as those who revered Ashe because it brought together entities that had for years been segregated, first by law

The Matthew Fontaine Maury Monument on Monument Avenue. Photograph by the author.

The J. E. B. Stuart Monument on Monument Avenue. Photograph by the author.

and later in lingering attitudes and practices. For others, however, this juxtaposition was seen not as disturbing but rather as reassuring in its symbolic potential for "suggesting that Richmond has moved on from its racist past."[15]

The juxtaposition of Ashe with the Confederates was not the only aspect of the Monument Avenue location to spark controversy, however. Some in Richmond's artistic circles were disturbed by the idea that DiPasquale's statue to the city would be placed on Monument Avenue without any sort of competition among artists for that privilege. Beverly Reynolds, a longtime local gallery owner, organized Citizens for Excellence in Public Art (CEPA), a group whose members believed that DiPasquale's rendering of Ashe neither matched the artistic quality of the other statues on the avenue nor did Ashe justice. CEPA advocated holding an international competition for another, permanent statue of Ashe to be placed on Monument Avenue. However, CEPA's proposal to the city council encountered resistance, in part because the majority African American council members thought, according to Mayor Young, that the "appearance of your group is that it's not inclusive."[16] Some council members may have believed that CEPA's aesthetic objections simply masked racial ones. Nonetheless, the juxtaposition of nineteenth- and early-twentieth-century statues with a late-twentieth-century piece—which some observers characterized as resembling a saguaro cactus or a man being held up at gunpoint and which others believed to be too small—created an additional layer of controversy.

Before the statue's location was finalized, the appropriateness of placing a statue of a twentieth-century African American best known for his athletic pursuits alongside statues of nineteenth-century "Confederate Americans" best known for their martial pursuits was the principal point of contention. When the site was selected, the issue shifted to aesthetics. Common to both strands of the debate over the Ashe statue (as well as the debate over the Lee mural) was a concern that the citizens' voices be considered when constituting the community's identity through the use of public space. The juxtaposition of these seemingly incongruous symbols enabled Richmond to see itself from a new perspective.

The debate over DiPasquale's statue of Ashe initially centered on location. When the various committees chose Monument Avenue as the most favored site, a public debate erupted because the site seemed to emphasize the disparities between Ashe and the Confederates: Ashe was widely known as a defender of human rights (as in his work to raise awareness of apartheid in South Africa) and as someone who broke racial barriers in the world of tennis whites, whereas the Confederates were generally seen as defenders of slavery and thus as people who wanted to maintain racial barriers. In addition, the idea of placing Ashe's statue on Monument Avenue brought to light the fact that, years after court-mandated integration, Richmond's most prestigious address remained segregated; up until 1996, all five of the avenue's monumental residents were Confederates. The issue brought back to the surface memories of segregation and emphasized the fact that it was not yet solely a phenomenon of the past. After placement was finalized, however, residents began to see how the juxtaposition of the Ashe statue with the Confederate statues created the possibility of new symbolism for Monument Avenue and Richmond.

There long existed a sense, particularly among the people of the South and inculcated through years of slavery and segregation, that whites belonged with whites and blacks belonged with blacks—and most certainly that whites and blacks did not properly belong together. The continued existence of "white churches" and "black churches" indicates that this attitude is not entirely one of the past, nor is it limited to displays of public art in the present. For all that the Civil War, Reconstruction, and the courts may have done (or attempted to do) to change this sense of what (or who) properly goes with what (or whom), the old piety of the separation of the races has persisted in many avenues of Southern (and American) life. Many progressive Richmonders saw the idea of placing a statue of Ashe alongside the Confederate statues of Monument Avenue as a way to change people's sense of what goes with what, to expand the sense of where it is appropriate and acceptable for African Americans to be in the life of the community. In the view of "Thelma Brooks, a 66-year-old from the East End who has vivid memories of segregation" and who attended the church at which Young served as pastor, "to deny Ashe a spot on Monument would mean 'they're still keeping you back, where they want to keep you.'" Likewise, "backing off the Monument Avenue plan . . . would sanction a 'separate but equal' policy for black and white heroes," according to Arthur Ashe's brother, Johnnie, and others.[17] In this view, blocking the Ashe statue's entrance to Monument Avenue would have been akin to preventing African Americans from walking or driving down that or any other Richmond street.

Thus, when Moutoussamy-Ashe and others suggested that Monument Avenue might not be the most appropriate place for the Ashe statue and that the city should revisit Arthur Ashe's original intention that the monument be featured at the yet-to-be-built African American sports hall of fame, some residents believed the pieties of segregation might be enforced once again. Having experienced the white establishment's delaying tactics throughout the years of the civil rights movement (as in Martin Luther King Jr.'s references to African Americans' years of waiting for equality in his "Letter from Birmingham Jail"), it made sense that African Americans feared that a plan to delay putting a statue of Ashe or another African American on Monument Avenue was a way to avoid ever placing such a statue there. Young recognized the presence of this sentiment in the community when he stated, "A number of individuals feared this (possible delay) was a move to keep Arthur Ashe off Monument Avenue." Further, as African American city council member Viola Baskerville argued, "To say a monument of this significance should be relegated to a sports hall of fame is to put Arthur back in the milieu he transcended." Planning commission member Terone B. Green, also an

African American, echoed the statement, describing himself as "offended that people think of the monument as not good enough for Monument Avenue but acceptable for an African-American Sports Hall of Fame."[18]

If an African American's statue could stand beside those of Confederates on Richmond's most honored street, then the symbolic sphere of African Americans' power and influence in Richmond would be significantly expanded. The statue constituted "the passion of an array of citizens—black and white, old and young—who argued that a street reserved for Civil War heroes had no place in modern Richmond." Consequently, the century-old piety of consecrating Monument Avenue only to Confederate heroes was set aside in favor of honoring heroes of various eras and allegiances there. As newspaper writer Margaret Edds observed, "For many, the placement of Ashe on a leafy boulevard long dedicated to white southerners who championed the lost cause of slavery and disunion is a seismic event. . . . It will be Richmond's, and perhaps Virginia's, visual confirmation that the era by which many outsiders identify the city and the state is dead."[19] Placing a monument to Ashe alongside memorials to white Confederates effectively ended Richmond's piety of venerating only Lost Cause saints with icons in its utmost shrine to heroes.

Once it was determined that Confederate-only Monument Avenue would change, people began to think more about how these statues would affect one another's meanings through their juxtaposition. On one level, just discussing the possibility of situating Ashe on the avenue exposed conflicts that had long been festering in the city. As Sylvester "Tee" Turner, the African American pastor of the New Jerusalem Missionary Baptist Church, observed, "The strife this monument has revealed needs to be ended. Arthur Ashe did that, he healed the (racial) rift." But at first Mayor Young "viewed the philosophical gap between Ashe and the currently honored individuals as too wide to justify their sharing space." This gap in philosophies brought before Richmonders' eyes the "racial rift" that existed within and among themselves. When "legions of city residents urged council members to place Ashe's statue among the white Confederate heroes," they voiced what white attorney and vice mayor John Conrad also articulated on behalf of the city council: "We need to reconcile Richmond's history with its future." Richmond's history as capital of the Confederacy makes the city distinctive and draws many tourists, but Richmonders also had to find a way to promote harmony among themselves so that they could ensure a stable future for the city, economically and otherwise. Placing a statue of Ashe, a symbol of Richmond's twentieth-century achievements, alongside statues of Confederate leaders, symbols of Richmond's nineteenth-century attainments, inspired writer Robert Little to note on the day of the groundbreaking, "Tuesday on Monument Avenue, Richmond looked more like a city of the New South. And still, it promised to remember the old days."[20] This juxtaposition of New South and Old South, though controversial at first, seemed to kindle confidence that the stated need to "reconcile Richmond's history with its future" could indeed be met—first through symbols and later through the dialogue those symbols sparked.

Indeed, the idea of situating a statue of Ashe alongside the Confederate statues on Monument Avenue was an exercise in "planned incongruity," designed specifically to "reconcile Richmond's history with its future." These words about reconciling past and future were articulated in the context of introducing the city council resolution to place Ashe on the avenue. Among the earliest and most vocal champions of the Ashe statue's eventual location on Monument Avenue was former governor Wilder, paraphrased by the Associated Press as stating, "Placing Ashe . . . on the city's most symbolic and arguably its most beautiful street is an important counterpoint to Richmond's legacy of slavery and segregation." While Young characterized Monument Avenue as "definitely representative" of "all the racial barriers [that] have not been broken down in the city," a white councilman, Timothy Kaine (who subsequently served as Richmond's mayor from 1998 to 2000 and was elected Virginia's governor in 2005), was paraphrased as saying that "a statue of a black American would symbolize a new dawn in the capital of the Confederacy." This juxtaposition created meaning beyond what either the statue or Monument Avenue could have conveyed in itself: together, the two entities created a symbol of a new beginning in Richmond's race relations. Situating the Ashe statue on Monument Avenue "says we have reached a new era in social affairs. It makes a positive statement about how people are able to get along" (according to Young), "shows that the old Confederacy is changing over time" (in the words of city manager Robert Bobb), and proves that "Richmond has finally turned a page in history" (as Johnnie Ashe put it).[21] Only when the symbols of Monument Avenue and Arthur Ashe were placed side by side, seemingly incongruous, could this new perspective be realized.

Paradoxically, when such seemingly incompatible entities as Ashe and the Confederate leaders were brought together, their previously unseen commonalities became more apparent. Rather than seeing only external differences such as race or citizenship, perspective by incongruity allows us to "hope that Monument Avenue at last can be identified with the internal strengths of the individuals honored there." Monument Avenue has long been considered a pantheon for heroes. With the addition of Ashe, the common identity of all those memorialized there as heroes has been emphasized. Addressing whether it was appropriate for Ashe to be on the avenue, DiPasquale asked, "Isn't it for monuments? Isn't it for heroes? No one questions that Arthur Ashe was a hero." Likewise, Johnnie Ashe declared at the unveiling, "Arthur Ashe Jr. is a true Virginia Hero, and he belongs." Indeed, advocates of placing the statue on Monument Avenue and of the positive symbolism thereby gained for Richmond put the idea of "belonging" at the crux of the matter. In what were perhaps the most cited words from the dedication ceremony, Wilder affirmed, "Monument Avenue is now an avenue for all people. . . . Today, I feel more pride and relevance in being here on

Monument Avenue than I have at any time in my life."[22] Situating Ashe on the avenue created a powerful symbol of belonging, especially for African Americans in Richmond. Even the most powerful of Virginians, the commonwealth's first elected African American governor, implied that he had previously felt irrelevant on Monument Avenue. But Ashe's statue made Wilder feel that he belonged there. Perhaps the most sacrosanct bastion of segregation in all of Richmond had finally been integrated, not by military force but by the powerful force of symbolism.

On the other side of the debate, as Wilder acknowledged at the statue's groundbreaking, "Some say Arthur Ashe doesn't deserve to be here, some say he deserves better." And as the Associated Press had already noted, the mayor and city council had received "complaints from black and white residents that Ashe would be out of place" on Monument Avenue, leading to a reconsideration of the site.[23] The symbolic objections to situating the Ashe statue on Monument Avenue fell into two basic categories: arguments that Ashe was too good to be placed alongside the Confederates, and arguments that the avenue's Confederate purity would be defiled by including a mere athlete alongside generals and statesmen. Those in the first camp found the proposed location incongruous because they did not see the Confederates as true heroes but believed that placing Ashe alongside those men would give credence to the long-held contention that defenders of slavery were indeed heroes. Those in the second camp saw Monument Avenue as dedicated to honoring the lives of Confederate heroes; including a twentieth-century man unrelated to the Confederacy in that setting would take away from the reverence that went with reserving a particular place of honor for the Confederacy's leaders. Both groups of Richmonders who argued against placing the Ashe statue on Monument Avenue on symbolic grounds did so because they viewed Ashe and the Confederates as incongruous, though for very different reasons.

Some of those who argued that the Ashe statue should not be placed on Monument Avenue did so out of deep respect and admiration for Ashe and his accomplishments, which they saw as inexorably incongruous with the actions of a group of men who had fought to maintain racial barriers and deny equal rights to African Americans. According to Arrelius D. Pleasant, a Church Hill resident and parishioner at Mayor Young's Fourth Baptist Church, "Arthur Ashe doesn't belong with those racists." As Little reported in the *Norfolk Virginian-Pilot*, "Some blacks said [Ashe] was too great a man to stand with the generals who fought for racism and separation." While some Richmonders, searching for some common bonds that would tie Ashe and the Confederates together, emphasized that all were "Virginia heroes," others, as Richmond resident Robert H. Lamb expressed, thought it was clearly "a flight of fancy . . . to suggest that Arthur Ashe viewed the Confederate heroes on Monument Avenue as kindred spirits." Another area resident, Medical College of Virginia graduate student Matthew

Craig, more bluntly articulated the difference between Ashe and the Confederates when he stated that Ashe was "a champion. Don't put him on a street full of losers. These guys can't win a war." And while not voicing her judgment of the Confederates, Moutoussamy-Ashe explained her stance against locating the statue on Monument Avenue, a stance she grounded in her deep respect and admiration for her late husband: "I have always felt that in all this controversy, the spirit that Arthur gave Richmond has been overlooked. I am afraid that a statue of Arthur Ashe on Monument Avenue honors Richmond, Virginia, more than it does its son, his legacy, and his life's work."[24] In Moutoussamy-Ashe's opinion, placing Ashe on the avenue to make a statement or send a transcending message honored Richmond's desired image as a racially reconciled city more than it honored Ashe's achievements. Those in this strand of the opposition shared a belief that Ashe transcended the personalities of the Confederates, the pieties of Monument Avenue, and the politics surrounding his placement there.

As Edds and Little observed, "Still others said Ashe would be incompatible with the Confederates." In the words of white *Richmond Times-Dispatch* columnist Ray McCallister, "Monument Avenue is far from the ideal spot for this statue. Arthur Ashe has no more business with Confederate heroes than Ulysses Grant." Richard Hines, an SCV member from Alexandria, stated, "The intent of the placement of the statue was to debunk our heritage." Hines and others like him clearly would have agreed that placing Ashe alongside the Confederates was an exercise in "planned incongruity" but would have done so from a paranoid point of view, seeing such juxtapositions as purposeful assaults intended to obliterate all Confederate commemorations. Adjacent to the statue dedication festivities, "men in suits and skinheads in T-shirts [held] Confederate flags and placards filled with overblown rhetoric [such as] 'STATUE LOCATION IS A HATE CRIME,' 'HERITAGE DESECRATION IS NOT A CIVIL RIGHT,' and 'CULTURAL BIGOTS DESTROY SOUTHERN HERITAGE.' . . . Another sign likened the monument to 'cultural genocide.'" For those displaying these messages, situating Ashe alongside the Confederates deeply offended their "sense of what properly goes with what." To place a non-Confederate's likeness—and an African American's at that—alongside memorials to revered Confederate heroes was not merely distasteful but was an act of war, an invitation to fight again on behalf of the Lost Cause. Former Ku Klux Klan leader David Duke of Louisiana stated in an appearance in Richmond three years after the Ashe controversy, in support of restoring the Lee mural to the city's Canal Walk, that he "chose the Arthur Ashe statue as the venue for his news conference 'to show the hypocrisy here.' He said it is unfair that 'we have to put up with a sports star on an avenue of Confederate heroes.' [City council member Sa'ad] El-Amin and his backers will not be satisfied until all those monuments are removed, Duke said."[25] And so the Confederate battle flag was once again unfurled as the defenders of Confederate heritage marched into the fight against those they perceived as trying desecrate or destroy their heritage, one monument at a time.

Those opposing the placement of Ashe amid the Confederates on the grounds that doing so would be anachronous offered less bombast and more tact than did Duke. Edward J. Willis III, a Chesterfield County businessman, argued before the Commission of Architectural Review's board of appeals that placing the Ashe statue on Monument Avenue "would historically fracture the identity of the neighborhood." Willis eventually attempted to file suit against the city in Richmond Circuit Court, claiming "that the monument site is within The Old and Historic District of Monument Avenue and is at an important location within the city's second line of defense during the Civil War. He says the city is failing to protect historic property. He also says the modern statue violates city code, undermines preservation and will harm tourism." An elderly Daughters of the American Revolution member, interviewed on the street by a reporter, "admired Ashe [but did not] see a statue to him in keeping with the theme of Monument Avenue. 'Our world has changed,' said her husband, who believes the tall pedestal and the stone wall around it were designed to thwart vandals. 'This is not part of our world,' the 75-year-old woman said." Another articulation of the anachronistic argument came from Edward Smith, director of the American studies program at American University in nearby Washington, D.C. (and an African American): "What I find most distasteful and disrespectful about the Ashe Memorial is that he is positioned so that his back faces the other monuments.... If his location on that street was for the expressed purpose of making the avenue more inclusive, then why is he facing in the opposite direction, thereby rejecting the presence of those who came before him?"[26]

While many Richmonders argued about the symbolic appropriateness of placing the Ashe statue on Monument Avenue, others questioned or defended the location based on aesthetic considerations. As Edds reported, "Art critics in Virginia's capitol [sic] have quietly mounted an effort to do what Confederate aficionados last summer could not: delay the placement of a statue of tennis great Arthur Ashe on Monument Avenue. Unlike last summer, however ... the issue is not location, but the statue itself." This strand of the debate concerned whether DiPasquale's sculpture was the most *appropriate* rendering of Ashe to be placed amid the avenue's existing monuments. Members of the general public, even those who prefaced their critiques with, "I'm not an art expert, but ...," commented that the statue was "not majestic enough. It is too small for its base. And despite improvements, it continues to look like a giant trophy.... Or a man being held up.... Or a saguaro cactus." The members of the city's artistic community who formed CEPA (which one columnist characterized as "a group of artistic snobs") circulated a petition and raised funds in support of an international competition to select a permanent Ashe monument for the avenue. Those who believed DiPasquale's statue conformed to Ashe's final wishes and consequently best captured the essence of how Ashe wanted to be remembered in his hometown challenged CEPA's arguments. Once again, incongruity lay at the heart of the controversy, with CEPA supporters emphasizing the aesthetic incongruity between DiPasquale's statue and the existing monuments and with dissenters attempting to trump CEPA's aesthetic concerns with appeals to Ashe's original intent.[27]

In the preamble to its petition in favor of holding an international competition, CEPA members argued, "For all the reasons Arthur Ashe should be honored, he should be honored with a statue that will be worthy of him and a work of which the city and its citizens can be proud. We therefore urge the City Council . . . to conduct an international competition among artists designed to produce a world-class monument to Arthur Ashe." One Richmonder, Sally Todd, characterized DiPasquale's statue as "commonplace and undistinguished. 'We've had world-class sculptors for all the other statues on Monument Avenue,' she said, 'so why should we have less than the best for one of Richmond's distinguished citizens?'" A white Monument Avenue resident, Mary Lou Carr, argued, "The statue should not be in casual dress or modern style." McCallister paraphrased the aesthetic opposition: "Don't let [DiPasquale] put his lifeless work on Monument Avenue. Works of majesty belong there, not stick figures with upraised arms. The [Jefferson] Davis statue may not be much, but at least it doesn't look like a deodorant commercial." In this view, a statue of Ashe in a sweat suit and tennis shoes and talking with children did not properly fit in with the existing Confederate statues, all of which were "majestically" arrayed in more formal garb and riding horses or contemplating the globe (in the case of Maury). This perception of incongruity—in terms of how the statues were clothed, in which activities they were depicted engaging, and how the sculptures were selected—can be explained by another of Burke's concepts, social mystery.[28]

Both sides of this aesthetic argument indicated the presence of perceptions of class division, not only between those depicted in the statues but also between those who disagreed about whether Ashe's clothing mattered. Regarding the perception of class division or incongruity between Ashe and the Confederates, CEPA members and other aesthetic opponents seemed to advocate having Ashe portrayed in such a way as to diminish the perception of class division between him and the Confederates. They argued that portraying Ashe in such a casual manner did not work to equalize people's perceptions of Ashe and the Confederates but rather reinforced certain factions' contention that Ashe was not good enough, that his accomplishments as an athlete were not significant enough, to merit placement alongside the more "majestic," less "commonplace" renderings of the Confederates. Thus, proponents of this view advocated portraying Ashe more formally, both in dress and in mode of sculpture, to send the message that Ashe was just as deserving of a place of honor on Monument Avenue as were the Confederates.

But CEPA's aims to more adequately honor Ashe were undermined by its inattention to racial matters. However well intentioned CEPA's efforts on behalf of a statue more "worthy" of Ashe may have been, the group's mostly white racial composition was central to its failure. In response to charges from the majority African American city council that CEPA was composed almost entirely of whites—and the implication that the group might have had a hidden, racially motivated agenda—CEPA responded that its concerns transcended race. As Reynolds noted in an opinion column published after CEPA's efforts had been derailed, "It was not until we reached the City Council for final approval that race entered into the effort.... This issue was never about race but about how to establish a process to ensure that this first Monument Avenue statue to an African-American be artistically and conceptually excellent—that it be more than just a symbol, that it be a great work of art also." Aesthetic opponents to DiPasquale's rendering of Ashe situated themselves not as *against* a statue of Ashe but rather as *for* a higher-quality depiction of him: "We had only one agenda: to honor a great African-American with a great monument." CEPA members did not want just any statue of Ashe; so that the Ashe statue would fit in and carry symbolic influence equal to that of the other statues, they wanted his statue to equal theirs in formality and artistic merit.[29]

Other opponents of DiPasquale's sculpture were concerned about aesthetic accuracy—whether DiPasquale's rendering was congruous with the essence of who Arthur Ashe was. Some observers found DiPasquale's depiction less than satisfactory in its portrayal of Ashe's physical condition. As one caller to the *Richmond Times-Dispatch*'s reader feedback phone line observed, "The statue looks like ET in glasses. It's not a very good likeness of Arthur Ashe." Another opined that "the informality and the depiction of Ashe as he looked near the end of his life [when he was suffering the effects of AIDS] create a less-than-dignified impression." One member of the Commission of Architectural Review, Douglas Harnesberger, advocated a middle ground between Ashe at the end of his life and Ashe in top condition.[30] These concerns seem to stem from many people's discomfort at seeing the gaunt figure of a man dying from AIDS juxtaposed with the more robust figures of the Confederate generals on their trusty steeds or the sculpture's juxtaposition of a sickly Ashe with the four healthy children.

Another possible interpretation of these expressions of uneasiness at seeing an AIDS-stricken Ashe immortalized in bronze is that the statue seemed incongruous with the widespread image of Ashe as a champion athlete in top physical condition. "What a clumsy effort to picture a man who's [*sic*] essence was speed, grace and intellectual presence," remarked one Richmonder, "It reminds me somewhat of the Soviet political statues except that they at least got the anatomical proportions right." *Richmond Times-Dispatch* writer Steve Clark argued that a tribute to Ashe should depict his "agility, grace and power. True, Ashe was much more than a tennis player. He also was an educator and a humanitarian. But . . . I say let the Ashe statue focus on the tennis hero in action. I want to see his muscles rippling and beads of sweat on his brow."[31] While most statues depict their subjects in idealized form, DiPasquale showed Ashe at the end of his life. Sculpting someone known most widely for his athletic achievements in less than vigorous form yet holding a racquet and wearing tennis clothes was too incongruous with the image of the more energetic and fit athlete many Richmonders wanted to honor with a statue.

While some observers argued that DiPasquale's Ashe was not athletic enough, others contended that Ashe should have been depicted in a more well rounded manner, reflecting more accurately the diversity of his accomplishments and the depth of his character. In the words of *Richmond Times-Dispatch* sports columnist Paul Woody, "Some make the argument that Ashe was just a tennis player and that depicting him in this manner is more than satisfactory. But that sells Ashe short." Likewise, Frances Lewis, a Virginia Museum of Fine Arts trustee characterized as "one of Virginia's premier art patrons," noted that "Arthur Ashe's lovingness, his energy, his intelligence . . . this championship man does not show in the statue and there could be an improvement." Rev. Sandi Stovall of the Commission of Architectural Review (also president of the Jackson Ward Historic Foundation, devoted to preserving an historically African American Richmond neighborhood once known as the Harlem of the South), noted that the artist's changes helped soften the statue but that Ashe needed to be shown making eye contact with the children. Stovall and others believed that the sculptor should strive to, as the *Richmond Times-Dispatch* paraphrased DiPasquale, "create more interaction between the Ashe figure and those of the children." These concerns regarding whether Ashe's statue adequately represented his greatness seem likely to have stemmed from its placement in the presence of the existing monuments on the avenue. As Moutoussamy-Ashe stated, "Given where the statue was supposed to be located [in front of the African American Sports Hall of Fame], Arthur requested that he be posed in a sweatsuit with a racquet and books, and with children around him. It is important to understand that had Arthur felt that the statue was to be used for other purposes or placed in a different location, he surely would have chosen a different pose."[32] Calling on the authority of Ashe's intentions, his widow echoed the argument that an athletically oriented sculpture of Ashe was not appropriate in the context of Monument Avenue. Once again, the Ashe statue was presented as incongruous. And in Moutoussamy-Ashe's view, not only was the statue incongruous with the context, it was also incongruous with the wishes of the man it depicts.

Though Jeanne Moutoussamy-Ashe drew on her late husband's intentions to bolster her argument against placing his likeness on Monument Avenue, most people who appealed to Ashe's original intentions did so in support of DiPasquale's rendering. Randy Ashe strongly contended that his cousin's wishes were best represented in DiPasquale's depiction: "Just one person in Richmond, Virginia . . . asked Arthur Ashe what message he wanted to say." In Randy Ashe's view, the existing statue showed "Arthur as he asked to be portrayed." For David Erhardt, who e-mailed his opinion to the *Richmond Times-Dispatch*, Ashe's desires were more deserving of consideration than the aesthetic concerns of others: "If Mr. Ashe had not participated in the basic design of the statue . . . there could be some excuse for the continued wrangling about the design." In the oft-repeated narrative of how the statue came to be, Edds explained that the "sculptor and Ashe had a phone conversation in which Ashe outlined his preferences . . . , including that he be informally dressed in tennis sweats, that his shoes be untied, and that he be interacting with children." Part of the reason for the effectiveness of these appeals to Ashe's original intentions is that they connected with some people's desire to determine how they will be remembered by others. As Chewning argued, "The best way to pay tribute to anyone is to remember them in the manner they want. [This statue] completely captures the spirit and messages Arthur wished to leave with us." Reader Allen J. Taylor called the *Richmond Times-Dispatch* to comment that the statue "captures the nature of Arthur Ashe as a scholar and great tennis player." Though many complained that the scale of the Ashe statue, especially in contrast with the other nearby monuments, was not grand enough to do him honor, Rev. Sylvester Turner contended, "I like the size of the monument. . . . I probably would like to see a larger statue. But Arthur Ashe never presented himself as larger than life. This monument exemplifies that fact."[33]

In the views of these and others advocating the placement of DiPasquale's version of Ashe on Monument Avenue, DiPasquale's mandate from Ashe and self-described faithfulness to Ashe's wishes imbued the statue with the authority of the man being depicted. Opponents found it difficult to argue against these claims that DiPasquale's statue was true to Ashe's wishes—and not just any wishes, but his last wishes. Only when Jeanne Moutoussamy-Ashe entered the debate in January 1996 did some people begin to reconsider DiPasquale's claims to be abiding by Ashe's original intentions. However, by the time Moutoussamy-Ashe made her opinions known, the momentum in support of placing DiPasquale's tribute on Monument Avenue was essentially unstoppable.

While the various factions debating the symbolic and aesthetic propriety of the Ashe statue on Monument Avenue were divided in their senses of "what properly belongs with what," a sense of identification was present in their division. Those who revered the Confederates shared with those who revered Ashe the desire to honor their heroes and their history. By defending the cause of an all-Confederate Monument Avenue, neo-Confederates and the like could identify with their Confederate forebears as they fought on behalf of the Lost Cause—or at least its symbols. And in their defense of Ashe's place on the avenue, African Americans and others could identify with their civil rights forebears as they fought on behalf of integration—or at least an artistic representation of it. In their defense of their respective heroes, advocates on both sides of the debate were joined in their concern for honoring the past and furthering their respective interpretations of history. Richmonders and others may well have gained perspective via what they once considered the incongruity of placing Ashe's likeness among those of the Confederate heroes.

Almost three years after the Ashe statue was unveiled, however, Richmond faced a similar controversy. The RHRF was installing on the city's Canal Walk floodwall a display of murals depicting events and people from throughout Richmond's history. Banners displayed a total of twenty-nine images reflecting thirteen themes: war, founders, floods, pleasure, power, transportation, labor, commerce, freedom, vision, enrichment, ruins, and renewal. Nine of the images featured individuals deemed of historic significance to Richmond and Virginia: William Byrd, Maggie Walker, Patrick Henry, Thomas Jefferson, George Washington, Bill "Bojangles" Robinson, Edgar Allan Poe, Chief Powhatan, and Robert E. Lee. The images were gleaned from three sources: the Library of Congress, Richmond's Valentine Museum, and New York Public Library's Schomburg Center for Research in Black Culture. The murals depicting Richmond's history formed part of an "outdoor museum . . . designed by consultant Ralph Appelbaum of New York" that was to be the crowning touch on the Canal Walk redevelopment project, which was scheduled to open soon thereafter with special dedication activities and events designed to bring area residents downtown to visit the city's latest step toward urban revitalization.[34]

Before the exhibition was even officially dedicated and opened to the public, the *Richmond Times-Dispatch* featured a photograph of workers installing the war-themed mural, which "included images of Chief Powhatan in 1607, Gen. Robert E. Lee in 1864, the Confederate evacuation and burning of Richmond in 1865, and World War I soldiers in about 1917." Richmond city councilman Sa'ad El-Amin became livid when he saw this image of Lee being displayed in the city's newly redeveloped public space.[35]

El-Amin, an African American born in New York and educated at Yale Law School, came to Richmond in 1969 to work as an attorney. Named Jeroyd W. Greene before his conversion to Islam in the 1970s, he worked briefly for the Nation of Islam in Chicago. A 2003 *Washington Times* article described him as having started his career with the goals of "wanting to change the world" and "stand up for the have-nots" by using "local events to speak his mind on racism" and noted that "he didn't mince words to get his message across." While El-Amin characterized his activism as "fight[ing] against white supremacy," others described him as "mostly fighting whites." When he was elected to Richmond's

A portrait of Robert E. Lee among several banners being hung on the downtown Richmond floodwall near the foot of Virginia Street in preparation for the official opening of the Canal Walk. Courtesy *Richmond Times-Dispatch*; photograph by Don Long.

Richmond police officers Doug Moore (left) and Eric Barden ride along the floodwall near the Canal Walk, near the foot of Virginia Street. The Lee mural has been removed but was located to the left of the large mural in the center, *War—The Confederate Evacuation*. Courtesy *Richmond Times-Dispatch*.

city council in 1998, El-Amin "used the seat to further his cause—and ruffle feathers."[36]

Thus, in the context of this history of social and political activism, El-Amin immediately contacted James E. Rogers, president of the RHRF, and James J. McCarthy, executive director of the Richmond Riverfront Development Corporation (RRDC), formed in 1991 "as a private, non-profit corporation to facilitate the redevelopment," in its first phase, of "32 acres of riverfront property stretching east from the historic Tredegar Iron Works site at 5th Street to 17th Street. Construction activities include restoration of the James River & Kanawha Canal and the Haxall Canal, with adjacent canal walks, and development of retail, restaurant, entertainment, office, residential and recreational space." A second phase would redevelop "the area from 17th to 26th Streets as a park where people might stroll along the course of the canal," while a "third phase would develop the area from Maymont to Ethyl. Residents and tourists could ride on reproductions of flat-bottomed James River batteaux, and a boat marina would be located at 16th and 17th Streets." As A. Barton Hinkle noted in a local newspaper editorial, Richmond Renaissance developed the project in 1991 in response to "visitors to Richmond [who] marvel at the James" River and to "Richmond residents [who] wonder why the city does not take greater advantage of the river's appeal." The redevelopment sought to make the riverfront "the crowning jewel of a revitalized downtown, drawing commercial investment to an underdeveloped part of the city." Construction to restore the canals, a crucial aspect of the project, began in 1995. Marc Hirth, the RRDC's director until 1996, predicted at the time that completion of the project would between twelve and fifteen years. By 2006, the Richmond Riverfront featured a Civil War Visitor Center at Tredegar Iron Works, a 1.25 mile Canal Walk, canal cruises, the Shockoe Slip shopping and dining district, and other commercial and residential development.[37]

Considering the Canal Walk murals in the context of the entire riverfront redevelopment project's economic and symbolic importance to Richmond as well as in the context of such previous controversies as the Ashe statue debate, it is easy to understand why displaying a mural of Robert E. Lee in the midst of a project meant to give Richmond a revitalized image was a move fraught with explosive potential. Consequently, when El-Amin first met with the RRDC's McCarthy, the city councilman demanded that either the Lee mural "comes down or we jam." Later the same day, El-Amin also met with the RHRF's Rogers and the RRDC's board president, Brenton S. Halsey. As a result of these meetings, the offending mural was removed on June 2, 1999, before the mural gallery opened to the public on June 4.[38]

News of the mural's removal spread quickly throughout the community. Among those most offended by the mural's removal were the members of the SCV. Although El-Amin had initially threatened a boycott of the Canal Walk, the removal of the Lee mural prompted the SCV to threaten one. Area residents did not hesitate to make their views, mostly in favor of restoring the Lee mural, known through the local newspaper's comment line and editorial pages. At the June 4 dedication ceremonies, Lee's mural may have been absent, but his supporters were not. SCV members and others, some wearing Confederate uniforms, waved Confederate flags and otherwise made their presence known. By the next week, the RHRF announced plans to form a citizens' panel to decide whether Lee's image should be returned in some form to the Canal Walk display. After several meetings, the panel decided to change somewhat the mix of images included in the mural gallery, adding images that would make the display more diverse, deleting the image of African American dancer Bill "Bojangles" Robinson, and replacing the previous image of Lee in uniform with an image of Lee, sans insignia, outside his Richmond home shortly after the Civil War. This new collection of images went on display at the Richmond Centre for six days in July, with forms available for comments and panel members present to talk with citizens.[39]

El-Amin decided to bring the issue before the city council for a vote, though there was some question regarding whether the matter fell within the council's jurisdiction. Organizations such as the Coalition for Racial Justice, the National Association for the Advancement of Colored People (NAACP), and the Baptist General Convention of Virginia issued statements opposing the restoration of Lee to the floodwall exhibition. Thus, when two African American council members, Bill Johnson and Gwen Hedgepeth, voted in support of a resolution calling for the mural's restoration, the Coalition for Racial Justice pledged that it would encourage other African American organizations to ostracize the council members and to assist in defeating them in the next election. Further heightening the level of controversy, David Duke announced he would visit the city to show his support for the Lee mural. Despite these developments, the RHRF citizens' panel decided in favor of displaying the revised set of murals, though having entirely new murals fashioned would cost the RHRF thousands of additional dollars.[40]

In December 1999, the *Richmond Times-Dispatch* declared, "Lee Likeness Returns to Wall without a Shot Fired." No protests had been made by individuals or organizations expressing their displeasure over the previous Lee image on the floodwall. However, a little over a month later, in the very early hours of Monday, January 17, 2000, an unknown person detonated a Molotov cocktail that burned Lee's image off its vinyl mesh mural. That the destruction took place on Virginia's annual holiday in honor of Lee, Stonewall Jackson, and Martin Luther King Jr. fueled SCV leaders' claims that the arson constituted a hate crime and should be investigated as such. However, local police and prosecutors noted that the hate crimes statutes address only offenses against persons, not against places or objects. Some discussion ensued about whether the RHRF should replace the mural that included Lee. However, in light of the effort the RHRF

At a June 13, 1999, Sons of Confederate Veterans rally on the grounds of the Virginia State Capitol to "demonstrate public sentiment towards the restoration of the Robert E. Lee mural on the Richmond Canal Walk," American University professor Edward C. Smith extols the virtues of Lee and defends him against Sa'ad El-Amin's comparisons of Lee and Hitler. Courtesy *Richmond Times-Dispatch*.

had expended on including Lee in the revised set of murals and of the fact that the only expense would be to have one new mural printed (using the existing design), the RHRF chose to replace the damaged mural. Moreover, as Rogers stated, failing to replace the mural "would condone that act of vandalism and ignore the city's public review and approval process for the floodwall gallery." Another community group, the Wednesday Morning Fellowship, described as "a biracial, nondenominational voluntary fellowship of laymen who live or work in the Richmond region," donated the $4,500 necessary to replace the banner, and the replacement mural arrived in a matter of weeks.[41]

In this controversy, a main point of contention involved incongruous interpretations of Lee's character and what the Confederacy was fighting for in the Civil War (or War between the States). Those who opposed Lee's inclusion in the display perceived Lee as a racist and a defender of slavery and saw the Confederates as having fought to preserve that peculiar institution. The SCV and Duke (whose involvement in the controversy the SCV did not welcome), in contrast, saw Lee as an honorable man who fought for the Confederacy more out of loyalty to Virginia than in defense of slavery. In their view, the Confederacy seceded and fought to protect states' rights in general—not solely the right to permit slavery—in the face of northern political and economic aggression. A third strand in this debate sought to bring the other two factions together by emphasizing that history provided a common ground both for those who admired Lee and those who questioned him.

The Richmonders and others most offended by the removal of Lee's image ardently admired him not just as a great general but perhaps even more as a great man. One common argument for restoring the Lee mural was that Lee's moral character was essentially stainless. As Michael Fellman observes of this veneration of Lee, "He was indeed duty bound, self-controlled, and deeply pious—that was his goal and his persona, which others took as the whole story, inflating him into sainthood, thus oversimplifying and dehumanizing him in the cause of sanctifying his name. . . . After his death, he could do nothing to prevent others from bleeding him of his humanity and elevating him into the pantheon for their social and political uses." Related to this belief in Lee's veritable sainthood was the contention that although Lee led the Confederate Army, he opposed slavery. But as Fellman further asserts regarding the sainting of Lee in the public memory, "To accept Saint Robert would be to accept the code of the white South at face value, to deny the reality of terrible historical questions by embracing the willful self-blinding of hero worship."[42] This antislavery depiction of Lee is, of course, intertwined with the related assertion that the Southern states seceded from the Union and fought the war not chiefly over the institution of slavery but rather to defend their economic and political sovereignty as states. And, countering accusations that Lee was a traitor to the United States, his defenders characterize him as both a loyal Virginian and a loyal American, emphasizing at times these aspects of Lee's identity rather than his role as a Confederate leader. Those opposed to the inclusion of Lee's image perceived him incongruous not only with the milieu of the Canal Walk redevelopment project, a symbol of the city's progress and place in the New South, but also with such images as those of a slave revolt leader and civil rights leaders. In contrast, supporters of the inclusion of Lee's image argued that Lee—a moral, antislavery, loyal Virginian and American—indeed fit with the Canal Walk environs as well as with the other images from Richmond's history that comprised the display. Furthermore, argued Lee's defenders, presenting a display of images of Richmond's history that excluded Lee would be incongruous with the facts of the city's history.

Lee's supporters saw him as much more than a Confederate general; from their perspective, he was a moral paragon. One editorial argued that Lee was "an honorable man who tied his fate to a Lost Cause that was well lost." McCallister explained the "flip side on Lee": "Historians judge him as a remarkable man, regardless of choosing to defend his homeland. Lee was brilliant and kind—and anti-slavery, by the way." Lee's defenders tried to make congruous the seemingly incongruous juxtaposition of a righteous leader with a cause widely agreed, from a contemporary perspective, to have been unrighteous. However, another

Lee defender called on the authority of renowned biographer Douglas Southall Freeman to make the point that "Lee was one of the small company of great men in whom there is no inconsistency to be explained, no enigma to be solved. What he seemed—he was—a wholly human gentleman, the essential elements of whose positive character were two and only two, simplicity and spirituality."[43] These Lee defenders encountered no moral or ethical incongruity in his decision to join the Confederate cause.

In answer to Lee's critics, who questioned his morality on the basis of his being aligned with the Confederacy's defense of slavery, Lee loyalists held him up as a model of virtue, "a man of . . . untarnished character and nobility," someone who deserved to be remembered with a place of honor on the floodwall. As Henry Kidd of the Virginia SCV stated, "I would ask those who are against this [picture] to study the man, to study the man's moral values." At a rally held on the State Capitol grounds, "a series of speakers portrayed Lee as a devout Christian, a key conciliator after the Civil War and a savior of Richmond." In short, wrote Andrew P. Bost in an e-mail to the *Richmond Times-Dispatch*, Lee was simply "one of the most ethical, moral and honorable men in our nation's proud history." As evidence of Lee's respectable character, Smith, the director of the American studies program at American University in Washington, D.C., who had also commented on the Ashe statue controversy, said that "Lee was so respected that President Lincoln initially invited him to lead the Union Army. Other admirers of Lee have included British Prime Minister Winston Churchill, President John F. Kennedy and civil rights leader Martin Luther King, Jr."[44] By citing other, more widely respected leaders, including those especially revered by Lee mural opponents, Smith sought to enhance Lee's ethos by association. Aligning Lee with such advocates for African American rights as Lincoln and King was an attempt to demonstrate that Lee was indeed congruous with leaders more commonly seen as racially progressive.

The main reason cited by those opposed to Lee's inclusion in the floodwall historical display was their revulsion at Lee's support of the institution of slavery. Consequently, Lee partisans knew that they had to prove that their hero opposed slavery. As Collin Pulley of the SCV pointed out, "Anyone who has even the slightest knowledge of General Lee knows that he did not stand for slavery." To counter any perceptions that Lee hated African Americans, Kidd observed, "Robert E. Lee loved everyone. . . . He was not a racist man." And as proof of Lee's amity toward African Americans, Gordon Hickey recounted, "While slavery was one of the issues that led to the Civil War, Lee had freed the slaves from his plantation prior to the war." Rebecca Previs, a youth correspondent for the *Richmond Times-Dispatch*, amplified this narrative: "Lee did not approve of secession or a divided nation and believed slavery was a 'moral and social evil,'" setting his father-in-law's slaves free as executor of his estate. Lee's own words that "there are few, I believe, in this enlightened age, who will not acknowledge that slavery as an institution is a moral and political evil," though not quoted completely by any of these advocates, may have been the most powerful (and underutilized) demonstration of his antislavery stance.[45]

Lee's defenders also articulated their version of why Lee and the Confederates seceded from and fought against the United States. Whereas Lee mural opponents characterized the Confederate cause as chiefly concerned with maintaining the institution of slavery, advocates provided a different narrative explaining why the Confederates left the Union and delineating Lee's role in that story. An editorial in the *Roanoke Times and World News* recounted that "Lee was a military genius who reluctantly applied his considerable gifts to the cause that his state had embraced in this nation's Civil War. He was a man of his time, a Virginian in an America that was not the cohesive, monolithic United States of today, but a loosely joined nation in which many citizens felt allegiance first to their state, then to the country of which the states were a part." In a similar vein, Robert Barbour, commander of the Virginia SCV, characterized Lee as "an honorable man who did not support slavery, but fought for the Confederacy to defend constitutional principles and states' rights." Bost similarly stated that "Robert E. Lee . . . did not fight to defend the institution of slavery but to win political and economic independence from an oppressive and tyrannical government." McCallister ultimately let Lee speak for himself on the topic of civil war, concluding a column with an 1860 statement: "If strife and civil war are to take the place of brotherly love and kindness . . . I shall mourn for my country and for the welfare and progress of mankind."[46] In so characterizing Lee and the Confederacy, Lee mural supporters sought to make the general and his cause more acceptable in light of contemporary pieties against slavery and secession, using an argument (states' rights) that audiences were likely to find more congruous with their late-twentieth-century political sensibilities.

Notwithstanding these depictions of Lee as an honorable man fighting for an honorable cause, Lee mural defenders knew that they had to go further. Some mural opponents characterized Lee as a traitor. To counter such accusations, Lee champions put forth numerous depictions of him as a loyal Virginian and American to counter the prevailing image of him as faithful only to the Confederate cause. Recounting the story of Lee's life, Previs noted that he was "reluctant to fight against family and friends . . . but he remained faithful to Virginia." Previs acknowledged Lee's "extreme loyalty . . . to Virginia" and asked, "Why wouldn't we want someone who loved his state as much as Lee did on our floodwall, which represents our history?" Not only was Lee a true Virginian, his supporters argued, but he also remained a true American—and an exceptional one at that. As Kidd contended, "He was one of the greatest Americans who ever lived. . . . He gave his talents, his life, and his devotion to this country." Previs characterized Lee as someone who "loved his country," "felt a great sense of loyalty and duty" to the Union, and even "applied to restore his U.S. Citizenship."

Especially notable among such depictions of Lee as loyal American was one put forth by Hill, who portrayed the Confederate general as a "healing force who urged his former followers to embrace their U.S. citizenship rather than look backwards toward their Confederate heritage."[47] These depictions of Lee conveyed a sense that his role as a Confederate general was not necessarily incongruous with his identity as a Virginian and an American. It was imperative for Lee's champions to prove that he did indeed fit in with Richmond's present status as Virginia capital and American city, not just with its past identity as the Confederate capital.

Those on the other side of the debate argued that Lee's was the most incongruous of images to be displayed in the context of the Canal Walk, a symbol of an evolving Richmond. Lee's detractors depicted him as unheroic and racist, not only disloyal to the United States but also with at best weak connections to Richmond. Many people, especially African Americans, could not conceive that Lee could have served as leader of the Confederate forces and not have been a defender and supporter of slavery and racism. The Richmonders most vocal in opposing the Lee mural also believed that if the general had succeeded in his endeavors, contemporary African Americans might still be enslaved. Most opponents perceived Lee as a symbol of slavery and other entrenched forms of racial oppression, a symbol utterly incongruous with contemporary Richmond, a largely African American city seeking to enter the new millennium focused on race-uniting goals such as economic revitalization.

The first and loudest voice in favor of removing Lee's image from the Canal Walk was that of city councilman Sa'ad El-Amin, who explained his position by stating that Lee "is offensive to the African-American community because of what he stood for. . . . He is a pariah in my community." What Lee stood for, El-Amin argued, was slavery: "If Robert E. Lee had accomplished what he set out to do, which was to win the war, then most of us would be picking cotton for free." As one newspaper paraphrased El-Amin's perspective, "The general supported and defended the Confederacy and that made him a supporter of slavery." El-Amin compared the public display of Lee's portrait with putting up a Hitler portrait in Berlin or Israel. Other community members shared El-Amin's view of Lee: Rev. Roscoe Cooper, head of the 125-member Ad Hoc Committee on Justice, a group of citizens "tired and beleaguered by the divisiveness," announced that "this group had watched a city divide and cannibalize itself over the symbol of a dead man" who had "trafficked in human cargo and owned my people." Eric G. Williams, an African American who grew up in nearby Petersburg, conceded "that many say the Civil War was about states' rights and [the] economic prosperity of the South" but noted, "one of those states' rights was the right to own slaves. In Virginia, and much of the South, the thriving economy was made possible by a cheap labor source—mainly enslaved Americans. Thus slavery was the main cause of the war." Another area resident,

Donald Minor, situated Lee in the effort to maintain a slave-based economy by depicting him as "a man who led military forces that would have preserved slavery." Overall, observed civil rights activist and Virginia Commonwealth University political science professor W. Avon Drake, who was involved in the civil rights and black power movements of the 1960s and today researches African American politics, opponents of displaying Lee's image perceived him as "the supreme symbol of their enslavement."[48] In Richmond, whose city council had included a majority of African American members since 1977, and when African Americans possessed equal rights under the law and increasing levels of social, economic, and political influence, adding yet another symbol of slavery to the city's already numerous Confederate memorials in the context of what was supposed to be a symbol of the city's progress seemed incongruous. To give added approbation to a man who symbolized slavery told many African American Richmonders that less progress had occurred than they had hoped; perhaps an image of Lee less incongruous with contemporary Richmond's political climate than they would have liked to believe.

Others averse to the Lee mural and its attendant symbolism of slavery couched their reservations by conceding their opponents' belief that Lee had not personally stood for slavery. One lifelong Virginian and fifty-year Richmond resident, eighty-three-year-old Florence Franklin, acknowledged, "'It does offend [black people] to think that Lee supported slavery. It does me, too.' . . . She said she knows Lee did not favor slavery and 'I know he considered fighting for the Union,' but his decision to support the Confederacy was also a decision to support slavery." Likewise, fifty-two-year-old Willie Pender, an African American who grew up in Richmond near Hollywood Cemetery, where Confederate President Jefferson Davis and General J. E. B. Stuart are buried, conceded, "I know Lee didn't have slaves and everything, but if he had won the war, slavery would have continued for a long time." *Richmond Times-Dispatch* writer Robin Farmer granted that Lee was "considered by many to be a noble man" but argued that he was, at minimum, "conflicted about the topic of slavery." In support of this contention, Farmer juxtaposed two seemingly incongruous quotations from Lee on the topic. On December 27, 1856, Lee wrote, "In this enlightened age, there are few I believe, but will acknowledge, that slavery as an institution is a moral and political evil in this country"; however, Lee later added, "The blacks are immeasurably better off here than in Africa, morally, socially, and physically. The painful discipline they are undergoing is necessary for their further instruction as a race, and I hope will prepare and lead them to better things. How long their subjugation may be necessary is known and ordered by a merciful Providence."[49] In exposing the internal incongruities within Lee's opinions about slavery, Farmer offered perhaps the most persuasive evidence that Lee's views of the peculiar institution were indeed incongruous with the image of a New South Richmond so coveted by city leaders.

Slavery was not the only reason offered for excluding Lee's image from the floodwall mural gallery. As King Salim Khalfani, executive director of the Virginia Conference of the NAACP, pointed out, "The Confederates were found to be traitors to the United States." Minor echoed this sentiment with his contention that "Lee should have been arrested for treason." Having turned his back on the United States in a time of war, Lee was a traitor and should not be honored in this celebration of Richmond's history. Others argued that Lee, who was not a native of Richmond and lived there for only a short time following the war, consequently was not very relevant in the big picture of Richmond's history. Thus, they argued, Lee should not be honored alongside those whose lives were more intertwined with and whose roles were more crucial to the city's development. African American Vice Mayor Rudolph C. McCollum Jr. voiced this argument when "he added that Lee really had little to do with the history of Richmond as a city." As area resident Ruth Hunter declared at the July 26, 1999, Richmond city council meeting, at which more than fifty people (most of them African American) spoke out against the Lee mural, "It's time to stop teaching . . . children that Robert E. Lee and Stonewall Jackson are heroes."[50] Those who posited that Robert E. Lee symbolized slavery, committed treason against the United States, and did not play a significant role in Richmond's development essentially argued that Lee and his image were incongruous with the picture of Richmond that city leaders wanted to project through the Canal Walk redevelopment project. A treasonous, pro-slavery, non-Richmonder was deemed irrelevant to a public art display that was meant to celebrate only the best of Richmond's long history.

In addition to the two main factions in this debate, which advanced disparate portrayals of Lee, a third, more loosely bound faction existed, emphasizing a unifying appeal to history. Proponents of this third perspective believed that the purpose of the floodwall was not to *honor* certain individuals and events from Richmond's history but rather simply to *conserve* a sense of the city's past. As fifty-three-year-old Henrico County firefighter Frank Bahen stated in comments on the local newspaper's call-in line, "Those murals represent who we are, good and bad." Mayor Kaine said that "Lee on the floodwall would serve as a history lesson—both good and bad—for everyone," thereby typifying this third basic stance.[51]

That there existed this third party promoting the depiction of history for its own sake, apart from particular factions' readings of it, is hardly surprising in "a city obsessed with its past." For those taking this stance, *history* was the "ultimate term." As Burke writes, "The 'ultimate' order of terms would thus differ essentially from the 'dialectical' . . . in that there would be a 'guiding idea' or 'unitary principle' behind the diversity of voices." Thus, according to Burke, "we can get a glimpse into a possible alternative, whereby a somewhat formless parliamentary wrangle can, by an 'ultimate' vocabulary, be creatively endowed with design. And even though the members of the parliament . . . may not accept this design, it can have a contemplative effect; it can organize one's attitude towards the struggles of politics, and may suggest reasons why one kind of compromise is, in the long run, to be rated as superior to another." In Richmond, the ultimate term is *history*; the city considers itself distinctive because of its veneration of the past even as it moves into the future. In his continued discussion of ultimate terms, Burke notes that Socrates sought "to define the human dispositions brought to the fore by each of the different political structures. . . . Each [political structure] has its own peculiar idea or summarizing term." Richmond, in Socrates' (and Burke's) taxonomy, is a timocracy, a state "governed on principles of honor and military glory." Richmond has certainly been ruled, at least until recently, by the principles of honor and military glory in its reverence of Lost Cause symbols. Those arguing for *history* as the Canal Walk display's ultimate term sought to unify the disparate concerns of Lee's supporters and his detractors under the banner of history, which appears to have been the shared concern of both these factions: Lee mural supporters wanted the city to continue to commemorate Richmond's role as capital of the Confederacy, while Lee mural opponents hoped people would remember the role of slavery in the Confederate cause. As one anonymous caller to the local newspaper opinion line advocated, "Declare the murals are there to tell the story of Richmond, be it good, bad, or ugly. [Slave revolt leader Gabriel] Prosser and Lee are both part of that history. For that reason alone, both should be on that wall."[52]

In Richmond, the "sense of what properly goes with what" has been determined in large part by the city's ultimate term, *history*. In the context of this debate, this ultimate piety of history was used to argue that figures as disparate as a Confederate general and a slave revolt leader *belonged* in the floodwall murals because both were part of Richmond's history. As a *Roanoke Times and World News* editorial argued, Lee's "place in such an exhibit is justified by his place in history." Those on various sides of the issue used this idea of Lee as a part of history as a way of establishing common ground. Former governor Wilder, a staunch supporter of the Ashe statue on Monument Avenue, also declared, "There is a place for Robert E. Lee on the wall." Eric G. Williams, who argued in a letter to the editor that there were enough memorials to Lee elsewhere in the city, conceded that "Robert E. Lee is a part of Virginia's history." Hedgepeth, derided by the Coalition for Racial Justice for her support for restoring the Lee mural, justified her vote by stating that Lee was part of Richmond's history. Edgar Toppin, a distinguished professor of American and African American history at Virginia State University (and an African American) whom the RHRF consulted regarding the content of the historical display, was surprised by the negative response: "The mural is about Richmond and the Civil War," he contended, "How can you talk about the Civil War without Lee?" Eric Penn, a thirty-four-year-old African American city employee, defended Lee's inclusion, saying, "He played a significant role in the history of America. We can't erase him from the history books." Or as Canal Walk business owner Andy Thornton observed, "Lee does belong . . . because he was a part of history."[53] In the Lee mural debate, those appealing to the piety of history sought to make room for everyone's heroes, even those as seemingly incongruous as Prosser and Lee, in Richmond's sense of what properly belonged in its communal history.

Just as those advocating the Ashe statue's placement on Monument Avenue did so out of a desire to belong, advocates of restoring Lee's mural to the floodwall argued out of their desire to preserve their sense of belonging in the narrative of Richmond's history. In both debates, advocates rallied around depictions of Ashe and Lee, which acted as symbols of African Americans and Confederate descendants, respectively. Both groups shared the desire to "properly fit" into Richmond's history through the approval of their symbols in the public space as well as the desire to determine what other symbols should be considered "proper" in the city's evolving piety of its history.

Two debates concerning symbols of the Southern tradition of division and the Southern change toward increased identification have been analyzed through the lens of perspective by incongruity. These public debates and their resulting compromises offer evidence that previously "mutually exclusive" or divided entities can indeed be "methodically merged" or identified with one another through their juxtaposition. The bringing together of such previously disparate entities allowed each to be seen from a perspective heretofore unknown, and thus these previously alienated entities could to be seen in terms of one another. Juxtaposing these previously segregated symbols of Southern tradition and change, of the orders of division and identification, allowed Richmonders to see these symbols, and in some cases themselves, in a new way—a perspective that allowed them to see through surface differences to a level of shared essences. By viewing themselves, their symbols, and their city through the perspective of incongruity, Richmonders could begin to attain a "maximum consciousness" through which they could transcend their segregated past by becoming aware of its "foibles." In the end, DiPasquale insisted that he was "glad his work generated so much debate. 'The dialogue exists on a social and spiritual level,' he said. 'That's what art is supposed to do.' He also said that because the Ashe statue is so different from the others on Monument Avenue, it will force people to think about all the monuments on the avenue. 'It does create sort of self-analysis of who are our heroes and why. That does more for the statues on Monument Avenue than anything else.'"[54]

Even as their debate proceeded, these proponents of Southern tradition and change, by their juxtaposition or combination within the same community, worked together, perhaps in spite of themselves, to create something beyond what either could achieve alone: the exchange of ideas, which enhanced Richmond through the conflict of its various factions.[55]

The opposing factions in both of these debates were in many ways divided in their interpretations of the city's history; however, juxtaposing Ashe with the Confederacy's president and generals and later Lee with the leader of a slave rebellion and civil rights pioneers revealed to Richmonders the possibility of identifying with one another through their shared valuing of history, albeit from quite distinct or divided perspectives. Similarly, South Carolinians juxtaposed divergent narratives to explain their interpretation of one symbol: the Confederate battle flag. South Carolinians as well as residents of other states debating Confederate flag issues found themselves at once divided from and identified with one another through the ultimate term, *history*—specifically, their shared history of racial struggle.

3

Stories of the War: The Confederate Flag in South Carolina

AS CONTENTIOUS AS the artistic portrayals of Southerners from Robert E. Lee to Arthur Ashe may have been in Richmond, no symbol has divided the contemporary South as widely and to such an extreme as the red field, blue cross, and white stars of the Confederate battle flag. This "rebel flag" has been displayed as a symbol of racist defiance by Ku Klux Klansmen and others of their ilk who continue to defend a racially divided South years after identification became the ruling order through federally mandated integration. Such divisive uses of this flag have imbued it with the symbolism of division or hate in the minds of many people, especially those who have pressed most to see this new order of identification enforced: African Americans, especially those living in the South and those associated with civil rights organizations such as the National Association for the Advancement of Colored People (NAACP). But some other Southerners—white neo-Confederates such as those associated with the Sons of Confederate Veterans (SCV)—take issue with the meaning of division or hate being associated with any Confederate symbol, especially the battle flag under which their forebears fought. For these Confederate descendants, the flag symbolizes their identification with the cause of their ancestors—the cause of states' right to secede and rule themselves. Given such division over what the battle flag symbolizes, it was not surprising when debates erupted at the turn of the millennium as to the propriety of displaying the flag atop the South Carolina Capitol in Columbia as well as within its legislative chambers. The way each side in this debate told its stories of the war, the raising of the flag, and the debate over lowering it revealed the way each interpreted the symbol of the flag.

Indeed, the two sides even referred to the war differently, with neo-Confederates tending to refer to it as the War between the States or the War of Northern Aggression and most other Southerners and Americans tending to refer to it as the Civil War. The flag's defenders portrayed the war as having been fought for states' rights and sovereignty in the face of a tyrannous central government, thus making their ancestors' fight honorable. The flag in turn became symbolic of a positive heritage of fighting for a just cause, and flying the flag atop the Capitol became a reminder of a noble heritage worth preserving. Conversely, the flag's critics depicted the war as having been fought over the issue of slavery and saw the flag as symbolic of those who wanted to keep African Americans in slavery, oppressors during the decades of segregation and since. Thus, people on this side of the debate attributed to the flag meanings of racial oppression and consequently wanted to see it removed from its position of prominence.

The positioning of the flag had much to do with its symbolism and thus lies at the heart of this controversy. A flag flying atop or within a seat of government symbolizes whatever entity holds power there. In fact, as James Forman Jr. suggests in explaining the theory of government speech as applied to the Confederate flag, "Because the government is the speaker, a balance of interests arises that is different from those normally presented in the battle between racist speakers and their victims. . . . [A] growing number of scholars [are] arguing that the First Amendment also limits the government's ability to speak."[1] Many South Carolina groups that passed resolutions in favor of removing the flag reasoned that since the Confederate States of America was not a contemporary, ruling authority in the state, its flag should not be flown along with the flags of those entities that do have authority: the United States (whose flag is always to be flown the highest) and the State of South Carolina. The controversy did not involve whether the Confederate battle flag (or any other Confederate flag, for that matter) can or should be flown by individuals or groups but whether it was appropriate for a state to fly a flag representing an entity that is no longer sovereign alongside the flags of two entities that are.

In the wake of the U.S. Supreme Court's decision in the case of *Brown v. Board of Education* (1954), many white Southerners became angered by the federal mandate for racially integrated public schools. In *Myth, Media, and the Southern Mind*, Stephen A. Smith states, "The *Brown* decision, like every force which has challenged the myth and threatened the security of the racist South, was blamed on outsiders." Looking for icons around which to rally their protest, however, white Southerners had difficulty appropriating traditional American symbols. As Francis Wilhoit points out, "From the outset the South's counterrevolutionaries suffered from the handicap of having their opponents preempt virtually all the national historic symbols of the United States. . . . [T]he South's leaders found themselves at a distinct disadvantage . . . for all they had left to manipulate were regional myths and icons discredited by the Great Rebellion." These Southern counterrevolutionaries would have been better off using no symbols at all than the defeated symbols of the Old South. Likewise, as Richard Weaver puts it, "Considerations of strategy and tactics forbid the use of symbols of lost causes. There cannot be a return to the Middle Ages or the Old South under slogans identified with them. The principles must be studied and used, but in such presentation that mankind will feel the march is forward. And so it will be." However, many white Southerners, whether protesting desegregation or commemorating the war, felt differently. Unable to associate the American

The South Carolina Statehouse from the rear. Courtesy South Carolina Department of Archives and History.

flag with their cause, they chose to resurrect the symbols of the Confederacy, which had persisted in Southern postbellum culture but achieved new prominence in the era of desegregation. As Smith observes, "The Confederate flag and the song 'Dixie' gained renewed popularity among the masses, especially in relationship with the rituals of intercollegiate football in the South and the countless ceremonies commemorating the Centennial of the Civil War." Further, according to Lewis M. Killian, "Homage to Dixie and the Confederate battle flag regained a significance they had lost over the years.... The white South was once again an embattled minority, with the forces of the Supreme Court, the NAACP, northern liberalism, and 'Yankee ignorance' arrayed against it."[2] In this cultural climate, the Confederate battle flag was hoisted to the top of the South Carolina Capitol in 1962 with the stated intent of commemorating the war's one hundredth anniversary. Flag opponents, however, believed that the real reason for beginning to fly the flag was to protest desegregation.

While much of the attention in the South Carolina flag centered on the top of the Statehouse dome, Confederate battle flags were also to be found within its legislative chambers. In 1938, the legislature passed a measure, sponsored by Union County representative John D. Long, that mandated that the Confederate battle flag—along with the U.S. and South Carolina flags—be displayed behind the speaker's desk in the House Chamber, arguably the room's visual fo-

The South Carolina Statehouse dome with the U.S. and South Carolina flags flying atop it. Courtesy South Carolina Department of Archives and History.

cal point. While, as K. Michael Prince notes, "Nothing in the resolution spoke of defiance against nationalist policies or federal interference . . . there is something about the timing of it that raises suspicions": Long's resolution came at a time of increasing tension in race relations and "shortly after the anti-lynching debate had ended" and "a senate reelection campaign in which President [Franklin] Roosevelt had 'intruded' into state affairs by advocating [Cotton Ed] Smith's reelection defeat." In April 1961, in the midst of celebrations of the war's centennial, John "Mr. Confederate" May, chair of the South Carolina Centennial Commission and a member of the state House of Representatives, "requested that the state agency responsible for State House maintenance add a Confederate flag to those already flying atop the state capitol, in observance of the Civil War centennial." At the time, however, "atop the state capitol" did not mean on a flagpole on top of the dome. The ladder to the dome's flagpole had been declared unsafe five years earlier, so a flagpole was put on top of a lower part of the building, visible only from the front side of the Statehouse, and the U.S. and South Carolina flags were on display there; the Confederate flag was added to that lower flagpole in April 1961. In February 1962, May proposed in a concurrent resolution that all three flags be moved to a flagpole atop the dome. According to newspaper columnist Elsa McDowell, Charleston lawyer and businessman

George Campsen Jr., a member of the South Carolina House from 1958 to 1964, recalled that "everyone knew the resolution was light-hearted. No one intended the flag to stay up beyond the centennial—not even John May. Had the intent been to make the flag a permanent fixture, . . . they would have discussed the propriety. Flags over a legislative body represent authorities sovereign over that body. No one was pretending that the Confederate States of America still existed and had sovereignty over the Legislature. Unfortunately, the resolution didn't state when it would come down. It was a mistake that the flag continued to fly long after the Centennial." The Confederate battle flag began flying atop the Statehouse dome in early April 1962 and remained there until July 1, 2000.[3]

Thirty years after South Carolina first raised the flag atop the Statehouse, similar controversies were taking place throughout the South as people discussed the appropriateness of continuing to display or use flags, monuments, and placenames connected with the Confederate States of America as well as its war heroes and political leaders. Many African Americans and others believed that government entities should not promote the cause and ideals of the Confederacy by maintaining these symbols on publicly owned property. On the other side of the debate, groups such as the SCV have worked actively to identify threatened flags, monuments, street names, and school names, featuring a monthly "Heritage Report" in its *Confederate Veteran* magazine, alerting members to "heritage violations," providing contact information (and even preaddressed postcards) for officials, and offering members a means of reporting new threats to their Confederate heritage.

In *Written in Stone: Public Monuments in Changing Societies*, Sanford Levinson details many recent conflicts in the South involving the public display of Confederate flags and monuments as well as the naming of public spaces such as streets and schools after Confederate heroes and slave owners. In October 1997, for example, the Louisiana's Orleans Parish School Board moved to change the name of George Washington Elementary School to Dr. Charles Richard Drew Elementary School and to change the name of General P. T. Beauregard Junior High to Thurgood Marshall Junior High, in accordance with the board's policy not to name schools for "former slave owners or others who did not respect equal opportunity for all." In Austin, Texas, a controversy raged over a plaque on the base of a statue located on the State Capitol grounds. The statue depicts members of each of the four branches of the Confederate military with Jefferson Davis in the center, standing above them, but the statue itself was not controversial. Instead, people argued about the plaque's interpretation of the war and the Constitution: "Died for state rights guaranteed under the Constitution. The people of the South, animated by the Spirit of 1776, to preserve their rights, withdrew from the federal compact in 1861. The North resorted to coercion. The South, against overwhelming numbers and resources, fought until exhausted." In Stafford, Virginia, judges required the removal of the Confederate flag from a courthouse exhibit of all the flags that had flown over Stafford, including the British Union Jack. The exhibit's curator took down all the historical flags, leaving only the current state and national flags, saying, "If you're going to take [the Confederate flag] down, take them all down. . . . You have to tell the history, warts and all."[4]

Georgia and Mississippi experienced controversy regarding the design of their state flags. In 1993, Georgia Governor Zell Miller tried unsuccessfully to convince state legislators to change the flag from its current design, which opponents argued had been adopted in 1956 as a protest against the *Brown v. Board of Education* decision. Miller advocated a return to the 1905 design, which was based on one of the Confederacy's less recognizable and thus less divisive national flags. By the time the South Carolina flag debate reached its climax in early 2000, Rev. Jesse Jackson Sr. said that Georgia would be next in line for boycotts if it did not change the design of its flag. In 2001, Georgia legislators adopted a new flag featuring a blue field on which were displayed the state seal surrounded by thirteen stars, the motto "In God We Trust," and a banner featuring the motto "Georgia's History" along with miniature versions of all the flags that have flown over the state, including the 1956 state flag. But though it offered something for everyone, this new design did not settle the flag issue. In the 2002 gubernatorial campaign, candidate Sonny Perdue promised that if elected, he would call for a statewide referendum giving voters a choice between the new design or the 1956 design. Perdue won the election, and when he took office in early 2003, state legislators, the media, and citizens across the state extensively discussed his proposed referendum. State legislators suggested yet another flag design, this one based on a less contentious Confederate national flag design (known as the Stars and Bars). This new flag featured two red bars on either side of a white bar with the words "In God We Trust." The upper-left-hand corner featured a blue field emblazoned with the state seal surrounded by thirteen stars. For a time, Perdue and like-minded state legislators continued to push for a statewide referendum offering voters the opportunity to return to the 1956 flag, but in the spring of 2003, state legislators adopted the most recent flag design without any provision allowing voters to bring back the 1956 flag.[5]

Mississippi voters, in contrast, received the opportunity to decide the flag issue by referendum in 2001. The present state flag, which features the Confederate battle flag in one corner, was adopted in 1894. In 2000, the Mississippi Supreme Court found that the law establishing that flag had been repealed— likely unknowingly—in 1906. Governor Ronnie Musgrove established a commission that studied the issue and held public hearings on the matter during the summer and fall of 2000. The commission ultimately recommended to the state legislature that a statewide referendum be held, giving voters a choice between the 1894 design and a new design that would replace the battle flag portion of the 1894 flag with a blue field featuring a circle of white stars. The legislature approved the referendum proposal, the vote occurred on April 17, 2001, and 65 percent of those who cast ballots voted to keep the 1894 design, Confederate battle flag and all.[6]

Momentum also began to build in South Carolina for a public debate about the Confederate flag's place atop the Capitol dome. In 1993, South Carolina attorney general Travis Medlock indicated that there was "no legal reason for the flag to fly." In May 1994, the chair of the NAACP's national board, William Gibson, a South Carolinian, announced that his organization would "organize economic sanctions to force the flag's removal." In response, South Carolina legislators came up with a compromise aimed at averting the NAACP boycott, but the state House of Representatives refused to take action on the bill. In response, Columbia mayor Bob Coble and some of the city's business leaders filed suit in the state Supreme Court to remove the flag, and in November 1994 the court agreed to hear arguments. But when state legislators passed a May 1995 law stating that only the General Assembly could decide to remove the flag, the lawsuit was dropped. In April 1996, Nelson Brown, a fifty-four-year-old law student from Greenwood, filed a lawsuit asking that the flag be removed until the General Assembly could decide whether to keep the flag flying.[7]

Republican governor David Beasley's willingness to publicly advocate removing the flag may have constituted a turning point in the continued debate. In July 1996, Beasley held a meeting of the Governor's Commission on Racial Relations at which the issue of the Confederate flag was discussed. On November 26, in his first televised address as governor, Beasley advocated removing the flag from the Capitol dome and relocating it to a less controversial location, a soldiers' monument on the Capitol grounds. During the gubernatorial campaign, Beasley had pledged that he would not disturb the flag, so some critics saw his shift as motivated by national political aspirations or as pandering to the state's growing international business presence. Beasley, however, located his change of heart and policy in a religious realization that led him to be more sensitive to the perspective of those South Carolinians offended by the flag: "I'm asking that we come together as a people—to honor each other and understand each other: to forge a ministry of reconciliation that extends to every citizen from the greatest to the least."[8] The matter subsequently became a hot topic in the state, especially in the 1998 gubernatorial campaign, which resulted in the election of a new governor, Democrat Jim Hodges. Some observers, including Beasley, attributed his loss in part to many flag supporters' perception that he had betrayed not only his initial promise but also the state's Southern heritage.

In July 1999, the issue again came to the fore, sparked mainly by the NAACP's threatened tourism boycott if the flag were not removed from the Capitol by the end of that year. When the new year arrived, the flag was still flying and the boycott began. The NAACP asked individuals not to vacation in the state, families not to plan reunions in the state, athletes and sports teams not to compete in the state, and corporations and organizations not to hold conferences in the state.[9]

The timing of the boycott overlapped with the presence in South Carolina of many high-profile candidates campaigning for the February 2000 presidential primary, the second of the primary season. The press asked all of the major candidates (Republicans George W. Bush, John McCain, Steve Forbes, Elizabeth Dole, and Alan Keyes; Democrats Al Gore and Bill Bradley; and the Reform Party's Pat Buchanan) to comment on the flag debate. The Republicans and Buchanan generally argued that the people of South Carolina should be left to decide the issue for themselves free from any federal pressure (reminiscent of the states' rights stance of old), while the Democratic candidates generally supported flag's removal.[10]

In late 1999 and early 2000, many groups and individuals from South Carolina as well as beyond the state's borders issued statements and resolutions calling on the legislature to take down the flag. Religious groups as diverse as Lutherans, Baptists, Seventh-Day Adventists, and African Methodist Episcopalians all supported the boycott either by moving their events or by calling for the flag's removal. The New York Knicks basketball team refused to hold pre-playoff practices in Charleston, tennis player Serena Williams withdrew from Hilton Head Island's Family Circle Cup, and the National Collegiate Athletic Association barred some competitions from taking place in the state. Nationally known South Carolinians from author Pat Conroy to fundamentalist college president Bob Jones III argued that the flag should come down. Rallies both for and against the flag's removal took place around the state. In early April 2000, Charleston mayor Joe Riley led a "Get in Step March" from Charleston to Columbia in support of bringing down the flag; among others, he was joined by University of South Carolina football coach Lou Holtz and Clemson football coach Tommy Bowden.[11]

In May 2000, the controversy remained unsettled and the boycott was still in effect. At that time, the South Carolina Senate and House passed legislation later signed by Governor Hodges to remove the flag from the Capitol and relocate it to the Confederate soldiers' monument on the front side of the Capitol grounds. The flag was finally lowered when the bill went into effect on July 1. Many observers came out to celebrate or protest the flag's ceremonious removal from the Capitol dome by two anonymous, uniformed Citadel cadets, one black and one white.[12] However, the NAACP and its allies continued to argue that although the flag no longer topped the Capitol, having it at eye level on a main downtown Columbia thoroughfare remained unsatisfactory. Some participants in the debate continue to argue, as they have since the controversy's beginning, that the Confederate battle flag should be removed from the grounds altogether and placed in the Confederate Relic Room.

All of these Confederate flag conflicts resulted from situations in which the

The Confederate battle flag flies by the Confederate Veteran Monument at the front of the Statehouse grounds at the intersection of Main and Gervais Streets. Courtesy South Carolina Department of Archives and History.

symbols associated with one group's interpretation of history were displayed in the public domain or were meant to represent the state as a whole. In all of these cases, government entities was perceived as affirming one version of history or constitutional interpretation—the Confederate version—to the exclusion of others, thereby offending anyone who dissented from that version. But perhaps more importantly, the various stakeholders involved debated their respective visions of what society should be and how shared public places should reflect those often divergent visions.

The fate of the South Carolina flag affected the status of Confederate symbols throughout the South. Thus, by looking at the conflict between these identity groups—change-seeking African Americans and other progressives, tradition-maintaining, neo-Confederate white Southerners, and those who sought a compromise between them—may provide a better understanding of all such conflicts over Confederate symbols.

The flag advocates included members of genealogical, history-oriented groups such as the SCV and the United Daughters of the Confederacy (UDC). The rhetoric of these groups emphasized their pride in the flag, their perception of it as a positive reflection of the state's Southern heritage and of their Confederate ancestors. J. Michael Martinez and William D. Richardson call this first set of flag advocates "'heritage preservationist' traditionalists," describing them as people who "defend continued displays of Confederate flags and monuments by arguing that we must remember and respect the history, traditions, and culture of the South," especially its "almost mystical faith in agrarianism, [its] fierce love of liberty, [its] mistrust of obdurate, centralized authority, and [its] unabashed appreciation of home and family." Other groups such as the League of the South and the Council of Conservative Citizens were more defensive in their approach, seeing the cause of the flag as an opportunity to refight battles of North versus South and black versus white. Martinez and Richardson describe this second strain of traditionalists as "extremists" whose "thought embraces the dark side of the Confederacy by deliberately espousing racist views" and for whom "political compromise on Confederate symbols is not an option" because "one does not compromise with an enemy in a race war."[13]

Flag opponents, in contrast, believed it to be a symbol of racist oppression and a valorization of the Confederate states' defense of slavery. Martinez and Richardson describe proponents of this interpretation as "reconstructionists" who "insist that Confederate flags and monuments are offensive reminders of the worst aspects of Southern culture: a degrading, paternalistic view of African Americans as racially inferior people and a belief that slavery was necessary to the economic and cultural interests of the antebellum South." Reconstructionists also associate the flag with "the views of racist groups that often have appropriated Confederate flags to express loathsome ideas contrary to the concept of equality within the American republic."[14] Flag opponents included groups such as the NAACP, the Rainbow/PUSH Coalition, the National Urban League, the Southern Christian Leadership Conference, the Assembly of African American Leaders, and the Congress of Black National Churches. Flag opponents first worked to remove the flag from the Capitol dome but later expanded their argument to include removing the flag from the Confederate memorial as well.

The third set of storytellers in this debate, the compromisers, was more loosely organized and received less coverage from the news media, which "tend to magnify the extreme positions and obscure the moderate positions to which most people adhere." Compromisers sought to protect South Carolina's business interests and educational reputation by moving the flag to the Confederate memorial or to a nearby museum. Examples of such middle-grounders seeking to protect the state's business interests include the Heritage Roundtable (HR), a group with an economic interest in the Upstate (the Greenville-Spartanburg area); the Palmetto Business Forum; the South Carolina Chamber of Commerce; and the South Carolina Travel and Tourism Commission. Faculty senates, trustees, presidents, and even coaches from some of the state's most well known colleges and universities, including Clemson University, the University of South Carolina, and the Citadel, spoke out in hopes of protecting their institutions' reputations in teaching and research. According to John Coski, "As the flag wars dragged on and as pollsters began asking more nuanced questions, more people answered that they believed the flag to be a symbol of honor but that they did not believe it should fly on state flags or over capitols."[15] These people understood pride in the flag, and some compromisers even felt some positive personal connections with the flag; however, they also understood that many others were offended by the flag and that its prominent display caused the state to be characterized as ignorant and behind the times, thus negatively affecting the state's economic and academic reputation and, more importantly, citizens' sense of unity and shared identity.

I will analyze public communications on behalf of all three of these camps from the rhetorical perspective of Walter Fisher's narrative paradigm. Statements to the press, speeches, Internet postings, and the like illustrate how public moral arguments proceed, how fantasy themes are generated "in group interaction out of a recollection of something that happened to the group in the past or a dream of what a group might do in the *future*." Each of these groups told its own stories of the war and desegregation as well as the state's future in terms of economic development and harmony among identity groups. These different stories explain these stakeholders' varying interpretations of the flag and its role and placement in the future of South Carolina. As Fisher explains, "Dramatic stories constitut[e] the fabric of social reality for those who compose them. They are thus 'rhetorical fictions,' constructions of fact and faith having persuasive force, rather than fantasies."[16] Thus, these public texts illustrate the contention that such public moral arguments are negotiated through the narration of stories that imbue contested symbols such as the Confederate flag with differing meanings.

Fisher's narrative paradigm explains why storytelling is an ideal means of persuading in the context of a public moral argument, which he defines as public in that it is "made available for consumption and persuasion of the polity at large" and "moral in the sense that it is founded on ultimate questions" such as "how persons should be defined and treated." The controversy over the flag in South Carolina indeed played out in the public forum and involved the question of "how persons should be defined and treated." The narratives told by all sides in this controversy were "descriptive," offering "an account, an understanding, of any instance of human choice or action" and involving "recounting and accounting"—that is, "stories we tell ourselves and each other to establish a meaningful life-world."[17]

The tellers of these narratives often talked past one another, telling stories that were "life-worlds" apart. Fisher addresses such stories told in the context of protest: "From the perspective of the narrative paradigm, the dynamic of this situation is that rival stories are being told. . . . If a story denies a person's self-conception, it does not matter what it says about the world. In the instance of protest, the rival factions' stories deny each other in respect to self-conceptions and the world. The only way to bridge this gap, if it can be bridged through discourse, is by telling stories that do not negate the self-conceptions people hold of themselves."[18] Herein lay the conflict between the various storytellers in this flag debate. In their rhetoric, flag advocates glossed over or totally ignored slavery's role in the war and thus attempted to delegitimate a significant part of African Americans' identity—their ancestors' struggles against slavery and segregation. Many flag defenders portrayed flag opponents as reverse racists, out to avenge past wrongs against their group, rather than as noble, nonviolent protesters in the tradition of the mid-twentieth-century civil rights movement. Likewise, flag opponents' rhetoric denied a significant part of white Southerners' identity—their belief in their ancestors' heroism, nobility, and valor in fighting a war for independence that they saw as paralleling the Revolutionary War. Opponents perceived proponents as racists, talking about heritage merely as a ruse to disguise a white supremacist agenda. However, the middle-grounders in this controversy seemed, as Fisher says, to bridge the gap between the two extremes in that their rhetoric did not negate anyone's self-concept. Instead, the compromisers attempted to value the self-concepts and stories of those in both of the extremist camps. Perhaps as a result of this rhetorical choice, the compromisers ultimately won the debate.

Though the opposing sides did not seem to be listening to one another, some good may have resulted from the debate. Such rhetorical conflicts as this give rise to what Kenneth Burke terms "'agonistic' or competitive stress," the product of arguing with an adversary. While such adversarial debates seem on the surface destructive, the competitive stress results in what Burke calls the "proving of opposites," a kind of purifying, refining fire of debate that results in the distillation not of one side's argument or the other but of the refined, purified truth of both, melded together through the heat of their debate. Says Burke, "The notion of rhetoric as a means of 'proving opposites' again brings us to the relation between rhetoric and dialectic. . . . [I]deally the dialogue seeks to attain a higher order of truth, as the speakers, in competing with one another, cooperate towards an end transcending their positions. Here is the paradigm of the dialectical process for 'reconciling opposites' in a 'higher synthesis.'"[19] By revealing the points of tension between the various narratives, we can come to an enhanced understanding of how the South came to be in this situation and of how the situation is symbolically constructed and maintained. A rhetorical analysis of this conflict will lead to an enhanced understanding not only of this controversy but also of the nature of the conflict between tradition and change—specifically, how the differing values of tradition and progress, division and identification, coexist and are negotiated in the context of the turn-of-the-millennium South. Only through increased understanding of such controversy can we hope to find a way out of it—if indeed we should find a way out of it.

Heritage was the term supported in the narratives put forth by defenders of the flag. Flag advocates merely had to say *heritage*, and they knew their intended audience of fellow, self-identifying white Southerners would think immediately of their Confederate heritage. Flag advocates centered their communications on the idea of heritage, focusing their actions on defending, commemorating, and celebrating their heritage as descendants of Confederate soldiers, officers, and citizens.

Addressing a January 2000 Heritage Rally in front of the Capitol, June Murray Wells, president-general of the UDC, sought to rally an audience predisposed to identify with heritage to take action by working with her and other leaders in defense of the flag. She spoke to reinforce her audience's extant attitudes about the Confederate battle flag and the heritage it represents. Heritage and its supporting narratives, working in conjunction with the myth of the Lost Cause, unified and strengthened Wells's intended audience of white, history-oriented Southerners, thus emboldening them to continue to fight for their flag.[20]

Wells began by characterizing herself as a Southerner: "I have spent my entire life in South Carolina and my entire adult life teaching the truth of Confederate history." Wells then went on to characterize the UDC, noting that its "objectives are historical, benevolent, educational, memorial, and patriotic." In particular, she wanted people to perceive her group as ameliorative rather than extremist in nature, pointing out that "the UDC has worked harmoniously on many projects with our Northern counterparts. We have worked toward forgiveness and peace." She explained why the UDC rarely becomes involved "in debates and arguments . . . in marches and protests": "The rules set by our founders and still in effect today require us to be non-political."[21] This explanation of the limits of her group's political activity emphasized the urgency of the flag situation and implied that the flag debate transcended the realm of mere politics. Wells's narration of her life as a Southerner and of the history of her particular group worked by analogy to reinforce and justify the attitudes and actions of her pro-flag audience. They could identify with her experiences; they too grew up revering the flag and listening to stories of their ancestors' sacrifices for the Confederate cause. Wells sought to persuade her audience to identify with those stories, with the values and good works inherent in them. In so doing, she reinforced the positive aspects of their identity so that they too would feel confidence in answering their opponents.

Wells saw the flag as representative of herself, and vice versa: "The Confederate States of America has several flags. They all represent me and I represent all of them. I'm proud to be an American, not just any old plain kind, but a Southern American, one still proud to be represented by that flag of the Confederacy on the dome."[22] Wells thus encouraged her listeners to equate themselves with the flag, giving them more of a stake in fighting for it. By using the present tense ("The Confederate States of America has several flags"), she conveyed that for her and many other flag advocates, the Confederacy still exists.

Therein lies the heart of this defense of the flag: South Carolina constituted the last vestige of the beloved Confederacy, the last Southern statehouse to display the flag at an official seat of government power. This fact may explain why not only South Carolina traditionalists rallied to the flag's defense but also those from around the South and the nation (as well as why so many others in South Carolina and beyond wanted the flag to come down). The fact that it was the last flag left in such a position of privilege imbued it with even more symbolic power, thus explaining the intense nature of this particular flag conflict. Adding to that intensity was the belief by people on both sides of the issue that a domino effect might ensue if South Carolina's flag came down, with changes in the Georgia and Mississippi state flags and perhaps the security of war memorials as well. Wells equated the flag with her audience's self-identity, implying that if the flag were taken down, a part of her listeners' identities would be defeated. As evidenced throughout her rhetoric, Wells aimed to increase listeners' sense of personal investment in the flag so that they would be more likely to come to its defense.

Though most of those who identified themselves with the Confederacy and its flag were white Southerners, one notable exception is H. K. Edgerton, a former head of the Asheville, North Carolina, chapter of the NAACP who now speaks out in defense of the flag. Edgerton characterizes himself as "a free man, ... an equal opportunity fighter for the people," and says that the flag "represents my heritage, my culture, my people's participation in this thing. ... That doesn't make me an Uncle Tom or lackey because I stand behind my heritage, because I understand the Confederate flag." In Edgerton's view, the Confederate flag bonds together the descendants of all those who suffered during the war, on the front lines and on the home front, white and black. Edgerton gave flag advocates an example of an African American who was "on their side," who identified positively with the flag and Confederate history (though not with slavery), and he thus became a case in point for such pro-flag groups as the Southern Legal Resources Center, based in Black Mountain, North Carolina.[23]

For flag opponents, a heritage of racial oppression summed up flag opponents' interpretation of the flag, its uses, its defenders, and its origins. Flag opponents merely had to say *hate*, and their target audience would understand immediately that they were referring to the hate of slaveholders, Ku Klux Klansmen, and all others whose racist views had denied equal opportunity through the years. Flag opponents focused their communications on depicting advocates as motivated by a heritage of hate and on defending their group against the oppressive hate of racists who continued to fly the flag of disrespect and violence toward African Americans. The NAACP depicted the flag as symbolic of racism because it had been "embraced as the primary symbol for the numerous modern-day groups advocating white supremacy." The NAACP also objected to the flag because its "placement . . . at the South Carolina State House with the flags of two existing governments . . . implies sovereignty and allegiance to a non-existent nation." Because of this negative symbolism, the NAACP hoped to gain "the removal and relocation of the Confederate Battle Flag to a place of historical rather than sovereign context."[24] This narrative translated into a belief that changing the context of the flag would change its meaning, making it less offensive to African Americans and thereby helping to create a less oppressive economic and social environment for African Americans living in South Carolina and the rest of the South.

NAACP representatives were not alone in articulating antiflag narratives. Jackson, founder and president of the Rainbow/PUSH Coalition, also spoke out about the controversy through his syndicated newspaper columns. On January 19, 2000, he offered a look at the conflicting interpretations of the flag, asking, "What is the confederate flag? It is the symbol, as Republican Senator John McCain stated on his good day, 'of racism and slavery.' One day later, McCain reversed himself to South Carolina reporters, saying the flag was a 'symbol of heritage.'"[25] Of course, the flag is a symbol of both—a symbol of heritage to some and a symbol of slavery and racism to others. Or in the case of McCain, the flag was a symbol of both to the same person, an incongruency Jackson used to point to the pandering nature of that year's Republican presidential contenders. Jackson used this narrative of McCain's Janus-like position on the flag to illustrate to his readers that the establishment-backed politicians of the Republican Party, even a supposed reformer such as McCain, could not be trusted. Even when apparently on the side of African Americans, Jackson argued, Republicans inevitably would take the side of the status quo—or of no other cause than their own political success. Sharing the McCain example, Jackson emphasized the need for his readers to analyze critically what people say in political situations.

Just as Wells explained what the flag meant to her on a personal level, so too did those opposed to the flag. James McJunkin, the ninety-one-year-old grandson of a former slave, told a reporter that when he sees the flag he sees "slavery, lynching, segregation, humiliation." As McJunkin emphasized, "I don't think we should have anything up on that building representing slavery. . . . It should be wiped completely off the map, cast into the sea of forgetfulness." Announcing that his group would honor the NAACP boycott and move its conference elsewhere, Timothy Downs of Atlanta, a minister with the Southeast Conference of the United Church of Christ, revealed that the "sight of the Confederate battle flag is like a stake through my heart, reminding me of the depth of the suffering of my parents and grandparents in a segregated South."[26] The meanings McJunkin and Downs attribute to the flag are rooted in the lived experiences of their parents and grandparents, in stories passed down about life under oppression rather than freedom.

For flag middle-grounders, the term *compromise* contained and summed up their belief that common ground was possible between the extremes of those who reverenced the flag and those offended by that same flag. The target audience of civic and business leaders on this middle ground saw the possibility of building a bridge over the deep ideological and cultural divide that would make it possible for roads of commerce and education to continue to connect South Carolina to the rest of the world. Flag neutralists focused on communicating the idea of compromise, finding an agreement that would benefit all South Carolinians economically and socially.

Thus, a capitalistic version of compromise was the strategy of choice for flag middle-grounders such as the HR, which characterized its membership as "a group of Upstate industry and business leaders, pastors, elected officials, lawyers, legislators and concerned citizens who have joined together to find a solution to the controversy . . . confident they will soon restore South Carolina's auspicious reputation and replace controversy with solution." Roundtable members interpreted the flag as "a symbol of the struggle between the North and South during the War Between the States. It stood for a nation's fight and has been transformed into the physical representation of the Southern heritage and way of life. . . . In recent years, the flag has been a source of much controversy—mainly because the flag means different things to different people." Based on this definition of the flag's meaning, the HR seems to have gone along with the traditional heritage interpretation yet recognized the fact that other interpretations existed and could not be ignored. Rather than stating that the flag symbolized the Confederacy, the group instead took the position that the flag signified the struggle between the North and the South rather than the ideology of one side or the other.[27]

Clemson University President James Barker characterized South Carolina as having "one of the nation's healthiest economies" and as "a rapidly growing population center" with a "future [that] seems undeniably bright." Barker thus emphasized the aspect of the state that he believed would most benefit from taking down the flag: its economy. He went on to list the many other "strong symbols" of South Carolina—"the palmetto tree, the state flag, revolutionary battlefields, and our natural scenic beauty"—that he saw as more appropriate (in terms of the state's economic interests) symbols for the state. Rather than debating whether or not the flag should remain, Barker constructed an alternative narrative when he proposed that "our debate should center on which of these symbols will best represent us and the kind of future we want to build for South Carolina."[28] Again, Barker redirected the focus of the debate from conflict over past narratives to the hope of an agreement that the future narrative of the state would focus on progress.

Governor Beasley's November 1996 remarks painted a similarly rosy picture of South Carolina life and his experiences of it:

> South Carolina is the only place I've called home. But even after growing up and being educated here, I have seen the fullness and richness of this state in a new light as your governor. We are a blessed people in so many ways. We possess the treasures of the honeysuckle and coral reef, the red clay of the mountains and the white sand of the beaches. We are stewards of vast natural resources to enjoy and protect. The land we live on is a gift. How we live on the land is a choice. And it is this—how we have chosen to live—that has inspired me in my travels. While we are not immune from the moral and social problems confounding the nation, we have not succumbed to them. In tens of thousands of households, children are being taught the difference between right and wrong. Against great odds, parents strive to be role models. The churches dotting street corners stand as beacons of hope and neighbor still helps neighbor. Ours is a good state with good people who have chosen to live honorably.

In telling this sunny story of nature and community, Beasley emphasized not only what is good about South Carolina (and by extension the South) but also what holds South Carolinians together in all their diversity. While Beasley acknowledged "church burnings and other hate crimes that have occurred," he stressed that "these crimes happened in South Carolina but do not represent South Carolina. Our people stand out against this backdrop of hate like stars against the midnight sky." Likewise, Beasley realized that "the Confederate flag flying above the State House flies in a vacuum. Its meaning and purpose are not defined by law. Because of this, any group can give the flag any meaning it chooses." Described as such, this flag is neutral, an empty signifier. Only the flags that "every South Carolinian can look up to with respect, admiration and the unshakable knowledge that the flag flies for them" should be flown at the Statehouse. Beasley painted this hopeful picture of a South Carolina whose people are joined together in the natural, communal glories of their idyllic, Eden-like state in hopes that the spirit of his story would be brought to life in a similarly peaceful ending to the flag debate.[29]

At the close of the flag debate in May 2000, Governor Hodges tried to set a similar tone in his depiction of South Carolinians as unified through their shared experiences of and valuing of history: "In South Carolina, history is more than just dates in a textbook. For all of us, white and black, history lives on in family traditions that are passed down from generation to generation.... We are proud to be South Carolinians. We have inherited a wonderful state from our ancestors. And we wish to make our state an even better place for our children." Again, the moral of the story was that history unifies rather than divides South Carolinians. Not only did Hodges try to rewrite South Carolina's experience as characterized by identification rather than division, he even attempted to tell the story of a South Carolina that was more progressive than other states (as opposed to a state still stuck in the quagmire of racism and its contentious symbols): "And our history will also be remembered in another significant way on our Statehouse grounds. In the last month, we have broken ground on a monument to honor the contributions of African-American citizens to this state—the only such monument on a statehouse grounds in the United States." In making this point as he was signing into law the bill that would remove the flag from atop the Capitol, Hodges co-opted the close of the Confederate flag chapter of South Carolina's history as a means of beginning the next chapter, in which South Carolina would take a role in leading the nation toward new heights of racial understanding.[30]

Central to flag advocates' positive interpretation of the flag is their similarly positive interpretation of the war. If the flag is to be portrayed as honorable, the Confederacy, its cause, and its defenders must also have been honorable. Wells's narrative of the war is typical: "South Carolina seceded first.... We would also be the only state to vote unanimously to secede.... The South did not leave the Union with animosity. They left simply because they wanted to be left alone to live in the way they chose. But this was not to be. A peaceful settlement could not be reached. The South did not invade the North. The North invaded the South[,] causing us to defend our homes, our way of life and even our lives." Wells made no mention of slavery, just an oblique reference to living "in the way they chose." Her narrative of events characterizes the South's motivations in leaving the Union solely as positive; the South assumed a defensive stance only after provoked by the North through the threat of invasion. In this telling of the war story, Wells reinforced her listeners' belief that their ancestors were on the right side of the war, that their heritage as Southerners was one of a peaceful pursuit of independence made violent only by the North's offensive action.

Other flag advocates echoed this theme. Helga Milsap, an eighty-two-year-old from Fountain Inn and the daughter of a Confederate veteran, told reporter Joseph Bryant that she did not "understand why some loathe the flag and are determined to see it removed. Looking at it, she sees the embodiment of pride and bravery demonstrated by men like her father.... With each wave, Milsap said the flag continues to salute men like her father who went to battle for their beliefs." As she stated, "Taking down that flag would mean their fighting didn't mean anything. Her father "wasn't better than anybody else, but he fought and lost, but they still fought." War reenactor Jim Ridge of the Palmetto Battalion opined, "We're here to celebrate our ancestors who died for what they believed in."[31] Both Milsap's and Ridge's comments clearly contain the narrative of ancestors fighting for an honorable cause to which they were sincerely committed.

In addition, Wells's war narrative counteracted any "false teachings" her audience may have received in the public schools. She answered any doubts created by opponents' version of the war, which blamed the South and situated its desire for independence in its desire to protect slavery. Wells negated this alternate view of the war by leaving out all mention of slavery and in so doing negated many African Americans' feelings of being oppressed by a flag that for them signified hate, first through slavery and later through segregation. In a similar vein, Edgerton offered an alternative narrative to the mainstream story of blacks as opposed to the Confederates' war effort. Rather, Edgerton explained, "If it hadn't been for the sweat of the black man, the Confederate army would have quickly come to a halt. [Blacks] were the folks who picked the cotton. They were the ones who prepared the foodstuffs. It was black hands working with white hands to till the soil.... It was trusted black hands left on the plantation to guard the mistress and her children. It was skilled black labor who worked in the factories, making the implements of war, and kept the Southern army in the field. Who else did it? ... It wasn't the lash that forced them to do this, it was love." Slaves in Edgerton's narrative of the war become loyal helpers to the families of Confederate men who have left home for the battlefields, assisting the cause not out of fear but out of love. In telling this alternative story of blacks during the war, Edgerton co-opts the slavery-based objections to the Confederacy and its flag, thereby recharacterizing slaves as heroes in the Confederate struggle rather than its victims.[32]

Flag opponents also told their own narratives about the war to justify the flag's removal. In its July 1999 emergency resolution, "Economic Sanctions for South Carolina," the NAACP included a war narrative typical of flag opponents: "The Confederate States of America came into being by way of secession from and war against the United States of America out of a desire to defend the rights of individual states to maintain an economic system based on slave labor." Thus, the NAACP depicted the purpose of the Confederacy as defending the institution of slavery rather than defending states' rights (as depicted by flag advocates). Kweisi Mfume, president and chief executive officer of the NAACP, offered his audience this version of the war and the raising of the flag to counteract historical narratives of these events promulgated by what his organization perceived to be the dominant culture, including the flag's defenders. Armed with their own version of history, Mfume's listeners were thus empowered to defend their pairing of the flag with a heritage of hate. This narrative resonated with the war stories passed down in McJunkin's family: his grandfather was threatened because "he told them that the North was going to whip the South and that the black man was going to be free. [An angry mob] said they were going to kill him. Too smart a man to live."[33]

Like others involved in arguing about the meaning and placement of the Confederate flag, Jackson shared his narrative of the war: "The confederate flag is not an insult to black people only. It is the banner flown by those who so strongly believed in racial supremacy and slavery that they turned to sedition, and tried to destroy the United States of America. A Republican president, Abraham Lincoln, was forced to war to preserve the union. More American lives were lost in that terrible war than in any other conflict in our nation's history. Slavery, sedition, savagery—that is some heritage." Like Mfume, Jackson offered African

Americans a reading of the events of the war and the raising of the flag that revealed flag advocates' beloved "heritage" to be a heritage of hate. In his version of Southern history, Jackson took the term *heritage*, emptied it of the positive connotations attributed to it by its defenders, and refilled it with his own interpretation of the Confederate heritage: "Slavery, sedition, savagery—that is some heritage." In so resignifying heritage with the meaning of a heritage of hate, Jackson claimed for his listeners the power to characterize their history and experience in their own terms. In addition, he sent a message to his opponents through the act of overturning the meaning of their revered heritage. James Gallman of the South Carolina NAACP took bit gentler approach than Jackson, acknowledging "that men fought honorably for the Confederacy" but holding to the narrative that "the cause they fought for was not honorable. Their attempt to maintain slavery was evil, and their attack on the United States of America was treasonous."[34] All of these reconstructionist war narratives associate the Confederate flag not only with the oppression of African Americans but also with disloyalty to the United States and all that it represented.

One group of compromisers, the HR, offered a solution to the flag controversy based in a shared narrative of South Carolina history and motivated by the hope of a shared narrative of future South Carolina prosperity. This group proposed legislation for the establishment of a Heritage Park, to be located on the site of the former Capitol, that would embrace various narratives of South Carolina's history from 1848 through around 1870. In a press conference unveiling the HR's plan for the park, State Senator David Thomas told his version of a shared narrative of South Carolina history: "I have always believed that if there was a common ground it had to be out of our common history and the heritage shared by us all. Black or white, if you are from South Carolina, your forefathers were affected and we all have been impacted forever by the outcome of the War Between the States. It is in that heritage that we have found the answer to this controversy." Thomas pointed to a history that was shared rather than divided or contested. By retelling the story of South Carolina race relations and history as one of shared struggles, Thomas hoped that the HR could, through its proposed park, rewrite the future of South Carolina in terms of improved race relations and continued economic growth. State Senator Ralph Anderson, also an HR member, literally characterized the situation as a narrative: "I am happy to stand today with Senator Thomas as we open a bright chapter in our state's unwritten history." Thomas's and Anderson's remarks conveyed to their audience the message that it is possible to rewrite history, to overcome past conflicts through positive, cooperative attitudes in the present. By offering a plan that they hoped would please those on both sides of the issue, HR members also were sending a message to business interests beyond South Carolina's borders that the voices of reason would prevail and that South Carolina would become an even more ideal place in which to do business.[35]

Wells also shared her narrative—typical of those of flag advocates—of why the Confederate battle flag came to be flown atop the South Carolina statehouse just over a century after the war: "The Battle Flag was chosen because it had been chosen by the living United Confederate Veterans as their symbol.... I was here at this same building in 1962 when the flag was raised. There was absolutely no negative intent. In fact quite the opposite. It was raised to commemorate the centennial of the war; to honor the memory of men, women and children; black and white, both military and civilian who lived in and defended the South during the War and came together after the war to rebuild the South they all called home." In Wells's narration, the flag signified the shared experience and achievement of all Southerners who endured the war and then rebuilt their region, countering opponents' accusations that the flag held positive meaning for only one segment of the state's population: whites descended from Confederate officers and soldiers. Wells again provided her audience with a quick answer to arguments that the flag did not represent the heritage of all South Carolinians and negated her opponents' interpretation of the flag in what she left out of her flag-raising account. Wells made no mention of the social upheaval in the wake of the 1954 *Brown v. Board of Education* decision, an omission of the social circumstances that did much to shape the self-concepts of her opponents as well as of members of her target audience. In the rhetoric of Wells and most other flag advocates, the heritage being defended was solely that of white Southerners with ancestral ties to the Confederate military, despite the lip service paid to the roles of other groups in their account of Southern history.[36]

Not surprisingly, flag opponents did not accept flag advocates' narrative of the flag raising at face value, substituting another perspective in which, as Jackson put it, "South Carolina's officials only raised the confederate flag over the capital in 1962 as a direct insult to the civil rights movement. It was the symbol of their commitment to legal apartheid and their opposition to equal rights for a race they considered inferior." This theme also appears in the NAACP's telling of the story: "The Confederate Battle Flag was raised in the States that comprised the defunct Confederate States of America for the supposed celebration of the Centennial of the War Between the States and as an unspoken symbol of resistance to the battle for civil rights and equality in the early 1960s." For flag opponents, the timing of the 1962 raising of the flag was significant not because it was the centennial of the war but because it was a time when the segregated institutions of the South faced increasing threats from federally mandated integration. This is a key element of flag opponents' contention that the Confederate flag atop South Carolina's Capitol was not merely an innocent memorial to the war dead but rather a symbol meant to flaunt whites' power over blacks at a time when whites feared that they might soon lose it.[37]

In addition, just as those on both sides used personal narratives to explain their connections with the flag and the Southern culture, opponents used such personal stories to explain their perspectives on why the flag had been raised atop the Statehouse dome. Gallman recalled growing up in Aiken in the years of segregation and the growing civil rights movement: "What I remember most as a child was the Ku Klux Klan riding through the streets of Aiken, on Sumter Street between Richland and Barnwell. They had their crosses and their bedsheets, and of course, they had their Confederate battle flags." Such memories cemented Gallman's conviction that the flag flew atop the Capitol for racist rather than commemorative reasons. As reporter Lane Filler observed, "While flag supporters say flying it shows reverence for the men who served with honor during the Civil War, Gallman's reasons to lower it go to the fear tactics he witnessed at the hands of whites. They stem from his perception that the Confederate flag was raised over the Statehouse in 1962 not to celebrate the Civil War centennial, but as a slap in the face to the civil rights movement that was gaining strength and to school desegregation that would hit South Carolina eight years later." Likewise, State Senator John Drummond, a white Democrat from the town of Ninety Six, also used a story from his past to explain his present view that the flag should be removed. As reporter Zane Wilson recounted, "Drummond tried to smooth some waters by recalling his time in a German prisoner of war camp with three black pilots. Until then, he had never been around blacks, and he learned much, he said. Those men came home to a segregated South where they had few of the rights they fought for, and just as the civil rights movement got under way, the flag went up on the dome, Drummond said. The flag was put up 'in defiance of civil rights,' not simply as a Civil War centennial celebration, Drummond said. The flag hurts people and it should come off the dome, he said. 'Love they neighbor,' he added." Drummond hoped that by sharing this personal narrative he might change others' perspectives on why the flag was raised and, importantly, on why it should come down.[38]

In his November 1996 speech promoting compromise on the flag, Beasley included a narrative about why the flag had been placed atop the dome: "By resolution in 1962, the General Assembly voted to fly the flag over the State House to honor the 70-thousand South Carolinians who served our state in the War Between the States, and the 20-thousand who died. It was—and is—proper to honor our heritage and the people who made it. But the plowshare has been turned into a sword. Hate-filled cowards cover their heads and meet under cloak of night, scattering their seeds of racism in the winds of deceit about the flag and its meaning." Beasley's narrative, typical of the compromisers' perspective, incorporated themes from both advocates' and opponents' narratives. From the traditionalists' flag-raising story, Beasley borrowed the theme that the flag had been placed on the dome to honor those South Carolinians who fought and died in the war. In like fashion, Beasley incorporated the theme of racism central to the reconstructionists' flag-raising story, though in Beasley's narrative, the racism had not necessarily been present when the flag was raised.[39]

In 1999, Barker related Clemson's narrative of balancing tradition and change during the 1960s:

> As I began my Clemson education in the early 1960s, the University was changing rapidly. We had successfully made the conversion from an all-military college for men to a coeducational civilian university. . . . However, other important changes were coming as Clemson prepared to change from an all-white institution to an integrated institution. African American students peacefully enrolled at Clemson. . . . It was a process that showed the best of Clemson University, and it was described in the national press as "integration with dignity." As Clemson's population became more diverse, we became more aware of existing symbols that represented our university at sports and other public events. These symbols included the playing of "Tiger Rag" and "Dixie," as well as the Tiger and the Country Gentleman mascots, and the confederate flag. Clemson listened carefully to our new, more diverse student body. It was clear that some of these symbols were stronger than others in representing the kind of place Clemson wanted to be and the kind of future Clemson envisioned for itself.

Barker concluded by noting that Clemson ended up "maintaining aspects of its traditions including 'Tiger Rag' and the Tiger mascot and letting the other symbols—the Country Gentleman mascot, the confederate flag and 'Dixie'—be part of Clemson's past." Barker offered an alternate narrative of South Carolina in the 1960s that depicted at least one pocket of the state in which more tolerant, progressive attitudes flourished even as the flag was being raised atop the Statehouse dome. His other purpose in sharing this story was to provide a precedent for the state to follow, a model for surveying its symbols and thinking about how those symbols not only relate to the past but also affect the present and the future. Barker's narrative of tradition and change showed that the two can coexist—and in South Carolina, at that—without negating each other. His narrative argued that the state as a whole could strike such a balance between tradition and change. The story of compromise at Clemson gave life and credence to the idea of a middle ground.[40]

Moving into the present even as she embraced the Confederate past, the UDC's Wells narrated her version of the contemporary flag controversy and boycott: "Now our heritage is being threatened by newspaper ads and a boycott, both scare tactics. . . . If we elected the right legislators, our symbols will be safe. If you see a newspaper ad that is designed to cause fear and division among Southerners, throw it in the trash where it belongs." This story paralleled Wells's narrative of the war: again the heritage of the South was being threatened, and again she characterized the South's defenders as passive victims not responsible for the conflict. But rather than admitting that South Carolina was being hurt by the economic sanctions, Wells turned the tables and spun an alternative tale in which the enemy was portrayed as hurting its own adherents: "It is a very sad thing that the NAACP is hurting their own people. I know there are many fine black people who own their own businesses and many who work at hotels, restaurants and other tourist oriented businesses. I think the NAACP should be working to help these people, not use them as pawns in a fight over a flag most of them have never seen. I am not particularly concerned over those events that have been withdrawn from South Carolina. It just leaves more time and space on the tourism calendar for our fine heritage groups and re-enactor groups to hold events that will attract tourists to learn about the truth of Confederate history."[41] Wells articulated this version of the boycott not only to answer her critics but also to help her audience feel better about the situation. If the boycott were hurting only those who were carrying it out, why should it concern Wells and her fellow flag defenders?

The syntax of Wells's characterization of the NAACP and those whose interests it represented, however, demonstrates that she was doing what she had accused the NAACP of doing: hurting her own cause. Phrases such as "their own people," "many fine black people," and "these people" betray a tone of condescension symptomatic of an attitude of white supremacy on her part. Wells could be seen as resituating African Americans in a servant role by emphasizing the idea that many African Americans "work in hotels, restaurants and other tourist related businesses"—in short, the service industry. And she characterized the NAACP as merely playing a game, thereby degrading its cause. But perhaps the clearest indicator of Wells's underlying racist narrative is her assertion that many African Americans in South Carolina had never seen the flag atop the Capitol, thus characterizing them as ignorant and ill traveled.

Wells closed her story of the boycott by privileging the tourist business of reenactors and other war enthusiasts (that is, whites), thereby minimizing the importance and effects of the boycott. The negative implications of this narrative took away from Wells's earlier credibility regarding the unifying nature of the flag as a symbol for all Southerners, not just whites. But pointing out the self-inflicted wounds of the boycotters provided her listeners with a sense of justice, with a sense that they had not been wounded by the enemy's fire inasmuch as the enemy had wounded its own.

Also characteristic of the pro-flag rhetoric in this debate were statements found on the Web site of the South Carolina Division of the SCV. This narrative also portrayed the contemporary controversy as paralleling the war. This served as an attractive and effective metaphor for rallying the troops, affording a chance to refight the war on behalf of their ancestors in the hope that this time they would emerge victorious: "We have once again been drawn into a battle over our Confederate flag. The forces of modernism and appeasement have determined to make another assault on the emblem of our ancestors. It is our duty to come to the defense of their good name. If we falter now, we will surely be faced with more and even greater demands for removing and relocating Southern symbols.

We have tried to be patient and conciliatory throughout this matter, but the other side will have none of it. Now is the time for action! There are three things you must do RIGHT AWAY." Words such as *battle, forces, assault, duty,* and *defense* framed the flag conflict as a reenactment of the war. In the same spirit, Edgerton said that the flag debate "is not the first time that carpetbaggers and scalawags have come into the South to try to separate white folks and black folks."[42] Such a characterization was appropriate for a group whose members focus on studying and reenacting the history of a war in which they situate themselves via genealogical ties. Not only did such syntax frame the contemporary flag conflict as a war, but the plot offered parallels with many SCV members' narrative of the War between the States. The assertion that "If we falter now, we will surely be faced with more and even greater demands for removing and relocating Southern symbols" paralleled nineteenth-century Southern secessionists' belief that if the South kept capitulating to northern-oriented policies, tyranny would not disappear but would instead intensify. Thus echoing their forebears, the leaders of the South Carolina SCV called the group's members to immediate action in the hope of victory in the war for a separate Southern identity.

Indeed, the writer for the South Carolina SCV continued his narrative elsewhere on the Web page: "I am often asked this question, 'when will all this controversy be over?' That is an easy answer: when we give up." This statement created another parallel with the war itself, with the implication that while the Confederacy gave up its fight too soon, modern defenders of the South could lose only if they stopped fighting for their cause. This narrative also reflected the belief that honor could be won in the process of fighting, an attractive idea to those who very much wanted to defend the honor of their ancestors' sacrifice on behalf of the Lost Cause. Even though those ancestors had lost the war, they gained honor simply by fighting. Drawing a parallel between defending the state's right to fly a particular flag and defending states' rights in the war was a very appropriate rhetorical strategy for rallying descendants of Confederate soldiers and officers. In portraying the flag debate as their chance to refight the war, advocates chose an especially appropriate means of inspiring their "troops" to keep up the good fight, to sacrifice their time, money, and other resources on behalf of the Confederate battle flag.

More pro-flag rhetoric appeared in materials from the national headquarters of the SCV on how to deal with "heritage violations" (perceived threats to Confederate flags, monuments, and the like) of all kinds. Group leaders offered members and other allies rhetorical advice for characterizing the SCV and its cause in a positive way: "Heritage violations are most severe. SCV members are reminded however to keep their cool. Those that cause a heritage violation sometimes take steps in an attempt to provoke us. Those that create heritage violation [*sic*] sometimes would like nothing better than for us to fly off the handle. Do not over react. Always handle yourself like the responsible Southern gentleman that you are.... [T]he SCV on a national level will respond when needed. We will respond with the truth, facts not fiction, and do it in a positive and calm manner." And on the "Heritage Issues" page, the SCV stated that it "promotes a positive resolution to all heritage violations. Correspondence to suspected violators MUST be dignified, thoughtful and polite."[43] The SCV clearly was not blind to the widespread narratives portraying Southern partisans as racist and ignorant in both their beliefs and behavior. Thus, the SCV countered such negative portrayals with what it believed to be the essence of its membership: the Southern gentleman. And just as it offered advice for positive self-presentation, the SCV conveyed a negative image of its opponents.

In contrast, Mfume offered a different narrative of the NAACP's boycott of South Carolina tourism. Speaking on February 19, 2000, at the group's annual board meeting, Mfume said, "The Black American economy is an unexplored treasure chest in a wrecked ship that must now be opened[,] inspected and liberated. We want as our forebears wanted throughout the twenties and the thirties and the forties, we want an end to the economic grandfather clauses, the perpetual contracts that have helped us simply as consumers. Too many industries have engaged in a process of systematically ignoring our buying power or boycotting our intelligence.... So when we talk ab[o]ut economic sanctions against South Carolina, we are boycotting it because our dignity has been boycotted by others." In telling this story, Mfume argued that the African American spending power has been underappreciated and that present NAACP members simply want what their forebears wanted. Therefore, they initiated the boycott of South Carolina not only to bring down the flag but also to highlight their right to equal opportunities in a capitalist society. Focusing his story in this way, Mfume appealed to the righteous indignation of his target audience of African Americans, many of whom felt they had been prevented from achieving economic success by the same people who stubbornly continued to fly the Confederate flag over the South Carolina Statehouse. When Mfume stated that "someone else's heritage is really our slavery," he not only redefined the heritage of the flag in his group's terms but also connected the economic realities of the slavery symbolized by the flag with the fact that African Americans are no longer commodities to be bought and sold. Contemporary African Americans, Mfume argued, are citizens who can buy and sell as fellow consumers and businesspeople in the American capitalistic system, and they were using those economic acts to make their voices heard in the flag controversy. He further detailed his group's interpretation of the flag as a negative, divisive symbol when he noted that "the folly of flying a flag that is symbolic of racism and anti-Semitism and bigotry and intolerance will simply not be allowed to occur." Mfume denied his opponents' idea of heritage and instead offered his audience a radically different interpretation for the meaning of the flag: hate. This hate was symbolized materially in the form of the flag and economically in the opportunities that remained closed to many African Americans.[44]

Similarly, Jackson told of a similar situation involving the Confederate flag in another Southern state: "Alabama took its confederate flag down in 1993 after a lawsuit by black legislators. It was only when its public romance with racism ended that it was able to attract major manufacturers like Mercedes and Honda." This story of breaking with the Confederate tradition resulting in positive economic consequences sent a clear message: Take down the flag and your state, too, will benefit. Moreover, the story also warned Georgia that it could face the same situation as South Carolina if it did not soon move to change its state flag: "That boycott will surely come to Georgia if the flag is not changed." To emphasize his point, he repeated himself, concluding, "South Carolina is reacting to growing outside pressure. If Georgia doesn't act soon, it will be next."[45] Jackson's narrative warned other states of the potential consequences of failing to meet flag opponents' demands and pointed out the benefits of embracing change. In addition, he encouraged his target audience of African Americans to persist in their efforts and thereby to reap rewards tangible (economic opportunity) and intangible (victory over former oppressors).

Rather than emphasizing the boycott's possible economic toll, Gallman stressed the social and emotional price black South Carolinians had already paid for living for years in the flag's shadow: "The fact is, it's not just about the flag. . . . It's about a group of people saying, 'We ain't gonna have a bunch of black folks tell us what to do.' And yet I think if those people had experienced what we had, they could understand that the flag has no business flying over a building that represents all the people of South Carolina." Or, as Rev. Sam W. Moore of Chester, the great-grandson of a Reconstruction-era black lawmaker, argued, "Legislators are supposed to be leaders and lead the people towards one direction. . . . All that flag does is keep us divided. It divides the blacks and the whites, and it divides us as a state. And anything we do that does that, we need to take a closer look at and evaluate it." South Carolinians Gallman and Moore emphasized the daily experiences of a state divided along color lines. To them, the flag was not a symbol or a rallying cry for some distant cause but rather vivid evidence of the past and present state of race relations in the state. In McJunkin's words, "I don't think we should have anything up on [the State Capitol] representing slavery. . . . It should be wiped completely off the map, cast into the sea of forgetfulness."[46]

Taking the middle road, Beasley tried to focus his narrative not on the past but on the present and the future:

> Do we want our children to be debating this issue ten years from now because we haven't resolved it? I say no. . . . I want to honor my ancestors. . . . But even more, I want to work for today's generation and those of tomorrow. I want us to leave for them a standard by which they measure themselves—a standard of respect, honor, integrity, and reconciliation. . . . Flag supporters say let it continue to fly over the State House. Flag opponents say take it down and stick

it in a museum. Tonight, I'm asking the leadership of both sides to meet me halfway. Let's end this debate once and for all. Tonight, I'm asking that we come together as a people—to honor each other and understand each other: to forge a ministry of reconciliation that extends to every citizen from the greatest to the least. I ask you to think about this and to pray about it.[47]

Beasley wanted his audience to think beyond the present and themselves to the future and others. He hoped to inspire his target audience of South Carolinians, especially legislators and leaders, to move from the political to the spiritual, to forsake stubborn arguments in favor of conciliatory prayers. By framing his speech in religious or spiritual terms, Beasley offered a parallel narrative in the form of biblical allusions to Jesus Christ's ministry of reconciliation as discussed in the Bible's New Testament. Realizing the appeal of the Jesus' example to South Carolinians in all three camps on the flag debate—advocates, opponents, and compromisers—Beasley hoped that all could find a common, shared narrative of reconciliation together in the next step of the flag debate.

In 2000, the HR succinctly summed up the narrative of the flag conflict, noting that, "The banner has put a strain on black and white relationships, not only in the public arena, but in the private sector as well. The issue is tearing friendships, relationships, businesses and communities apart." As Hodges noted in his January 2000 State of the State address, "Let's resolve this issue. And let's resolve it right now. . . . We must move the flag from the dome to a place of historical significance on the Statehouse grounds. The debate over the Confederate flag has claimed too much of our time and energy."[48] Middle-grounders' message to their audience of citizens concerned about the state's economy and reputation was that it did not matter which side was right in the war or now. Instead, compromisers argued that what mattered was the conflict's negative impact on the state's internal and external relationships. South Carolinians should agree that what mattered most was not the past but the present and future and should support any compromises necessary to ensure a positive future. In other words, compromisers advocated shifting the focus of the debate from intangible ideals and interpretations of history to the tangible benefits to be had by moving beyond the flag conflict.

Underlying the compromisers' narratives was a concern for polishing the state's reputation, which had to be maintained so that the state could continue to grow economically. Barker, as president of a university with many financial and relational ties to industry, which provided grants, internships, and jobs for graduates, and with a stated goal of rising in the national rankings, had an enormous stake in the flag debate. Thus, he offered the narrative of Clemson's change in philosophy and image in the hope that legislators would follow suit. The moral of Barker's story is that "much of Clemson's success can be traced to the decisions made more than three decades ago regarding the symbols that would represent Clemson University in the future."[49]

At the close of the 2000 flag debate, when Hodges signed the bill to move the flag from the dome to the Confederate Soldiers' Monument, he offered a hopeful narrative for life in post-flag South Carolina:

> Today, we bring this debate to an honorable end. Today, the descendants of slaves and the descendants of Confederate soldiers join together in the spirit of mutual respect. Today, the debate over the Confederate flag above the Capitol passes into South Carolina history. . . . The debate over the Confederate flag has claimed a great deal of our time and energy. We must now heal the wounds of this divisive debate. We must strive for reconciliation. We must now work together on the other challenges that confront our state. . . . We must meet these challenges with willing hearts and ready hands. Only then can we lead South Carolina into the bright promise of this new century. Only then can we truly be one South Carolina under two flags that unite us all—the American flag and the Palmetto flag.[50]

Hodges's concluding chapter thus offered a story of reconciliation, of present and future unification for South Carolinians via acknowledging and overcoming past divisions.

All sides in this conflict would agree that their stories of the war and its consequences were central to their distinctive Southern identities, whether as Confederate descendants, civil rights activists, or capitalistic compromisers. All involved cared about what the flag's absence or presence conveyed about their state, and the existence of this debate stemmed from their unacknowledged consensus that, for better or worse, the Confederate battle flag reflected the way those on all sides viewed themselves and others as Southerners. Fisher's narrative paradigm provides a valuable means by which to understand these texts because considering "that public-social knowledge is to be found in the stories that we tell one another [enables] us to observe not only our difference, but also our commonalties, and in such observation we might be able to reform the notion of the 'public.'"[51] By allowing us a means to discover not only the dynamic of division but also the presence of identification, the narrative paradigm offers some hope of understanding in an otherwise seemingly polarized field of conflict.

Therefore, even though division existed regarding the flag's meaning and history, identification also stemmed from the fact that the flag's existence and the historical narratives it symbolized were important to all participants in this debate. All of those involved agreed that the war, its outcome, and subsequent events constituted a narrative crucial to understanding Southern identity, but that narrative took many forms, depending on the experiences of those telling the story. These distinctive narratives of the war, race relations, the flag raising, and the debate about lowering it explain the equally distinctive meanings attributed to the symbol.

Considered together in the agonistic crucible of this conflict, the meanings and messages of these divergent narratives ignited a fire that purified and refined both sides' messages. In the end, when the fire of controversy had burned out, what remained was what was common to all stakeholders: a shared concern for their distinctive identity as Southerners. These debates and conversations about the diversity of the meanings Southerners attach to the Confederate flag could not and did not take place in 1962, when the flag was first raised atop the Capitol. At that time, no debate occurred—the flag was raised without question. But many lively, invigorating, and contentious debates about the flag and its meaning have taken place in the ensuing years, a fact that should cause the people of the South joy. As Coski observes, "The battle over the battle flag represents one of the most intensive and extensive ongoing public dialogues about U.S. history." Rather than being a sore spot or source of shame, these debates should be seen as a source of a reconciling, reinvigorating pride that all South Carolinians and all Southerners can share and from which Americans at large can benefit. In Coski's words, "Continuing controversy over the battle flag could be healthy for America's public dialogue. . . . If the public dialogue about the flag were intelligent and free of dogma and unrestrained emotion, it might generate genuine insights into the complex issues of race and states' rights in the American past, present, and future."[52]

Of course, the debate over the Confederate battle flag in South Carolina would not be the last conversational skirmish in the ongoing unfinished civil war for Southern identity. Other public debates would also purify and refine Southerners' shared identity. One such debate occurred in December 2002, when equally divergent stories would be told in the accusations and apologia that constituted the Trent Lott–Strom Thurmond debacle.

4

Senator Trent Lott: Southern Sinner, Scapegoat, and Sacrifice

IF THE CONFEDERATE battle flag was the most divisive of Southern symbols throughout the twentieth century, the causes with which it has most often been associated during that century, segregation and racism, have been just as divisive in practice. At the same time that formerly segregated Southern institutions such as the Virginia Military Institute were beginning to admit women, Southern cities were making room for depictions of a more diverse array of heroes than Confederate generals, and symbols of division such as the Confederate flag were being taken down, a new controversy arose when questions surfaced about whether one of the most powerful Southern political leaders on the national scene was a supporter of racial segregation. When Trent Lott made remarks at Strom Thurmond's one hundredth birthday party that could be interpreted as supportive of Thurmond's 1948 segregationist presidential bid, many people associated the Mississippi senator with segregation, the twentieth-century South's chief manifestation of the order of division. Lott's accusers looked for evidence not only that his recent remarks had been divisive but that his entire career had been filled with instances in which Lott chose to associate himself with the causes of division rather than the causes of identification. In response, Lott needed to prove that he had moved away from the order of division and toward the order of identification. At the resolution of this controversy, however, Lott was forced to resign from his post as incoming Senate majority leader, another instance in which the new order of identification triumphed over the old order of division in the turn-of-the-millennium South. A scapegoat needed to be sacrificed to expiate the race relations sins of the South, the political establishment, the media, and the nation. Accusers singled Lott out as a worthy sacrifice because of his controversial remarks and his position of power. However, it is unlikely that Lott provided a sufficient sacrifice for the South's entire history of segregationist sins.

Prior to December 5, 2002, most Americans probably would not have known that South Carolina senator J. Strom Thurmond had been a candidate for president in 1948, let alone what party he had represented. But the family, friends, staff members, and Senate colleagues who gathered for his one hundredth birthday party surely knew of Thurmond's candidacy as standard-bearer for the States' Rights Democratic Party, in which he garnered thirty-nine electoral votes and made a name for himself on the national political scene. Thurmond believed that he and his party had sent a message to the Democratic Party that it should no longer take for granted the South's support on Election Day. Furthermore, the exposure brought by the presidential bid laid the groundwork for the former two-term governor of South Carolina's election to the U.S. Senate in 1954, an office he still held forty-eight years later.

Lott was among those who knew of Thurmond's 1948 presidential run as well as of his subsequent "personal and philosophical transformation," as Lott puts it in his 2005 autobiography, *Herding Cats: A Life in Politics*. Lott recounts that as Thurmond closed in on the centennial of his birth, he "slipped easily into bouts of depression," and Lott found that "one way to brighten his spirits instantly was to spin jokes about his run for president in 1948.... I was only seven when Strom was barnstorming the South, and I remembered nothing about the election or the furor that surrounded it. So I'd kid him, 'You know, you would have made a great president.' His eyes would light up, and you could sense that he savored the compliment. I never mentioned the segregationist platform ... and neither did he. I was aware that he had evolved over the years, broadening into a minority-oriented politician. But we didn't talk about that either."[1] Similarly, at Thurmond's Senate-hosted birthday party on December 5, 2002, the focus was not Thurmond's distant, sometimes controversial political past and his transition from Democrat to States' Rights Democrat to Republican. Instead, the mood was jovial, and in this atmosphere of levity, Lott took the floor to share his thoughts on and good wishes for Thurmond.

According to Lott, the preceding speaker, Bob Dole, gave "a typically sarcastic speech packed with just about every joke in the Strom Thurmond repertoire—including all the ones my staff had used in mine." "Hard pressed to come up with a batch of fresh compliments and gags to match Dole's performance," Lott was forced, "in desperation," to begin "talking off the cuff." He joked about Dole "dang near" winning the presidency by telling Thurmond jokes and "Thurmond never leav[ing] the Senate until the Capitol froze over." In a similar vein, Lott told "of that great debate in 1850, when John C. Calhoun . . . whirled around to face Daniel Webster . . . to declare, 'Dan, I know Strom Thurmond. He's a friend of mine. And, Dan, you're no Strom Thurmond.'" For his conclusion, Lott "revived a bit I'd done back in 1980 at a campaign rally for Ronald Reagan in Mississippi." These forty words would come to have very serious consequences for Lott: "I want to say this about my state: When Strom Thurmond ran for president we voted for him. We're proud of it. And if the rest of the country had of followed our lead we wouldn't of had all these problems over all these years." The transcript indicates that both laughter and applause followed the first two sentences; after the third line, however, the audience neither laughed nor applauded but fell silent. Lott recalls the moment somewhat differently: "The stag-party mood all but drowned out those forty words. There was no stunned silence as I concluded, as no gasp from a rapt audience—though both would be reported thousands of times during the next three weeks."[2]

Lott moved on to the rest of his jokes and compliments about the guest of honor. But when the first of much mainstream media reporting focusing on Lott's controversial comments appeared two days later, in a *Washington Post* article by Thomas Edsall, Lott could only pray that the press, the public, and his political colleagues would move on just as quickly.[3] Instead, however, Lott's remarks sparked a two-week-long mass-mediated exchange of accusations and apologia in which Lott became the scapegoat for the South's—and perhaps even the nation's—unatoned sins of segregation and racism.

I will detail the events of this rhetorical situation, creating a timeline of the various accusations and apologia that constituted this debate. I will then provide background on Thurmond's 1948 presidential campaign and his subsequent decades on the national political scene, giving a historical context to the controversy surrounding Lott's comments. I will briefly summarize Lott's life, paying special attention to race-related issues from his college days through to his terms as a U.S. senator. Having established a thorough understanding of the rhetorical situation, I will survey the literature on *kategoria* and apologia as well as scapegoating, victimage, and mortification, thereby explaining the theoretical underpinnings of this section. These discussions prepare the way for a detailed rhetorical analysis of the various accusations leveled against Lott in the midst of this controversy as well as of the various apologia Lott (and his few defenders) articulated in response to these accusations. This rhetorical analysis will ultimately lead to some overarching conclusions regarding the scapegoating of Lott for the sins of segregation some forty years after the civil rights movement resulted in segregation's legal demise.

From the first media coverage of Lott's remarks on December 6 through the senator's resignation from the post of majority leader–elect on December 20, many accusations and apologies were articulated. Lott's spokesman, Ron Bonjean, offered a brief explanatory (but unapologetic) statement soon after the event, stating that "Senator Lott's remarks were intended to pay tribute to a remarkable man who led a remarkable life. To read anything more into these comments is wrong." This explanation, however, was not sufficient to prevent public criticism of Lott. Rev. Jesse Jackson Sr. of the Rainbow/PUSH Coalition issued a statement on December 8 calling for Lott to step down as incoming majority leader. The following day, former vice president Al Gore, in an interview with Judy Woodruff on CNN's *Inside Politics*, described Lott's words as "a racist statement" but did not go so far as to call Lott a racist. Gore recommended that Lott withdraw his remarks or face formal censure by the Senate. Also on December 9, Lott issued his first apology: "A poor choice of words conveyed to some the impression that I embraced the discarded policies of the past. . . . Nothing could be further from the truth, and I apologize to anyone who was offended by my statement." However, many observers found this brief, emotionless apology unsatisfactory. On December 10, two interest groups from opposite ends of the political spectrum spoke out against Lott and his remarks. The National Association for the Advancement of Colored People (NAACP) called for Lott to resign as incoming majority leader, while the Family Research Council issued a statement asking whether the Republican Party should consider someone else to be its Senate leader.[4]

December 11 brought information from Lott's past that made his latest comments seem less isolated and extemporaneous than the senator and his spokesman had indicated. Carl Hulse reported in the *New York Times* that Lott had made a very similar remark on November 3, 1980, in a Mississippi appearance with Thurmond on behalf of Reagan's presidential campaign: "You know, if we had elected this man 30 years ago, we wouldn't be in the mess we are today." Also on December 11, Lott gave his first interview on the topic. Speaking to Sean Hannity in a conservative-friendly radio forum, Lott went into more detail than previous statements issued through his press office had contained. Lott admitted his mistake, asked forgiveness, and expressed hope that he would be able to move on and turn the mistake into an opportunity for growth. Of particular note was his repeated use of the phrase that his was "a mistake of the head, not of the heart," a simplified version of Jackson's 1984 apology at the Democratic National Convention for negative comments he had made in reference to New York City's Jewish community. The same day, Lott was interviewed by telephone on CNN's *Larry King Live*, and another interest group, the Anti-Defamation League, issued a brief statement denouncing Lott's comments.[5]

On December 12, a week after Lott made his controversial remarks, President George W. Bush made a statement addressing Lott's situation. In a brief aside in a speech devoted to other matters, Bush observed that "recent comments by Senator Lott do not reflect the spirit of our country. He has apologized, and rightly so. Every day our nation was segregated was a day that America was unfaithful to our founding ideals." In addition, the Congressional Black Caucus, through its outgoing chair, Texas Democratic representative Eddie Bernice Johnson, and its incoming leader, Maryland Democrat Elijah Cummings, called for "a formal censure of Senator Lott's racist remarks." Further, national media published two articles calling attention to Lott's questionable history regarding issues of race. A *Time* magazine article by Karen Tumulty detailed Lott's successful bid in the early 1960s to keep his fraternity, Sigma Nu, segregated—not only his chapter at the University of Mississippi but nationally. The same article noted, however, that as a college senior, Lott was responsible for convincing his fraternity brothers not to participate in the riots protesting the integration of Ole Miss. An Associated Press article by John Solomon released the same day highlighted Lott's association with the Council of Conservative Citizens (CCC), his push to restore Jefferson Davis's U.S. citizenship, his statement to the Sons of Confederate Veterans (SCV) that "the spirit of Jefferson Davis lives in the 1984 Republican Platform," and his votes against the Martin Luther King Jr. national holiday and the Voting Rights Act. The Associated Press article quoted Bonjean as saying that Lott "repudiates segregation because it is immoral" and explaining that the efforts to keep Sigma Nu segregated occurred "years ago in a different time, in a different era. [Lott] repudiates segregation and supports integration in his old fraternity." And, foreshadowing developments in the week ahead, December 12 also brought a brief statement in which Republican senator Bill Frist of Tennessee agreed with Bush's comments and accepted Lott's apology.[6]

Not surprisingly, given the many crucial December 12 developments in the situation, Lott held a news conference the following day. Speaking in his hometown of Pascagoula, Lott began, "Segregation is a stain on our nation's soul. . . . It represents one of the lowest moments in our nation's history, and we can never forget that." Lott described Thurmond as "a friend, a colleague, and conservative who came to understand the evil of segregation and wrongness of his own views. He's said as much himself." Moreover, Lott clarified, "In celebrating [Thurmond's] life, I did not mean to suggest in any way that his segregationist views of 50 years ago were justified or right." Lott ended with a pledge "to undo the hurt I have caused and [to] do all that I can to contribute to a society where every American has an equal opportunity to succeed."[7]

As is often the case in the weekly news cycle, Saturday, December 14, brought no major developments in the Lott situation. However, the next day saw the first public statement in which a Republican senator raised the possibility of someone else becoming majority leader. Oklahoma's Don Nickles accepted Lott's apology but stated, "This is bigger than any single senator now. I am concerned [he] has been weakened to the point that it may jeopardize his ability to enact our agenda and speak to all Americans. There are several outstanding senators who are more than capable of effective leadership and I hope we have an opportunity to choose."[8] The press suggested Nickles, Frist, Kentucky's Mitch McConnell, and Pennsylvania's Rick Santorum as possible alternatives.

On December 16, Lott sat down for another interview, this one with Ed Gordon of Black Entertainment Television (BET). Answering Gordon's questions, Lott frequently emphasized themes of forgiveness and redemption: "The important thing is to recognize the hurt I've caused, and ask for forgiveness, and find a way to turn this into a positive thing, and try to make amends for what I've said and for what others have said and done over the years. I'm looking for this to be not only an opportunity for redemption, but to do something about it." Gordon asked Lott not only about his comments regarding Thurmond but also about his college fraternity, his votes against the King holiday and the Voting Rights Act, his views on affirmative action, his connection with the CCC, and his support of controversial judicial nominee Charles Pickering. This interview featured the most in-depth apology Lott offered during the two-week uproar.[9]

Frist released another statement on December 17, this one in response to media reports that he had endorsed a new election for Senate majority leader. Frist acknowledged that Senate Republicans were considering their options but stated that he had "endorsed no specific proposal at this time." The next day, Lincoln Chafee of Rhode Island issued the first statement in which a Senate Republican publicly declared the hope that Lott would step down as majority leader. In a radio interview, Chafee talked at length about the situation, the procedure necessary to elect a new majority leader, possible candidates, and his contention that Lott's apologies weren't "connecting" with the public and that Lott should leave. Another blow to Lott's chances of becoming majority leader came during a news conference at which Secretary of State Colin Powell noted, "I was disappointed in the senator's statement. I deplored the sentiments behind the statement. There was nothing about the 1948 election or the Dixiecrat agenda that should have been acceptable in any way to any American at that time or any American now."[10] The day also featured media reports of negative comments by former president Bill Clinton; Florida's Republican governor, Jeb Bush; and outgoing Oklahoma representative J. C. Watts, an African American Republican.

On December 19, Frist released a third statement, acknowledging that some of his fellow Senate Republicans had approached him about becoming Senate majority leader. Following this signal, Lott proffered his resignation as majority leader–elect the next day: "In the interest of pursuing the best possible agenda for the future of our country, I will not seek to remain as majority leader of the United States Senate." On December 22, Lott gave his first postresignation interview to Sheila Hardwell Byrd of the Associated Press. Speaking at his Pascagoula home, Lott vacillated between taking responsibility for his words and blaming others for his fate. On the one hand, he stated, "I don't think there's any use in trying to say I'm disappointed in anybody or anything. An inappropriate remark brought this down on my head." On the other hand, he also voiced his belief that "a lot of people in Washington have been trying to nail me for a long time. . . . When you're from Mississippi and you're a conservative and you're a Christian, there are a lot of people that don't like that. I fell into their trap and so I have only myself to blame."[11] The following day, Senate Republicans elected Frist as the new majority leader. Few observers would have predicted that Thurmond's one hundredth birthday party would come to have such far-reaching effects.

Understanding why Lott's comments were controversial enough to force his resignation requires a brief look back at Thurmond's campaign. In December 1946, just a month after Thurmond won his first South Carolina gubernatorial election, Harry Truman formed the President's Committee on Civil Rights and issued Executive Order 9008, which instructed the committee "to enquire into and to determine whether and in what respect current law-enforcement measures and the authority of and means possessed by Federal, State, and local governments may be strengthened and improved to safeguard the civil rights of the people." On October 29, 1947, the committee issued its report, *To Secure These Rights*, which included "calls for abolition of poll taxes, enactment of antilynching legislation, legal proscriptions of discrimination in interstate transportation, and guaranteed voting rights in federal elections for qualified voters."[12]

In February 1948, at the Southern Governors' Conference in Wakulla Springs, Florida, Thurmond spoke in response to what he perceived to be "the spectacle of the political parties of this country engaging in competitive bidding for the votes of small pressure groups by attacking the traditions, customs and institutions of the section in which we live." He stated his opposition to "a so-called anti-lynching bill" on the basis that "lynching has been virtually stamped out in the South without outside interference" and that such "legislation would be an unconstitutional invasion of the field of government of several states." He similarly argued against "a so-called anti–poll tax bill" because it would be "an unconstitutional infringement on the right of the several states to prescribe voting qualifications." These constitutional arguments against federal encroachment on states' rights became a common theme in Thurmond's political rhetoric of this era. Another common idea was his contention that on a day-to-day basis, segregation was beneficial to the lives of whites and blacks alike: "They talk about breaking down the laws which [the] knowledge and experience of many years have proven to be essential to the protection of the racial integrity and purity of the white and negro races alike. . . . [T]heir sudden removal would jeopardize the peace and good order which prevails where the two races live side by side in large numbers."[13] These two arguments, along with the beliefs that the Truman administration and other Democrats were promoting civil rights legislation purely for political advantage and that the Democratic Party had for too long taken the South and its political support for granted, became the basis of the States' Rights Democratic Party, which grew out of this conference.

At the 1948 Democratic National Convention in Philadelphia, the party passed a civil rights program inspired by *To Secure These Rights*. The inclusion of this plank in the official Democratic Party platform caused all of the convention delegates from Mississippi and half of those representing Alabama to walk out and nominate their own candidates for president and vice president—candidates who would defend the sovereignty of states' rights to protect "custom and tradition" in the area of race relations and civil rights. Just three days later, these rebel delegates joined other like-minded Southerners for an already planned meeting in Birmingham, Alabama, where the States' Rights Democratic Party was officially formed. Meeting in Houston on August 11, the new party selected Thurmond and Mississippi governor Fielding Wright as its presidential and vice presidential candidates.[14]

Throughout his campaign, Thurmond continued to emphasize the three themes he had promoted since his remarks at Wakulla Springs: (1) the unconstitutionality of federal laws mandating employment, voting, and criminal justice practices in the states; (2) the subsequent loss of community peace and individual freedoms for those affected; and (3) the political motivations behind civil rights legislation. On November 1, Thurmond delivered a radio address, broadcast across fourteen Southern states, in which he made one last effort to urge those who believe "the South is right in this fight [to] go to the polls tomorrow and vote your honest convictions." In addition to his political and constitutional arguments, Thurmond included his usual emotional appeals to listeners' fears of anything that might disturb their way of life, painting a vivid picture of how "the so called civil rights program would bring about the end of segregation in the South, forcing the mixing of the races in our hotels, in our restaurants, in our schools, in our swimming pools, and in all public places." He emphasized that "a vote for Truman, for Dewey, or for Wallace is a vote that says 'We want the [Fair Employment Practices Commission] and the mingling of the races.'" In the end, the States' Rights Party candidates carried their home states plus Alabama and Louisiana. Thurmond and Wright carried those states while running "under the official Democratic party label," a sign that many Southerners, even in the heart of Dixiecrat country, were not ready to break their adherence to the mainline Democratic Party.[15]

Thurmond went on to win a U.S. Senate seat as a write-in candidate in 1954, winning reelection seven times and serving until January 2003, when he retired from public office. In his eight terms as a U.S. senator, Thurmond's public views and Senate votes on issues of race reflected the changing mores of the nation. By the 1990s, Thurmond voted in favor of civil rights legislation and supported the nomination of an African American, Clarence Thomas, to the Supreme Court. As Thurmond observed shortly after winning reelection in 1990, "If you can't change with the times when it's proper to change, you'd be lost in the shuffle. I don't think I've sacrificed any principle in my career, but times change." Thurmond biographer Nadine Cohodas concludes that although "he never rose up in indignation and vowed to help change the rules, his long career had shown that few knew better how to adapt once those rules were changed." Perhaps Lott would have benefited from a refresher course in such adaptation to the times, a course based on the political life lessons of his "hero," Thurmond.[16]

Like Thurmond and many other politicians, Lott has his own rags-to-riches story that he uses to emphasize his working-class roots and how he has, by his own efforts rather than through family wealth or prestige, succeeded in life. Though Lott lacks the proverbial log cabin origins, he often tells the story of where, how, and by whom he was raised. Born Chester Trent Lott to parents Chester and Iona Lott on October 9, 1941, in Grenada, Mississippi, Lott emphasizes his identity as a "sharecropper's son." According to his official Senate biography, "Trent Lott's early years were shaped by the no-nonsense values of hard-working parents in hard-working times. More than once, the family moved to take advantage of a job opportunity and a chance at a better life. He grew up in a home where frugality countered economic uncertainty and where personal advancement had to be based on personal achievement." The family eventually moved to Pascagoula, where Lott's father worked as a pipe fitter at the local shipyards and his mother taught elementary school.[17]

Lott went on to Oxford to attend the University of Mississippi, where the sports teams and fans are known as the Rebels. When Lott was a student during the 1960s, it was tradition for fans to wave Confederate battle flags and sing "Dixie" at football games. Lott's extracurricular activities included being a cheerleader and a member of Sigma Nu, a traditionally Southern fraternity. In the early 1960s, when some northern chapters of Sigma Nu wanted to integrate, Lott and his Ole Miss brothers argued for retaining an all-white brotherhood, and their argument prevailed—African Americans were not admitted to the fraternity until the late 1960s. During Lott's senior year, Ole Miss made national headlines as Governor Ross Barnett and others attempted to prevent the first African American, James Meredith, from enrolling at the university, even in the face of federal troops. Perhaps somewhat surprisingly in light of the Sigma Nu episode, Lott persuaded his fraternity brothers not to participate in the riots protesting the university's integration.[18]

After receiving a bachelor's of science degree in public administration in 1963, Lott stayed on at Ole Miss for law school. He financed his legal studies by working in the university's alumni affairs office and received a juris doctorate in 1967. Five years later, Lott was elected to the U.S. House of Representatives, where he eventually ascended to the role of Republican whip. In 1988, Lott was elected to the Senate, and in 1996 he became majority leader when Kansas senator Bob Dole left to run for president. After a shift in the balance of political power in the Senate, Lott became the minority leader. However, when Republicans regained control of the Senate in the 2002 election, Lott was poised to return to the post of majority leader.[19]

The remarks at Thurmond's birthday party brought to the public's attention a side of Lott that had, for the most part, escaped mainstream press and public attention. Solomon and organizations such as Fairness and Accuracy in Reporting (FAIR) noted Lott's longtime association with the CCC, which Solomon describes as "advocat[ing] the preservation of the white race." Other observers describe the CCC as "the successor to the notorious white Citizens Councils, whose history dates back half a century to the 1950s when the groups were referred to as the 'uptown Klan.'" Solomon reports that in 1992, Lott delivered a keynote address at a CCC gathering in which he stated that "the people in this room stand for the right principles and the right philosophy." In addition, Solomon and others observe that Lott has had columns on policy issues included in official CCC publications and that he has hosted representatives of the group in his Washington, D.C., office. The CCC describes itself "as a nonprofit organization to work for the rights and collective interests of true conservatives" and notes that "on some issues, such as forced busing, quotas and immigration, the Council does indeed speak out for white European-Americans, their civilization, faith and form of government, but we do not advocate or support the oppression or exploitation of other races or ethnic groups." However, the CCC goes beyond this benign self-description with statements articulating a stance "against the tide of nonwhite, Third World immigrants swamping this country" and the belief that "there is no acceptable substitute for the civilization that has evolved through the Greeks, Romans, Celts, and Anglo-Saxons."[20] Lott's association with the CCC; his involvement with a less controversial group, the SCV; his voting record (which received a failing grade from the NAACP); and previous positive remarks about Thurmond's presidential run caused many observers to wonder whether Lott's comments were a more revealing gaffe than Lott and his advisers wanted the public to believe.

This controversy can be understood as a set of accusations and apologies. While some might prefer to focus solely on the apologia offered by Lott and his few defenders, I agree with Halford Ross Ryan's contention "that the critic will better understand both accusation and defense by evaluating them as a speech set." Informing Ryan's work on *kategoria* and apologia are B. L. Ware and Wil A. Linkugel's studies of apologia. They posit that self-defenders use denial and bolstering to "reform" their audience's image of them while using differentiation and transcendence to "transform" their audience's vision of them. Similarly, Noreen W. Kruse draws on Maslow's hierarchy of needs as another psychologically based avenue for understanding apologia. She groups nondenial apologia according to what human need they address. Ware and Linkugel's four factors of verbal self-defense and Kruse's three need-based responses are instructive in that they remind critics, as Ryan also advises, to be ever-mindful of persuaders' motivations. Whether accusing or defending, communicators always have motivations, external and internal, that must be considered in any well-rounded analysis of their texts.[21]

As will be elaborated in the rhetorical analysis to follow, *kategoria* and apologia are intertwined with spiritual motives of purification and redemption, motives that can be understood through application of Kenneth Burke's theory of scapegoating. Throughout his writings, Burke returns again and again to the idea of the scapegoat—one upon whom the sins of others are placed or blamed who is then in turn sacrificed to purify all those whose sins he or she now contains or represents. Burke delineates three ways in which such a scapegoat is made "'worthy' of sacrifice."[22] Lott was "made worthy" of sacrifice in two ways. Legalistically, some of Lott's accusers gathered evidence of a pattern of sinful behavior (support of segregation and segregationists, lack of support for civil rights initiatives) to prove that he was worthy of sacrifice in the form of giving up his position of Senate leadership. Fatalistically, some of Lott's accusers and defenders argued that he was a "marked man" because of his identity as a Southern conservative, and Lott used this argument in his postresignation interview with the Associated Press; from this perspective, Lott was sacrificed for the sins of all Southerners, of all "true" conservatives (that is, paleoconservatives). Lott's tragic personal flaw may have been his continued identification with paleoconservative, neo-Confederate ideologues in a political environment in which such associations were considered worthy of punishment.

As the rhetorical analysis to follow will illustrate in more detail, those who would make Lott their scapegoat—his accusers—came from many ideological and political camps. In addition to the more obvious accusers from civil rights organizations, left-leaning political action groups, and the Democratic Party, Lott was also sacrificed by his fellow Republicans (mainly by those in the party's neoconservative mainstream) and his fellow Southern paleoconservatives. This phenomenon of equal-opportunity scapegoating proves what Burke believed to be "a related process of dialectic: unification by a foe shared in common."[23] Though their motivations for guilt varied as widely as their ideological and political views, all who participated in the scapegoating of Lott were brought together by their guilt and were redeemed together in his sacrifice. An analysis of the various strands of accusation in this debate in concert with an analysis of the various apologies offered by Lott and his few defenders should lead to a more thorough understanding of the rhetoric of race as a rhetoric of sin, sacrifice, and redemption in contemporary American (and especially Southern) political culture.

Lott's accusers came from a variety of political and ideological perspectives, but they can be roughly categorized into three basic groups: (1) African Americans (such as representatives of the NAACP, Rainbow/PUSH, and the Congressional Black Caucus) and those sympathetic with their perspective in politics in general and on the Lott situation in particular (such as the editors of *Roll Call* and the *Nation*), Democratic politicians, and some moderate (neoconservative) Republicans; (2) Republicans, in particular the more moderate face of the party establishment as personified by the White House (not only President Bush but also such leaders as Secretary of State Powell), Lott's fellow Republican senators, and prominent pundits (such as Peggy Noonan and David Frum); and (3) white Southern conservatives, many of whom could be considered paleoconservatives (such as the League of the South) and the less rational among them perhaps unreconstructed racists (such as the CCC).

With such a wide range of perspectives, the accusers generated an equally wide range of accusations against Lott. The accusations fall into eight basic headings: (1) Lott was a racist segregationist; (2) Lott simply gave the impression of supporting racism and segregation; (3) Lott's life provided evidence that his remarks were part of a pattern of behavior; (4) Lott meant what he said; (5) Lott's remarks and underlying attitudes were unbefitting a Senate majority leader; (6) Lott damaged the Republican Party; (7) by apologizing, Lott was cowardly and weak; and (8) Lott was more concerned about himself than his constituents. None of these accusations was made by a single group of accusers; rather, overlap existed between the various groups' accusations (sometimes in unexpected ways). Following Ryan and Burke, my rhetorical analysis of all of these accusations is guided by four basic questions: (1) Who was carrying out the scapegoating/accusing? (2) What aspect of Lott was being scapegoated? (3) How were they going about scapegoating, and which strategies were being used? and (4) What motive lay behind this scapegoating?

Perhaps the most obvious of the accusations against Lott was that he is a racist who still believes segregation was just. Through their interpretations of the meaning of and attitudes behind Lott's comments, his accusers concluded that these words proved that Lott held racist, segregationist views. Some of Lott's accusers were motivated to accept this interpretation of his remarks because they, as African Americans, were members of the main group that experienced the negative effects of segregation in America. Jackson argued that Lott "is supposed to be the Senate Majority Leader for all Americans, but he has once again shown he is interested only in Confederates." Jackson thus accused Lott of representing only whites rather than all the citizens of Mississippi and the United States, thereby leaving many without the political representation—and influence—that is their right. Powell, perhaps the most popular and powerful African American Republican, also voiced his disappointment: "I deplored the sentiments behind the statement. There was nothing about the 1948 election or the Dixiecrat agenda that should have been acceptable in any way to any American at that time or any American now." When a fellow Republican (albeit a much more moderate one) such as Powell joined in accusing Lott of accepting the Dixiecrats' agenda, his accusation held particular weight, in part because of his personal identity as a widely respected African American and because of his position of power as the sitting secretary of state. However, Powell did not speak out against Lott's comments until December 18, almost two weeks after the remarks were made, and just two days later Lott resigned.[24]

Accusers charged Lott with racism and support of segregation not only in his initial comments praising Thurmond's presidential bid but also in the language he used to apologize. Democratic representative Jesse Jackson Jr. of Illinois argued that Lott's explanation that he was praising Thurmond's other policy stances, such as in the areas of the economy and national defense, can be read as proof of the racism Lott was denying in this explanation: "He said he wasn't praising Senator Thurmond's past racial stance, but he liked his commitment to a 'strong defense' and his 'fiscal conservatism.' Before the Civil War the Democratic slave masters used to have anti-black conventions where they called us 'out-our-names.' But after the Civil War, when they had lost power and were trying to get it back, they knew they had to change their language." Jackson went on to explain that during Reconstruction, racists would gather for what were billed as "anti-taxation" rallies but had the true purpose of serving as forums for opposition to Reconstruction policies: opposition to increased taxes existed only because whites believed the monies were used to fund social programs benefiting former slaves. The phrase "tax-and-spend liberals," Jackson asserted, originated with these Reconstruction-era racists as code words for those who promoted civil rights and the enforcement of Reconstruction initiatives.[25]

Former Reagan speechwriter Peggy Noonan wondered if "maybe it was the kind of thinking mistake politicians sometimes make," recalling, "Way back in the 1950s and '70s and even '80s some Southern politicians of Mr. Lott's generation—in both parties—employed the 'thinking mistake' to talk about race. So when Mr. Lott the other day emphatically but nonspecifically declared that if Strom Thurmond had been elected president, 'we wouldn't have a lot of the problems we've had,' a lot of people, including me, wondered if he were not making a thinking mistake." Thus, when Lott defended his ambiguity by saying his intent was to praise Thurmond's fiscal policies and the like, Jackson, Noonan, and others wondered whether this explanation provided additional evidence of Lott's inherent racism. In other words, both Jackson and Noonan argued that Lott's supposedly innocent bumbling instead represented an instance of strategic ambiguity (what Noonan calls a "thinking mistake"). By using the vague phrase "a lot of the problems we've had," Lott could encode a meaning of racial problems to some audience members (fellow Southern conservatives in the good-ol'-boy tradition). Edsall, one of the first print journalists to report on Lott's comments, called Bonjean late on December 6 to ask, as Lott recounts, "whether I had used any 'code words' in my Thurmond remarks." However, having used sufficient ambiguity in his wording, Lott and his aides could easily reinterpret the phrase in his subsequent explanations as meaning more widely agreed upon problems such as the economy or national defense.[26]

Similarly, writers for two journals of political opinion and observation, *Roll Call* and the *Nation*, also accused Lott of being a racist and a segregationist. These authors offered interpretations of the meaning behind the seemingly vague terms *we* and *problems* in Lott's original statement. In an editorial, "Lott's Disgrace," the editors of *Roll Call* posited, "The 'problems' Lott apparently thinks would have been 'avoided' include integration of the schools, the right of blacks to vote, anti-lynching laws, and equal access to jobs, housing and public accommodations." Likewise, in "Lott Should Resign," the members of the *Nation*'s editorial board offered their interpretation: "Who is the 'we' in Lott's declaration? The white people of the South who used the powers of the state and local governments to impose the racial caste system called Jim Crow upon their fellow citizens. What were 'all these problems' Lott wished to avoid? The triumph of legal equality for African-Americans, including, in the South, the long-denied right to vote."[27] The editors of these two journals clearly accused Lott of loading seemingly vague and innocent words with bigoted, exclusionary meaning, thereby accusing Lott of being quite specific and far from innocent in the coded meaning he conveyed.

While many of Lott's critics charged that his words betrayed his true identity as a racist, others chose to accuse him of simply giving the *impression* of being racist. Those most likely to accuse Lott of this lesser sin were his fellow politicos. In his initial public response, for example, outgoing Senate majority leader Tom Daschle stated, "It is clear that Senator Lott's remarks left many people with the impression that he felt the segregationist policies of the past would have been preferable to the equality under law that so many fought for in the civil rights movement. When Senator Lott called me . . . he indicated he did not mean for his statement to be interpreted to condone segregation, and I accept that. That does not mean, however, that I found the statement appropriate. Regardless of how he intended his statement to be interpreted, it was wrong to say it and I strongly disagree with it." Frum, one of the first conservative pundits to comment on Lott's situation and a former speechwriter for President George W. Bush, commented, "I for one do not believe Trent Lott is a racist or a segregationist. My guess is that his speechwriter gave him note cards with a few jokes, and that when Lott finished reading them, he launched himself into what he probably intended to be nothing more than a big squirt of greasy flattery. But that's not what came out of Lott's mouth."[28] Early on in the controversy, when Daschle and Frum made these observations, the possibility that Lott simply had misspoken and been careless with his words was a more widely held interpretation of the incident than later in the controversy. However, in the days immediately following Daschle's and Frum's comments, the major media outlets circulated accounts of Lott's earlier such comments and his efforts to keep his fraternity segregated; when these accounts became common knowledge, contentions that Lott had merely given the impression of racism all but disappeared, and Daschle and others stepped up the severity of their accusations.

In addition to using close readings of Lott's word choice to accuse him of promoting racism and segregation, Lott's accusers also sought to prove a pattern of racist behavior throughout his personal and political life. They cited other incidents to prove that his December 5 remarks had not been an isolated incident but simply the most recent occasion in a lifetime of racism. As Jesse Jackson Sr. argued in one of his syndicated opinion columns, "Lott's comments were not an aberration. Once the sleepy press started to look, they found amble [*sic*] evidence of Lott's racial attitudes and policies." Jackson concluded that Lott's "rhetoric fits his record. The pronouncement is part of a pattern, a practice and a policy." Jackson and FAIR not only accused Lott of a "long history" of racist words and deeds but also faulted the mainstream media for not devoting sufficient attention to Lott's racist record, even in the wake of the Thurmond controversy. As FAIR observed, "Lott's public record on race going back more than 25 years indicates that the incoming majority leader has consistently preferred the legacy of Lincoln adversaries such as Jefferson Davis to that of Lincoln. Lott's long history of support for racist and neo-Confederate causes is generally missing from coverage of the Thurmond controversy."[29]

Many people who accused Lott of a pattern of racist behavior detailed a litany of his sins, as in the case of the chair of the NAACP's board, Julian Bond: "From his college days until today, Trent Lott has consistently and aggressively opposed accepted remedies for discrimination, opposed integration of his own fraternity, celebrated the Confederacy, successfully supported restoring the citizenship of war criminal Jefferson Davis, embraced, praised and endorsed the goals of a white supremacist organization and hosted its leadership in his Senate office, and in statements 22 years apart, expressed regret that racist candidate Strom Thurmond had not been elected president in 1948 and his policies adopted by the nation. No apology can change the attitude and work of a lifetime." Other accusers emphasized Lott's congressional voting record as evidence of this pattern of racist behavior, as did *New Republic* writer Michelle Cottle when she noted that "during his 16 years in the House, Lott cast more than a few votes that showed the esteem in which he held the vestiges of his home state's racist past." Kweisi Mfume of the NAACP called attention to controversial votes often referenced by other Lott accusers, emphasizing that the Lott of December 5 "is the same Trent Lott who voted against the extension of the Voting Rights Act, extension of the 1964 Civil Rights Act and against the Martin Luther King Jr. Commission and the federal King Holiday." Bond questioned the sincerity of Lott's contention in his BET interview apology that the controversy concerning his comments had been a "wake-up call": "It could only have been a wake-up call for someone who was sound asleep from his college days 40 years ago until last week. Upon awakening, he's surprised to find he's been in bed with racists and white supremacists, and cannot explain how he got there. Lott kept saying he'd made a mistake, but he didn't make just one; his whole public life has been a mistake, and he compounded the mistake" in the BET interview.[30] By charging him not only with racist words but also with racist deeds, Lott's accusers strengthened their case against allowing him to retain his position of power and influence.

However, just as Lott's accusers exposed the long litany of his failings on racial issues, they simultaneously revealed their knowledge of those shortcomings—and their failure previously to have curtailed them. Denouncing Lott as "a racist—actually an unreconstructed segregationist," the editors of the *Nation* admitted, "We knew the truth about this man long ago, since his career in Washington is littered with the evidence of his reactionary views on race." Their explanation for their failure effectively to call attention to Lott's "reactionary" record contended that he was "particularly dangerous" in December 2002 because, "buoyed by postelection Republican triumphalism, the Mississippi Senator found the audacity to crow about his racist opinions in public."[31] Overall, providing evidence of Lott's record on racial issues from throughout his life gave weight to accusations that his December 5 comments were not isolated but rather were indicative of a lifelong pattern of behavior and a long-held set of beliefs. However, revealing that Lott's racism and segregationism were nothing new may have also served to accuse Lott's critics of not taking action to prevent such a person from rising, practically unchecked, to such a position of influence.

As I will detail in the analysis of the apologia, Lott's initial strategy was to explain his comments as "intended to pay tribute" to Thurmond and as nothing more than "a poor choice of words [that] conveyed to some the impression that I embraced the discarded policies of the past." In answer to this explanation, Lott's accusers sought not only to provide evidence of his pattern of racist behavior but also to prove that his remarks were the product of intent rather than accident. Many accusers backed up claims of racist "authorial intent" by pointing to, as Mfume did, the fact that the "senator made comments praising segregation in the 80s similar to the ones he made last week," leading Mfume "to believe that those were not a 'poor choice of words,' they were his favorite choice of words." Others, such as the editors of *Roll Call*, saw not only his past comments as evidence of Lott's authorial intent but also his delivery of the remarks: "Lott's offensive words were in fact expressed forcefully and with apparent deep conviction—and, it turns out, he's expressed them before. So we think further explanation on the history of his racial attitudes is required." Neoconservative columnist Charles Krauthammer questioned Lott's explanation: "It was not 'a poor choice of words,' as he later pleaded. It was a perfectly clear choice of words articulating a perfectly clear idea. Had Lott stopped with Thurmond-for-president, 1948, this might have been written off as idle and presumably insincere birthday flattery for a very, very old man. But Lott did not stop there. He added, fatally, that America would have been better off had it embraced Dixiecrat segregation. With that, Lott cut off any retreat." Krauthammer thus offered Lott's elaboration as additional evidence that he meant what he said. Similarly, paleoconservative Samuel Francis refused to let Lott off the hook, pointing out that "what Mr. Thurmond's States Rights Party mainly stood for was racial segregation, and Mr. Lott knows that," thus arguing that Lott also knew the implications of praising that campaign. As Cottle observed, "The problem with Lott's little birthday tribute wasn't that he thoughtlessly misspoke. It's that, as even the most cursory review of Lott's history on racial issues suggests, the senator's toast was a textbook gaffe as defined by former [*New Republic*] editor Michael Kinsley: The case of a politician accidentally saying what he really believes." In response to Bob Novak's defense that "Trent Lott got out there and he winged it. That's one of the dangers of not having a text. He thought it was a social occasion.

He's thinking what comes to his mind," FAIR argued, "That sounds like a perfect reason to continue investigating Lott's racist connections."[32] Overall, Lott's accusers offered evidence that Lott was not a victim of a mere "poor choice of words" made by an ill-equipped extemporaneous speaker but rather of more of a Freudian slip that revealed racist beliefs left over from the Old South lurking beneath Lott's New South facade.

While the accusations previously discussed were concerned more with proving that Lott's words, actions, and intentions marked him individually as a racist, other accusations focused on how Lott's racism or impropriety (depending on one's terministic screen) affected his relations with others, especially in the political realm. Lott's accusers expressed their concern that someone who would utter such words, whether intentionally or unintentionally, was not worthy or capable of holding a position of power and influence such as Senate majority leader. As the NAACP's Mfume argued, such "callous, calculated, hateful bigotry . . . has no place in the halls of the Congress. His remarks are dangerously divisive and certainly unbefitting a man who is to hold such a highly esteemed leadership role as the majority leader of the senate." In the words of Anti-Defamation League national director Abraham H. Foxman, "The Senator's praise for a candidacy based on segregationist policies was irresponsible and unacceptable, and unbecoming of a leader of his stature in Congress." While Hannity and other Lott defenders reminded his detractors of equally controversial, racist words uttered by fellow senator Robert Byrd, a Democrat from West Virginia, and mentioned Byrd's association with the Ku Klux Klan, Lott accusers differentiated between Byrd's and Lott's sins based on their distinct Senate roles. As *Roll Call*'s editors noted, they did call "on Byrd to make a full and complete apology on the Senate floor (which he didn't)." However, the editors believed, "It's more incumbent upon Lott to do so because he is Majority Leader." Taking a more harsh stance, Krauthammer called not only for an apology but for Lott's resignation: "Trent Lott must resign as Senate majority leader. It's not just that no one who has said this can lead an American political party. It's that no one who *could* say something like this should be an American leader." Like the *Roll Call* editorial board, Krauthammer pointed out that "backbenchers might be permitted such a lack of vision. Leaders are not. Lott must step down." Whether Lott was guilty of racism or just political clumsiness, his accusers made the case that his controversial remarks disqualified him from the top Senate leadership post. That Lott could exhibit such "historical blindness" to the national significance of segregation and the civil rights movement, observed Krauthammer, "utterly disqualified" him from leading the nation, through the Senate, toward future progress.[33]

Some participants in this debate argued that Lott's comments damaged his political party, and some expanded charges to include allegations that the party itself was guilty of racism. Looking back at the controversy in a December 24 opinion column, Jesse Jackson Sr. argued that "Lott embarrassed Republicans with his fervid endorsement of Strom's pro-segregation, pro-lynching party. But he outraged them by apologizing on Black Entertainment Television and announcing that henceforth he would support affirmative action. It was bad enough that he exposed the racial politics behind the Republican rise as the party of white sanctuary in the South. It was worse when he expressed opposition to the next chapter in their playbook—the assault on affirmative action." In this accusation, Jackson simultaneously exposed the sins of Lott and those of his party, using the debacle as a way to lay bare what he perceived as the GOP's inherently racist strategies. Likewise, the editors of the *Nation* hypothesized, "The reason the White House turned on Lott had little to do with distaste for the Mississippian's remarks at Thurmond's 100th birthday party; it moved only when it appeared the controversy might expose a penchant to play the race card when convenient."[34] Here again, accusers outside the Republican Party used the sins of Lott the individual as an opportunity to reveal the sins of the system of which he was a part (Republican leadership as personified by the Bush administration).

While those outside the Republican ranks used Lott's sins as an opportunity to reveal how he had damaged his party by revealing its racism, most of the accusations that Lott's words had damaged his party came from within it. As Noonan complained in one of her syndicated columns, "Of course the Republican Party is damaged by having as one of its leaders a man who, half a century after Jim Crow's long death began, makes statements that can be construed as meaning segregation was better than its demise." Noonan also argued that "a man who does that should not, half a century into the modern movements for civil rights, be allowed to continue as the face of a major political party in politics."[35] In other words, Lott's racist face, now revealed, would cause his party damage—in the media, in elections, and in its policy initiatives. The image of a racist or even a seeming racist as Senate leader was not the image the GOP wanted to convey to the press or the larger public because it would tarnish public perceptions of Republicans' principles as well as their political agenda.

Participants in the public debate from both within and without the Republican Party repeatedly referred to the "party of Lincoln." External accusers, such as FAIR, alluded to Lincoln as a means of highlighting the unfavorable contrast between the party's first and most widely admired (across party lines) leader and Lott: "The incoming majority leader has consistently preferred the legacy of Lincoln adversaries such as Jefferson Davis to that of Lincoln." FAIR pointed to Lott's espousal of Davis's policies and principles as evidence that Lott and thus his party had strayed from the purer ideals of party founders such as Lincoln. Meanwhile, internal accusers such as former senator Jack Kemp, described by Thomas Edsall and Dan Balz as a longtime "advocate for the GOP to return to its roots as the party of Abraham Lincoln," maintained that until Lott "totally repudiate[d] segregation and every aspect of its evil manifestation," the party would continue to suffer damage. "The party can't duck it," Kemp said.[36]

Many other Republicans deemed Lott's remarks sinful because they were at odds with the principles the Republican Party espoused or wanted the public to believe it espoused. When President Bush finally spoke out about Lott's remarks on December 12, he carefully emphasized that in contrast to Lott's suggestion that the segregated past was acceptable or positive, "the founding ideals of our nation and, in fact, the founding ideals of the political party I represent was, and remains today, the equal dignity and equal rights of every American." On a more pragmatic level, Frum theorized that Lott's remarks indicated that he did not stand for the principles of Lincoln or of Davis: "This week, the only principle he stands for is the principle of careerism. And that's just not enough to qualify for the leadership of the party that remains after all these years the party—not of Davis—but of Lincoln." For more mainstream, neoconservative Republicans and those concerned with the party's image and continued livelihood, even the appearance of deviating from the preferred image constituted a transgression worthy of punishment. Republican strategists and pundits wanted to prevent the stigma of this sin from staining their collective image and influence. As Noonan interpreted the president's remarks, "Mr. Bush hit Mr. Lott hard . . . [b]ecause he wants to separate himself and his party from Mr. Lott and his mouth." Likewise, Frum argued from the earliest days of the controversy that if Lott did not offer a more substantial apology "than a curt 'I am sorry if you were offended' [then] Republicans need to make it clear that Lott no longer speaks for us."[37] Those concerned with safeguarding the GOP's image—if only its self-image—as the "party of Lincoln" knew early on that they would need to differentiate and separate themselves as moderate, modern Republicans from the increasingly prevalent view of Lott as an extremist throwback.

Many Republicans intent on differentiating themselves and their principles from Lott and his principles were motivated by the idea of saving the party's political agenda. Kemp, speaking from a more idealistic perspective, observed that Lott "set back what President Bush is trying to do to broaden the Republican Party." Frum, ever the pragmatic political operative, foresaw a future in which "the Republican party will be led in the Senate by a leader who owes his survival to the sufferance of his political opponents. . . . All those bold, unapologetic conservatives who believe that Republicans should rally around Lott and not yield the Democrats an inch should understand: The party will probably be able to save him—but only by selling *you* out." Frum feared not only that the party would have to sacrifice its policy initiatives to save Lott but also "that Lott will try to save himself by jettisoning the conservative agenda in the Senate." Lott faced charges—explicit from Frum, more subtly from other Republicans—that he would jeopardize the party's hopes for overturning affirmative action in the coming year: "Lott could hardly have chosen a more inopportune time to hand his opponents proof that the Republican party is an updated version of the Dixiecrats. The Supreme Court this term will take up the issue of racial preferences in education. Conservatives and Republicans have spent two decades denouncing preferences in the name of color-blindness and legal equality for all. Lott's words will be used to question the sincerity of our commitment to this high principle."[38] Lott tainted the image of a pure "commitment to . . . principle" that moderate Republicans such as Frum were trying to associate with attempts to overturn racial preferences in areas such as college admissions and hiring.

Later in the controversy, Lott's fellow senators began to come out against him in the hope of saving the party's image and agenda—and in the hope of replacing him as majority leader. On December 15, Nickles issued a statement in which he not only differentiated Lott from the party's mainstream ("His comments did not represent Republican ideals") but went on to suggest that Lott, because of his transgression, was "weakened" and thus should be purged for the greater good of the GOP: "This is bigger than any single senator now. I am concerned Senator Lott has been weakened to the point that it may jeopardize his ability to enact our agenda and speak to all Americans. There are several outstanding senators who are more than capable of effective leadership and I hope we have an opportunity to choose."[39]

Despite Noonan's assertion that "normally Republicans rally around when they think one of their own is being unfairly smeared," it seems more accurate to say that in this case, Republicans circled around a weakened Lott not as in protectively circling the wagons but rather as opportunistic circling vultures out to fill their stomachs off his politically weakened carcass. Some, like Nickles, sought to gain political position, while others, like Bush, sought to gain prestige by using the incident to enhance their standing with African Americans. In addition to what Republican politicians and pundits said publicly, much political strategizing and power brokering took place behind the scenes. Lott and his staff fairly quickly began to sense "the complicated, Byzantine, and incessant political games that . . . were happening within the White House." Though White House press secretary Ari Fleischer stated on December 10 that the "president has confidence in him as Republican leader, unquestioningly," by the next day, Lott recounts, "many on my staff had grown certain that some powerful Bush staffers had launched a power play to replace me as Senate majority leader. While Bush was professing deep support, several Capitol Hill journalists had warned us, some of his key advisers were telling another story." By December 12, Bush, to use Lott's words, "struck out at me. . . . When Bush said, 'He has apologized *and rightly so*,' his voice hammered away at those last three words in a tone that was booming and nasty." As Lott later learned, Bush had told some present on Air Force One on the way to a speech in Philadelphia, where he chastised Lott, "This is going to be painful. . . . But we have to do it. It's like lancing a boil."

The media began to speculate about Lott's job security as majority leader, which overshadowed Lott's subsequent attempts at apology—in particular, his December 13 statement from Pascagoula, a speech Lott describes as being "as close to a manifesto on racism as I would ever give." On December 18, Florida governor Jeb Bush spoke out against Lott, who later learned that "Bush had spoken with the president's chief political adviser, Karl Rove, the morning he informed the world of his views on my situation." When Lott finally resigned, the media was quick to report the story of the behind-the-scenes intrigue and political maneuvering orchestrated by Rove. On December 21, the day after Lott's resignation, both Mara Liasson of National Public Radio and Elisabeth Bumiller of the *New York Times* released stories implicating Rove and the White House as the instigators of Lott's quick demise. As Ron Hutcheson of Knight Ridder newspapers noted, "Bush and Lott never really hit it off on a personal level, which didn't help Lott when times got tough. With no strong personal bond, no compelling reason to keep Lott in power and a growing need to be free of his racial baggage, Bush let Lott fend for himself until he was engulfed by controversy." Lott's troubles provided the Bush White House with a convenient opportunity to remove Lott and replace him with Frist, described as "a staunch ally of President Bush," especially after having served as the White House liaison to senators during the 2000 campaign.[40]

While mainstream, mostly neoconservative Republicans accused Lott of being weak and thereby weakening his party, more extremist, paleoconservative Southerners accused Lott of being weak and thereby weakening those in his region with his many apologies. Lott's constituents in these more right-wing Southern circles were initially pleased by his very public praise of Thurmond and by association his policies and perspectives of 1948: As paleoconservative columnist Samuel Francis opined, "For one brief shining moment, it was beginning to look like Senate Majority Leader Trent Lott was taking hormone shots." Or, as the CCC's chief executive officer, Gordon Baum, declared, "God bless Trent Lott." As Lott began to apologize for his comments, however, his former allies in this camp, which included such groups as the League of the South and the CCC, quickly lost hope that Lott would continue to defend their extremist views and saw his weakness as indicative of wider decline. As one paleoconservative commentator articulated, "There is no fight left in the white public sector. That is why we saw immediate disavowals and apologies from Trent Lott." So disgusted were these Southerners at Lott's apologies that he was characterized as no better than a cowardly Yankee, a severe punishment for a fellow Southerner and Confederate descendant such as Lott: "Not since General Pierre Gustave Toutant Beauregard sent Yankees reeling back over Bull Run Creek has America witnessed such a reversal of fortune as that displayed by Senator Lott's pitiful and puerile reaction to liberal criticism."[41]

Aside from this likening of Lott to fleeing Union troops, most of the imagery evoked by Lott's unreconstructed accusers was of a religious bent, focusing attention on issues of ritual sacrifice, repentance, and submission. Greg Kay, in an opinion piece linked to the CCC's Web site, painted a vivid image, recounting that "when Lott backed down and began his penance of crawling on his knees to the Jerusalem of political correctness, endlessly repenting while accepting the ritual scourging from the self-appointed watchdogs of society, he proved . . . to be an abject coward. A man, a Southern man in particular, would have stood up on his hind legs and defended his beliefs, whatever they happened to be, and not apologized for them." Similarly, CCC representatives observed that "Lott continues to flagellate himself with a tar brush. Next he will be singing 'We Shall Overcome' at NAACP headquarters." Flogging was also evoked by Lew Rockwell, who, in a column linked to the CCC site, wondered, "Why would a conservative Republican suddenly find himself embracing the full panoply of the left-wing racial agenda and flog himself so mercilessly?" Rockwell's explanation was more charitable than Kay's, likening Lott to "a Chinese political prisoner under Maoist Communism. . . . [T]he accused was already guilty as charged so he had only one right: to repent of his errors. If he appeared insufficiently repentant, the attacks were renewed until the accused was completely destroyed." From these perspectives, apologizing—with Lott often described in such terms as on "his wobbly knees"—was portrayed as submitting to the reigning political and cultural order, as permitting the War of Northern Aggression to be lost all over again with each new apology. Apologizing for one's politically incorrect, unreconstructed beliefs was portrayed as weak and therefore sinful. As Kay, among others, argued, Lott should resign "not for telling the truth, but for apologizing for it, thus calling that truth a lie, and agreeing with his detractors' insults against Dixie and its people. Besides, if a man can't stand for something, what good is he?"[42] From this point of view, Lott's apologies became transgressions worthy of further repentance.

Why did Lott succumb to the pressures of political correctness? A number of Lott's accusers attributed his sudden about-face to the further sin of being tempted by the fruits of political position and power. Late in the controversy, the neoconservative Frum noted, "This week, the only principle [Lott] stands for is the principle of careerism. And that's just not enough to qualify for the leadership of the party." However, most of those who charged Lott with being overly concerned with protecting his political position were from the paleoconservative camp. Feeling that Lott had betrayed not only them but his "true" beliefs, Lott's fellow (or formerly fellow?) Southern paleoconservatives longed for the days before Lott sold himself to the devils of what they called "Cultural Marxism": "Would that Trent Lott had cared more for his integrity than his position as Senate leader. If he really believed in the things embodied in the compliment given to a 100-year-old man on his birthday, then Lott would be worth a whole lot more to Mississippi and the rest of us as a simple Senator who just might be representing a majority of white people who have no one to speak for them." In their eyes, Southerners of their ilk would have been better served by a non-majority leader Lott who was true to their (formerly) shared beliefs than by a majority leader Lott whose position had been maintained (as it was at that point) only by sacrificing his Southernness at the altar of political correctness. As Kay asserted, "It could be even worse if he maintains his leadership position. If he manages to pull it off with his continuous butt kissing, he will then owe the people who hate the South for their allowing him to continue to exist, and he will owe them big-time! When they come to collect, it's going to be hard on Dixie—if we sit back and allow it."[43]

Viewed from the perspective either of neoconservative Republicans or of paleoconservative Southerners, Lott's "willingness to jettison all political principle for the sake of saving his status as Majority Leader" was a transgression that hurt not only Lott's personal integrity but also the agendas of these two constituencies. Lott's quest for political survival at the expense of his neo-Confederate beliefs was particularly hurtful to those who continued to hold those convictions. Many of these unreconstructed Southerners considered "Lott's playing to his opponents at the expense of his natural constituency . . . a form of betrayal." As is often the case with those who feel abandoned politically, they lashed out with threats of nonsupport: "I'm certain that he will feel their displeasure sharply during the next election, unless he bows out completely as many of his detractors demand." Or, as the CCC threatened none too subtly, "Whatever direction Lott takes, he better keep in mind that Beltway liberals and black harpies did not elect him to office. The conservative white vote in Mississippi sent Lott to Washington, and that same vote can retire him."[44] Having been denounced for the sake of Lott's political future, the members of the CCC and their ilk believed they had no other recourse but to sacrifice Lott as they perceived he had first sacrificed them.

More traditional accusation and defense speech sets typically consist of one accusation text answered by one apologetic text. However, twenty-four-hour television and Internet news coverage has created a rhetorical situation in which more back-and-forth exchanges occur between accusers and defenders, as in the Lott debacle. Accusations were levied against Lott nearly every day for two weeks. Lott thus could not offer one isolated apology and be done with it; the nature of the rhetorical situation required multiple apologies in answer to the evolving charges against him. Lott made six different apologies throughout this controversy—the December 9 prepared statement, the December 11 Hannity and King interviews, the December 13 Pascagoula news conference, the December 16 Gordon interview, and the December 22 Associated Press interview. (Bonjean's December 6 statement regarding Lott's remarks was more of an explanation than an apology; Lott's December 20 statement announcing his resignation as majority leader did not constitute an apology per se.) In addition, the apologia under analysis include a few offered on Lott's behalf, such as the one by Pat Buchanan. All of the apologia are grouped according to Ware and Linkugel's four factors of apologetic discourse: denial, bolstering, differentiation, and transcendence.[45] In particular, Lott was found to be (1) denying accusations that he had racist intentions and had taken racist actions; (2) bolstering his image through attempts to establish common ground with his accusers; (3) differentiating by separating Thurmond, himself, and the South from segregation; and (4) transcending his situation by "fetching good out of evil" and pointing to a conspiracy against him and those like him.

In his initial explanation and in his first official apology, Lott denied that his words were anything but kindness and respect shown to Thurmond on a momentous occasion. In fact, Lott even denied the plausibility of interpretations to the contrary. As Bonjean stated, "Senator Lott's remarks were intended to pay tribute to a remarkable man who led a remarkable life. To read anything more into these comments is wrong."[46] This statement did not so much constitute an apology as it did an explanation, as it admits of no wrongdoing—except perhaps on the part of those "read[ing] anything more into these comments."

Lott's first apology, also issued as a prepared statement, addressed the accusations of racist intent, albeit obliquely: Lott admitted to a "poor choice of words" but denied that his remarks did anything more than leave him open to misinterpretation. He avoided acknowledging the interpretations of support for "racism" and "segregation" per se, choosing instead to refer to the accusations more vaguely as concerning "the discarded policies of the past" (and he did not, as some accusers noted, condemn those "discarded" policies as wrong). He firmly denied the legitimacy of such interpretations in his statement that "nothing could be further from the truth." And with that firm denial of racist meaning or intentions, Lott should have ended his apology. However, as in his initial remarks about Thurmond, Lott continued to talk himself into further trouble. In closing his statement, Lott apologized "to anyone who was offended by my statement." Though Lott admitted to "a poor choice of words," this first apology could be read, in conjunction with Bonjean's initial explanation, as more of an accusation of those hypersensitive few who read too much between the lines or were too easily offended. These statements put the onus more on Lott's audience of interpreters than on himself as the speaker who made the "poor choice of words" that opened his comments up to such interpretation. Lott next apologized for the impression of blaming the audience given in his first apology, telling Hannity that "it was not intended just to say, 'I'm sorry if you didn't like it.'"[47] Thus, beginning with this second apology, Lott began to take more direct responsibility for the "impression" given through his "poor choice of words."

In addition to apologizing for his first apology, Lott's second apology began to articulate more clearly his denial of racist meaning or intent in his comments about Thurmond. In both December 11 apologies, Lott repeatedly referred to his transgression as a "mistake of the head, not of the heart." Early in the Hannity interview, Lott stated, "I can almost say that this was a mistake of the head, not of the heart, because I don't accept those policies of the past at all." Later in the interview, Lott reiterated, "The main thing I want to say to [the accusers], and people all across the country, [is] that my comments conveyed things that I did not intend, and I regret it. And, you know, I apologize for it." By his fourth apology, given as a news conference in Pascagoula, Lott realized that he had to do more than simply deny racist intent and tiptoe gingerly around words such as *racism* and *segregation*. Lott now stated, "Let me be clear: segregation and racism are immoral. . . . In celebrating [Thurmond's] life, I did not mean to suggest in any way that his segregationist views of 50 years ago were justified or right. Segregation was immoral then and it is wrong now."[48] As the accusations of racist intent increased in number and intensity, Lott began to deny them in more unequivocal terms.

Perhaps the strand of accusations that put the most pressure on Lott to take up the apologetic strategy of denial was the strand in which evidence from Lott's past was offered as proof of the racism behind his remarks. In his interview with Hannity, Lott denied any racism in either his earlier or his more recent comments by explaining them as "typical of a friendly relationship with Strom Thurmond." Also in his conversation with Hannity, Lott denied that his appearance at a CCC event proved racism on his part, repeatedly describing the event in question as "an open forum for candidates" at which he was but one participant. In his fifth apology, given during an interview on BET, Lott admitted that it "was wrong" for his fraternity to remain segregated but denied accusations that he had led the movement that kept Sigma Nu open to whites only, stating that he "was not as active a participant as some people would have said." Also in this interview, Lott denied that supporting Pickering's judicial nomination constituted racism, defending Pickering as "a good man who . . . is not a racist or a segregationist in any way. . . . [M]any of the things said against him he was not guilty of." Moreover, said Lott, Pickering was "a fine man with an outstanding record who actually took risks with his own life in actions against the Klan."[49] In each of these instances, Lott denied allegations that he was racist or had supported racist causes by offering alternative explanations for his allegedly racist actions and associations.

Lott, like many other apologists before him, not only denied the accusations against him but also attempted to bolster his reputation with his audience by "identify[ing] himself with something viewed favorably by" them or by "reinforc[ing] the existence of a fact, sentiment, object, or relationship."[50] One bolstering strategy that appeared repeatedly in Lott's apologia was identifying himself with those of his accusers in the African American community by emphasizing (1) his connections with African Americans and (2) commonalities between his life experiences and theirs. Another of Lott's bolstering strategies involved emphasizing positive motivations for his comments, such as friendship and respect, with which a broad spectrum of audience members could identify, and reinforcing the fact that he was not alone in praising Thurmond on his one hundredth birthday.

The main way in which Lott attempted to bolster his image in his various apologies was identification with one of the most crucial parts of his audience: African Americans. Many of Lott's Mississippi constituents are African Americans. Further, the controversy over Lott's remarks centered on how they reflected his attitudes toward racism and segregation; therefore, many of Lott's accusers were either African American activists or those sympathetic to their reaction to Lott's words. Thus, to repair his image as perceived by members of this key group of constituents and accusers, Lott needed to emphasize those aspects of his life he shared with them rather than those aspects of his life that had so repulsed them. One such shared life experience or belief was the American dream. In his interview with Hannity, Lott argued that "the best thing to do [is] to help all people, regardless of their ethnic, religious, or racial backgrounds, to give them an opportunity to live the American dream. Which I have lived, by the way. I'm the son of a sharecropper myself. . . . I grew up in a blue-collar . . . family, and I understand that you need economic opportunity in America, you need a quality education everywhere, regardless of race or background." In his Pascagoula news conference, Lott again referred to his blue-collar roots: "I am humbled by the American dream because I have lived the American dream. To those who believe I was implying that this dream is for some and not for all, I truly apologize."[51] By alluding to the broadly held idea of the American dream, Lott endeavored to identify his own experiences and aspirations with those of his audience, thereby attempting to span the political divide with a bridge of shared experience.

Lott also sought to identify with his audience through his religious faith. Realizing that many Southerners, white and black, are Protestant Christians, Lott drew on this aspect of his life in several of his apologies. In addition, emphasizing themes of repentance, forgiveness, and redemption with an audience that he perceived as sympathetic to these concepts provided another way to connect with listeners' values and persuade them to practice forgiveness toward him. The day after a number of high-profile accusations against Lott surfaced—President Bush's comments, the Congressional Black Caucus' statement, and *Time*'s article revealing the Sigma Nu incident—the senator concluded his Pascagoula news conference by emphasizing his faith and citing scripture: "As a man of faith, I have read the Bible all of my life. I now fully understand the Psalm that says 'a broken spirit: a contrite and humbled heart.'"[52]

In his December 16 interview with Gordon, Lott similarly referred to his church attendance and alluded to a passage from Ecclesiastes when he recalled,

"When I went to my home church on Sunday, the preacher talked about the seasons of life—the good times, the bad times, and a time for correction." Earlier in the same interview, Lott had pointed out, "I feel strongly about my faith, and I have grown over the years," as part of an explanation that "to be a racist you have to feel superior. I don't feel superior to you at all. I don't believe any man or any woman is superior to any other man." When Gordon asked if Lott had always held that view, he framed his response in religious terms: "I think I did. I grew up in a religious family, and I had concerns about what I saw over the years. I didn't act on it." A few exchanges later, Lott gave additional evidence for his increased faith and ultimate redemption by recounting a conversation with his daughter: "Who among us does not mature? You know, my daughter a few years ago said, 'Dad, you know, you've changed.' Me. She said, 'Well, you used to be quicker to anger, you wouldn't spend as much time. You didn't talk as much about your faith. What happened?' . . . And I said, well, as you get older you learn from your mistakes. You begin to love people in a different sort of way."[53] By identifying himself as a religious man—through references to his reading of the Bible, church attendance, and personal spiritual growth—Lott sought to establish common ground with many of his listeners: his Mississippi constituency, African Americans throughout the nation, and the influential Religious Right within the Republican Party. Further, through these and numerous other allusions to the tenets of repentance, forgiveness, and redemption, Lott hoped to inspire forgiveness of his sins and a subsequent redemption of his image and influence in the political sphere.

Another way in which Lott attempted to bolster his image with African Americans in particular was through frequent references to reaching out to their leaders and practicing of affirmative action or diversity as an individual. For example, when Hannity asked about the Congressional Black Caucus, Lott responded, "I have talked with them, and I think we've had good conversations. I've answered questions and pointed out . . . what I have done in my own office and in my own career in terms of making sure we had involvement and participation by African-Americans in my own staffing and in my appointments." In his interview with King as in other apologies, Lott highlighted specific individual actions intended to further diversity in his home state: "I do have a long record of trying to involve African-Americans and supporting our historical black colleges and universities [and] making sure we had an active intern program to bring African-Americans into the [Senate]. We have a leadership program at the University of Mississippi that probably has half of its students are minorities; not all African-Americans, . . . Vietnamese and others. So I think . . . the programs I've supported, indicate that I'm not insensitive to the need for fair elections and community renewal." On December 16 on BET, Lott again underscored his efforts to "reach out" to African Americans in particular: "I've been reaching out, talking to a lot of different people—African Americans—seeking their advice—pastors, media, business leaders—and looking for their suggestions of what we can do. J. C. Watts has been very helpful in making sure that I understand how people feel about what I said. . . . Even today I talked to John Lewis, Congressman Lewis from Georgia." Lott referenced Lewis's invitation (made on *Meet the Press*) to take a tour of civil rights sites throughout the South and described a plan under which Lott and Lewis would develop "a task force of reconciliation" in which they would "sit down and talk" in "a bipartisan way, bicameral and multi-racial" with "young and old men and women from all sections of the country."[54] By reinforcing his efforts to increase diversity on his staff and leadership opportunities for minorities and identifying himself with African American leaders, especially Lewis, a former civil rights activist, Lott sought to shore up his weakened image on racial matters by offering evidence that would enhance his image with the constituency that he had most offended.

Appealing to a broader audience, Lott also sought to explain his comments in terms of widely held and practiced values of friendship and respect. On December 11, Lott explained to Hannity and his largely conservative radio audience that the birthday comments had been part of a tradition in which he had "kidded" Thurmond "about the kind of job he has done and what he has stood for, and it is basically saying, 'You know, you would have made a great president.' He lights up, he smiles at that. That's the vein it was in. It was never intended to say, 'Because of the policies you were advocating in 1948.' It's because of a lifetime of service. . . . [W]hat are you going to say, 'I wish you'd lost'? But really [it] is just typical of a friendly relationship with Strom Thurmond." Similarly, in the King interview later that day, Lott stated, "This is a guy that's 100 years old, and I've been in the Senate with him . . . since he was 86. And I've always . . . been nice to him and . . . tried to honor him every way I could."[55]

In addition to defending his comments about Thurmond as indicative of his friendship with and respect for the elder statesman, Lott also pointed out in the Gordon interview that he was not the only senator to have praised Thurmond on the occasion of his birthday and retirement from the Senate: "Let me tell you what I said on the floor of the United States Senate about him in a serious moment, thinking about what I was going to say. . . . I was one of 36 senators that spoke praisingly. Not one condemned his past, but six of us did comment on it. And I said Senator Thurmond is a different case in many ways. He is of course a different generation, and he exemplifies its strengths, just as he has worked to leave behind its shortcomings."[56] With such comments, Lott defended his remarks as well intentioned, springing from the widely held and approved values of friendship and respect for one's elders. Further, the fact that nearly three dozen other senators had made similarly respectful and friendly statements about Thurmond on the Senate floor made Lott's comments seem less of an aberration and more like one praise among many; Lott's statement became clothed with additional respectability because the senators who lined up to pay homage to Thurmond came from both the Democratic and Republican Parties. Noting that he was among the minority of those who did remember to couch their commendations with recognition of Thurmond's weaknesses further enhanced Lott's ethos as one who was not offering unqualified praise for Thurmond and his controversial past.

Similarly, speaking with Hannity, Lott drew a parallel between his remarks about Thurmond and his comments at the death of Democratic senator Paul Wellstone of Minnesota: "I went to the floor of the Senate not too long ago and said words of praise for Paul Wellstone. Now, did that mean I was endorsing his positions in the Senate? No. What it meant was, this was a man who served the people, he was killed in a plane accident, and he was always courteous to me and friendly, and so that was . . . the human and right thing to do." Framing his praise for Thurmond as emanating from a spirit of friendship and respect, Lott likely hoped to evoke audience members' memories of similar remarks they had made about friends, relatives, or colleagues; indeed, he continued his remarks about the Wellstone analogy, "Quite often we do become too exuberant in our endorsements of people that perhaps we work with or that are retiring or it had been birthdays, in this case."[57] Setting his remarks in the context of similar comments by himself and many others added a level of credibility and respectability to his explanation.

While Lott indeed sought to make his comments about Thurmond seem more respectable by allying them with the values of friendship and respect as well as the credibility of the Senate, he also realized the need to answer the accusations of racism by separating Thurmond, himself, and their region from the sins of segregation. In so doing, Lott practiced the apologetic strategy of differentiation, "separating some fact, sentiment, object, or relationship from some larger context within which the audience presently views that attribute."[58] Throughout his several apologia, Lott differentiated Thurmond's present from his past, arguing that the praise had referred to Thurmond the man and not to his segregationist background. Along these lines, Lott also repeatedly pointed out that Thurmond long ago had repudiated segregation, thereby offering evidence that he had separated himself from his past segregationist ways. Lott not only emphasized Thurmond's changed stance regarding civil rights and race but also underscored changes in Lott's attitudes regarding such issues. Finally, Lott argued that the South as a whole had also changed. By emphasizing the changes in attitude and policy he, Thurmond, and their region had made, Lott sought to differentiate all three from their less than respectable records on issues of race.

From the very earliest of his apologies, Lott sought to differentiate praise of the man (Thurmond) from praise of his past policies (support of segregation). As Bonjean explained on December 6 and as Lott clarified on December 11, "When I think back about Strom Thurmond over the years, what I've seen is a man who was for strong national defense and economic development and balanced budgets and opportunity, and that's the kind of things I really had in mind." He similarly explained his 1980 remarks about Thurmond, noting that "when I talked about Strom again, we were talking about the problem in Iran, talking about deficits over the years, strong law enforcement speeches. . . . So those are the kinds of things we've had problems with over the years with defense, budgets, . . . law enforcement. I think we could have done a better job." Lott made similar comments to both King and Gordon in which he differentiated the Thurmond of the 1980s and 1990s with the Thurmond of 1948. As Lott said on December 13, "By the time I came to know Strom Thurmond—40 years after he ran for President—Strom himself had long since repudiated these repugnant views." By specifying Thurmond's less controversial and more recent policies, Lott sought to differentiate clearly the racist, segregationist Thurmond and the elderly, more moderate, and even "progressive" Thurmond. As Lott told King, Thurmond "has changed over the years and I think that . . . he has developed . . . a progressive record in many ways."[59]

Lott also sought to differentiate his own past and present selves: "My positions have changed over the years. I have changed my emphasis—greater emphasis on things like education and economic development and . . . opportunity for community development." Speaking with Gordon on BET, Lott described his personal and political evolution: "Part of it is when you get outside of a cocoon, when . . . you begin to live other places. [At] law school, I started studying civil rights suits and [the] Civil Rights Act of 1964. . . . But I think it really happened when I started to move around statewide, and I went into the poorest part of the state. I saw poverty I had never seen before. [By the 1990s,] I was very much changing, but it wasn't complete. In fact, it's never complete. You never—I am not a perfect person. I have made mistakes, and I am sure I will make more. Gordon went on to ask Lott about a number of race- and civil-rights-related issues. Responding to the list of "transgressions" as a whole—including votes against the federal Martin Luther King Jr. holiday, the Civil Rights Act of 1990, and the 1992 extension of the Voting Rights Act—Lott argued, "There are a number of things that I have done in recent years that I think would show that I have been changing: the legislation I have sponsored, bills that I moved." Explaining his vote against the King holiday in particular, Lott admitted, "I am not sure we in America—certainly not white America and the people in the South fully understood who this man was, the impact he was having on the fabric of this country . . . but I have learned a lot since then . . . and I now . . . would vote for a Martin Luther King holiday."[60] In these and other instances in his apologies, Lott worked to differentiate the Lott of the present and future from the Lott of the past.

Lott also sought to show how the South had evolved over recent decades. Lott told Larry King, "We're way beyond those policies of the past, Larry. They were bad at the time; we've made huge progress since then. My state has more

African-American elected officials than any other state." Two days later, in Pascagoula, Lott recounted, "I grew up with segregation. I grew up in an environment that condoned policies and views that we know were wrong and immoral. . . . I have seen what it did to families, to schools, and to communities. I have seen personally the destruction it has wrought on the lives of good people. . . . I lived through the troubled times of the South, and along with the South I have learned from the mistakes of the past." And in the BET interview, Lott pointed out specific changes of which he was proud at the University of Mississippi: "I think you should reach out to people . . . across the board. That's why I am so proud of my alma mater now, University of Mississippi, that obviously had a difficult time in the '60s and '70s—now led by an outstanding chancellor, Robert Khayat, that has gotten rid of the Confederate flag, that has now got an Institute of Reconciliation."[61] Lott thus set himself and Thurmond in the context of a changing, progressive South. Lott hoped to persuade his wider audience that he and Thurmond had changed by showing that the region that had voted in 1948 to elect Thurmond and preserve segregation had changed significantly in years since.

Especially in his later apologies, Lott attempted to transcend the boundaries of his quandary by "cognitively join[ing] some fact, sentiment, object, or relationship with some larger context within which the audience does not presently view that attribute." The two strands of Lott's apologies that furthered such transcendence were (1) efforts to "fetch good out of evil" by rhetorically changing his political problems into political opportunities and (2) contentions that in the world of national politics, people were out to get him or to sacrifice him rather than his party's agenda and image. Throughout his apologia, Lott repeated his hope that everyone would "move on" or "move past" this incident to achieve greater good and understanding. In his later apologia, these "moving on" statements came to be stated in ways very reminiscent of Ernest Bormann's fantasy theme of "fetching good out of evil." In Lott's final apology, his postresignation interview with the Associated Press, Lott seemed to resign himself to (or finally express openly) a more paranoid interpretation, reminiscent of Richard Hofstadter's articulation of the "paranoid style in American politics," in which his situation was explained not by some greater, immaterial good but rather by the darker, overarching mechanisms of political life.[62]

In the fantasy theme of fetching good out of evil, as Bormann explains, "Evil always has a purpose since God does not afflict his chosen people with troubles unless they are failing to live up to the covenant he has with them. The community members and their spokesman must, therefore, search the evil and discover the good that is within it. . . . [T]he participants in [this] fantasy type ask, 'How have we sinned? What must we do to be saved?'" This is an apt way to understand Lott in the wake of his comments about Thurmond. The earlier manifestations of this theme in Lott's apologia take the form of "moving on" statements. After telling Hannity that the "comments conveyed things that I did not intend, and I regret it. And, you know, I apologize for it," Lott expressed his "hope that we could move on from that and move on to things that we can do to help the people all across the country" through initiatives that would ensure "economic opportunity for everybody, community renewal, . . . election reforms, . . . and put[ting] more money in education." At his Pascagoula news conference, Lott similarly stated, "In the days and months to come, I will dedicate myself to undo[ing] the hurt I have caused and will do all that I can to contribute to a society where every American has an equal opportunity to succeed." In his later apologia, Lott's wording more clearly evoked Bormann's "fetching good out evil" fantasy type, as on December 16, when Lott stated, "I hope that maybe this bad experience for me, the mistake I made, will wind up helping lead to better relationships and improvements." Lott elaborated on this theme at the conclusion of his interview with Gordon, articulating his belief that "this actually can help us move an agenda that will be good for America—all Americans—equal opportunity for everybody, and improved society. And I am going to work to make that happen." Shortly after his resignation, Lott told an Associated Press reporter, "I feel very strongly about my faith. God has put this burden on me, I believe he'll show me a way to turn it into a good."[63] Such statements seemed to express Lott's simultaneous hopes for political and spiritual redemption. By explaining his situation in such terms, Lott seemed to seek to convince his audience to take up a similarly rose-colored terministic screen of forgiveness, a perspective from which they would be more inclined to forgive him his sins and allow him the opportunity to make amends by "fetching good out of evil" or turning lemons into lemonade.

But were such repentant, optimistic statements sincere? Perhaps only Lott and his God will ever know for sure. However, after a long string of such hopeful comments, Lott appeared to give in to a more accusatory, pessimistic, and even paranoid perspective. While Lott had consciously attempted throughout his apologies to avoid responding to specific accusers (although various interviewers asked him to do so), in the end, after resigning as majority leader–elect, Lott voiced a seemingly paranoid reading of his situation in which his accusers were more at fault than he was: "A lot of people in Washington have been trying to nail me for a long time. When you're from Mississippi and you're a conservative and you're a Christian, there are a lot of people who don't like that. I fell into their trap and I have only myself to blame."[64] Lott, however, was not the first or only participant in this exchange of accusations and apologia to voice such a conspiracy theory.

While few people came to Lott's aid, one person who consistently defended him throughout the controversy was Pat Buchanan, who argued in a December 13 opinion column, "The words were said in gracious tribute. But the malicious saw opportunity. Tom Edsall of the *Washington Post* dug up 54-year-old Thurmond quotes . . . , then phoned around to elicit the 'outrage' he had sought to incite. As ever, the left and a few neoconservatives were delighted to contribute." Buchanan further developed this conspiracy theory as one of intraparty betrayal on December 18, arguing, "When the official autopsy is performed on the corpse of Trent Lott, it will be revealed that he died of a stab wound that came from above. This time, Caesar knifed Brutus." Buchanan portrayed Bush's December 12 comments as "throw[ing] Lott . . . to the wolves." Adding further fuel to the fire of Bush's betrayal, Buchanan contrasted Bush's actions with what Buchanan imagined Reagan would have done in the same situation: "Ronald Reagan would have never knifed a friend and ally like this, even if he were guilty! It is a failing of the Bush family that they believe in loyalty up, but not loyalty down." Buchanan added another level to his conspiracy theory by observing that Lott's "own president cut him dead and collaborated, almost surely at the instigation of 'Boy Genius' Karl Rove, with his assassins." Buchanan concluded that had Bush framed his comments about Lott with more loyalty, "Lott's enemies would have scattered like the jackals they are. Now, with Bush's assist, they have horribly wounded his majority leader. Trent Lott is the victim of a hate crime, not the perpetrator of one." On December 30, Buchanan reflected on "the squabble among neoconservatives over who among them was the first to stick his nail file in the back of Trent Lott," observing that "their collusion in ruining Lott, their relish in the pats on the head they are receiving from the left, confirm the suspicion: Neoconservatives are the useful idiots of the liberal establishment."[65]

A number of Lott's paleoconservative accusers also accused the Republican Party of disloyalty to Lott and thus to its Southern base. The CCC accused Lott's "fellow Republicans" of "joining the hyena pack of blacks and liberals who are demanding his ouster." Walter D. Kennedy, coauthor of *The South Was Right*, asked rhetorically, "Did anyone notice how quickly the President and the National GOP tried to distance themselves from the South? . . . The South is encouraged to jump on the Republican bus and take a ride. As soon as Dixie gets on board, she is told to 'go to the back of the bus, sit down, shut-up, and for goodness sake, don't wave that Confederate flag!'" In short, Kennedy explained, "the media could not have caused Lott's demise without a lot of help from the beleaguered senator and the Republican Party." In a similar spirit, Kay laid out a very specific conspiracy theory whereby President Bush, after his December 12 comments chastising Lott, "immediately crawfished . . . after Lott's staffers informed him that if Lott was forced to resign from the Senate leadership, he would likely resign from his seat as well. . . . Faced with his greatest fear—a 50/50 Senate that might cease to be a rubber stamp—Dubya prudently shut up about the whole thing. His great moral outrage be damned; the possible frustration of his dictatorial powers was just too high of a price to pay."[66] While these same pundits had harshly accused Lott of weakness, cowardice, and disloyalty to the South through his many apologia, they situated Lott in a bigger picture in which he, as representative of Southern conservatives such as themselves, had been betrayed by the Republican Party's national establishment in the person of George W. Bush. While the GOP's betrayal of Lott did not absolve him of his sins against his (former) brethren, it framed his transgressions within the overarching political system, which was proven, through this controversy, to be conspiring against the South and its defenders.

In addition to these right-wing Southerners, some more moderate and liberal commentators who had been among Lott's accusers discerned a conspiracy at work in his situation. A December 19 *Roll Call* editorial summed up this more mainstream version of the White House conspiracy to get rid of Lott: "Despite formal pronouncements by White House spokesman Ari Fleischer that President Bush does not think [Lott] should resign, the newspapers are filled with unsourced—but authoritative-sounding—statements that Bush does not think that Lott can, will or should survive. The evidence suggests that Fleischer's statements are vain attempts to remove the White House's fingerprints—or bootprints—from Lott's back." The writers argued quite bluntly and vividly that "Bush is not just letting Lott 'twist slowly in the wind,' in the cruel phrase from the Nixon era, but is actively building the scaffold and tying the rope." Frum shared this perspective, asking, the day after Bush's public comments, "It couldn't be clearer if the president actually pulled the lever on the trap door himself, could it?" Likewise, the editors of the *Nation* opined in January 2003 that "Lott's fate was sealed when the White House decided it needed a smoother, and smarter, son of the Confederacy running the Senate." Jesse Jackson Sr., also looking back on Lott's resignation, argued that the "Bush White House helped push the drive to dump Republican Senate Majority Leader Trent Lott.... Echoing unnamed White House advisors, Republicans argued that Lott would be an 'impediment to the passage of the president's agenda,'" which Jackson argued was the overturning of affirmative action laws.[67] While these accusations that the White House had ultimately decided Lott's fate from behind the scenes did not defend Lott, such more mainstream conspiracy theories helped legitimize the idea that Lott was a victim of (somewhat) unseen political forces beyond his control.

Hofstadter argues that in "The Paranoid Style in American Politics," "the feeling of persecution is central, and it is indeed systematized in grandiose theories of conspiracy . . . see[ing] the hostile and conspiratorial world . . . directed against a nation, a culture, a way of life whose fate affects not himself alone but millions of others." Lott stated that he was being targeted because of his identity as a Christian conservative from Mississippi. Implicit in this statement is the belief that all Christian conservatives from Mississippi—and perhaps the South in general—were being victimized by those outside their region and belief system. Joining his fate with those of his fellow Southern Christian conservatives may have been a rhetorical strategy to reidentify with the constituency Lott had jettisoned (perhaps only temporarily) via his apologia. As Hofstadter observes, "The paranoid disposition is mobilized into action chiefly by social conflicts that involve ultimate schemes of values and that bring fundamental fears and hatreds, rather than negotiable interests, into political action. Catastrophe or the fear of catastrophe is most likely to elicit the syndrome of paranoid rhetoric." Having lost precisely the position he had sought to preserve through his apologia, Lott needed to save face with his previously loyal constituency of like-minded white Southerners to avoid his ultimate political demise: the loss not only of his leadership position but of his Senate seat in the next election. If Lott could not rebuild the bridges he had burned by the end of his next term or build amazingly strong new ties with African Americans in his state, political catastrophe might well have been at hand. Having failed in his attempt to transcend his mistake by articulating the hope that good could come from his evil, Lott resorted—whether through rhetorical strategy, genuine fear, or both—to the conspiracy theories to which the contemporary right wing so often turns.[68]

On one level, Lott served as the scapegoat for all the old-school Southern politicians whom the press and the political establishment had neglected to punish adequately for their sins. Lott's remarks at Thurmond's party brought back before the public eye the sins of Lott and his Southern political forebears and cohorts—Strom Thurmond, Robert Byrd, William Fulbright, Bob Barr, and others. This time, the media and the political establishment would not let the opportunity for victimage pass them by. In particular, Lott's celebration of Thurmond's most segregationist moment reminded Lott's accusers that they had never punished Thurmond, or he would not have gone on to serve eight terms in the Senate. Wrinkled, weak, and immobile at age one hundred, Thurmond was no longer a candidate for sacrifice, perhaps too close to a natural death to be an acceptable kill—though his segregationist sins were, it could be argued, worse than Lott's. But Lott, comparatively young (at sixty-one) and ascendant in power, had something that could be sacrificed (his position as majority leader) and had made himself vulnerable to attack through his remarks. Therefore Lott was made a victim both by others (homicidally) and by his own actions (suicidally).[69]

On another level, Lott was made a scapegoat to bear the burden of the sins of his accusers. Lott's controversial comments brought to light not only his own sins in matters of race but also the sins of other people of influence (Thurmond and others) that had gone unpunished. The fact that such racism in the halls of Congress had for so long gone unchecked, with no one paying the price, may have made Lott's accusers experience feelings of guilt at not having done enough to expose the sins of the Lotts and Thurmonds of the political realm and not having done more to remove such sinners from positions of influence. As *Salon* columnist Joe Conason opined, "The attitude that ignores or downplays Lott's remarks is what used to be called institutional racism."[70] By sacrificing Lott in the press, in the public estimation, and among his political colleagues, the senator's accusers could in turn experience a feeling of redemption—at last they had done something to remove their feelings of guilt at having let such entrenched institutional racism remain unchecked. By their own inaction or ineffective actions, Lott's accusers had allowed him and others like him not only to stay in positions of power but to survive and thrive. Accusing Lott again and again until he became their sacrifice helped them to purge their guilt, resulting in their feeling that they had been redeemed.

But Lott's political and ideological rivals were not the only people sacrificing him. President Bush and other Republicans allowed Lott to be attacked as a sacrificial lamb left unguarded in a political landscape populated by hungry wolves in the media and from across the political aisle. By failing to come to Lott's defense, Republicans essentially made Lott their sacrifice, too, though seemingly in a more passive manner than did Lott's more obvious political rivals and ideological enemies. Republicans allowed Lott to become their sacrifice, their scapegoat, to avoid sacrificing any more of their flock. At a time when Republicans had been making overtures to recruit African Americans and other minorities, Lott's comments constituted a major sin against the party's growth strategy. Further, Republicans could not allow the general public to think of them as the party of racists and old-time segregationists, even though they had given safe haven for more than thirty years to Thurmond as well as to CCC sympathizers such as Lott and former Georgia representative Bob Barr. And, perhaps most crucially, many Republicans believed that Lott's remarks would hurt, in terms of press coverage and public opinion, their hope of overturning affirmative action.

Looking at Lott as a Republican Party scapegoat allows us to see that, at least for Republican Party power brokers, the sacrifice of Lott was more strategic move than heartfelt penance for the party's racial failings. On the one hand, the Republicans wanted to be seen as welcoming to African Americans, frequently touting J. C. Watts, Colin Powell, and Condoleezza Rice as the faces of a more diverse party elite. On the other hand, however, Republicans needed to appease their more traditional base by taking clear actions against affirmative action policies. Because Republican opposition to affirmative action would bring charges of racism against the party, some observers believe that sacrificing Lott because of his alleged racism was a calculated move of triangulation (in the strategic tradition of Dick Morris) to make the party seem less racist and more mainstream. Republicans thus allowed Lott to be sacrificed to the media and political wolves yet managed to save face with their Southern base by selecting as his successor Tennessee senator Bill Frist, a younger Republican from the South whose medical profession shrouded him with a sense of scientific purity and rationality, a stark contrast to Lott, who was seen as allowing his emotions, passions, and prejudices to overwhelm him.

Finally, Lott was also sacrificed by the people whose taint had resulted in further accusations from others—that is, Southern paleoconservatives from such groups as the League of the South and the CCC. These former Lott defenders did not see his comments about Thurmond as sinful; rather, Lott's apologies caused his sacrifice in these circles. When Lott not only apologized for his remarks but began to pledge his support for civil rights initiatives, Southern paleoconservatives no longer saw Lott as a brother and fellow unreconstructed Confederate but instead perceived him as a coward and a traitor to what they believed were his true convictions. Lott was sacrificed by his former brothers to pay the price of disloyalty not only for his own sins but also perhaps for those of the neoconservatives, whom the paleoconservatives believed had betrayed true conservatism in return for political influence. And, though any CCC member worth his salt would never admit it, on a deeper level, Lott likely was sacrificed as a burnt offering for the group members' sins of racism, anti-Semitism, and other practices of hate.

That Lott became a scapegoat for the sins of the South because of his remarks about Thurmond seems appropriate, since Thurmond's life essentially spanned and therefore symbolized the history of race relations in the twentieth-century South. The close coincidence of Lott's sacrifice (in December 2002) and Thurmond's death (in June 2003) may in a way signify division's demise as the South's distinctive order. These two events may be harbingers of a new order of distinctiveness on the Southern horizon. Nonetheless, when Lott reclaimed a Senate leadership position in November 2006, "lifted from disgrace" when his Republican colleagues elected him minority whip, they sent a message that there may in the end be "Redemption for the Pariah from Pascagoula."[71]

Conclusion: Dialectical Rhetoric as the New Rhetoric of Southern Identity

A STRONG CASE may be made that if any one person embodied the changing order of the South in the twentieth century, it was Strom Thurmond. As Delaware senator Joseph Biden noted in his July 2003 eulogy, "Strom Thurmond was the only man I knew who in a literal sense lived in three distinct and separate periods of American history. . . . Born into an era of essentially unchallenged and unexamined mores of the South, reaching his full maturity in an era of fully challenged and critically examined bankrupt mores of his beloved South, and living out his final three decades in a South that had formally rejected its past on race—in each of these stages . . . Strom represented exactly where he came from." Thurmond was born in Edgefield, South Carolina, in December 1902, and died there just over a century later. The son of a small-town lawyer, Thurmond grew up in the shadow of Edgefield's other famous political son, the populist but virulently racist Ben "Pitchfork" Tillman, a family friend. In 1925, Thurmond fathered his first child, Essie Mae Washington, with the daughter of his family's African American housekeeper. He started his political career as a Democrat, moved to the States' Rights Democratic Party in 1948, returned to the Democratic Party fold, and then, during the 1960s, in the days of Barry Goldwater, switched to the Republican Party. In the 1970s, he became the first Southern senator to hire black staff members, and in the 1980s and 1990s he cast votes in support of the Martin Luther King Jr. holiday, the renewal of the Voting Rights Act, and Clarence Thomas's confirmation as a Supreme Court justice.[1]

At the peak of his political career, Thurmond ran for president on a platform rooted firmly in the defense of the Southern states' right to remain segregated. And as Diane McWhorter observes, "Thurmond has always been an ornery redemption project. He did not repent. Even so, his illegitimate daughter further complicates the moral picture. . . . We need not dwell on the obvious mind-boggling hypocrisies here: that someone who ran for president on an anti-pool-mixin' platform was party to an integrated gene pool." McWhorter argues that this aspect of Thurmond's life story was not more widely reported because the "particulars of this family saga simply do not fit into the 'redemption narrative' Americans tend to impose on our more regrettable bygones: Better that ol' Strom 'transformed' from the Negro-baiting Dixiecrat presidential candidate of 1948 to One of the First Southern Senators To Hire a Black Aide in 1971."[2]

So whose interpretation of Thurmond's life is more believable—Biden's more hopeful narrative, or McWhorter's more skeptical one? According to Biden, although "it's fairly easy to say today" that Thurmond's evolution resulted from "pure political expediency," he believes instead that "Strom knew America was changing, and that there was a lot he didn't understand about that change. Much of that change challenged many of his long-held views. But he also saw his beloved South Carolina changing as well, and he knew the time had come to change himself. . . . Thurmond was doing what few do once they pass the age of 50: He was continuing to grow, continuing to change." McWhorter argues, however, that Thurmond's racial demagoguing "was just 'bidness,'" a fact that "may account for why Strom Thurmond never felt compelled to ask the forgiveness of a race he devoted so much public capital to making miserable—a race that included members of his own family. Then again, he had always been an integrationist."[3] Biden argues that as America and the South shifted their paradigms from that of division to that of identification, Thurmond in turn adjusted his paradigm accordingly—not for "political expediency" but rather because he, like his nation and his region, over time had come to accept identification as the more moral order. McWhorter argues that Thurmond's racist rhetoric of his earlier career was politically expedient for a politician representing a South that valued the order of division, while Thurmond's personal life and even some of his political actions of that period bespoke someone who embraced, at least on some levels, the order of identification.

There may be some truth in both Biden's and McWhorter's interpretations of Thurmond's life. Since we are not privy to the inner workings of Thurmond's heart and mind, we will never know for sure why he acted as he did in the area of race relations over the many years of his life. And yet it does seem accurate to say, as Biden did, that "Strom represented exactly where he came from." Thurmond's actions in the first part of his political career largely sought to conserve the existing Southern order of division—in particular, the division of the races. As his long career progressed, the rhetorical situation changed in such a way that Thurmond began to take political actions not to defend the order of division but to move forward (or at least not hinder the progress of) the order of identification. Whether this evolution proceeded for moral or political reasons, we do not know. But as McWhorter points out, Thurmond had on one level "always been an integrationist." Perhaps this seeming paradox best "represented exactly where [Thurmond] came from." Though the South long had promoted and defended the order of division in public, the private reality was that identification was not so much the exception the rule. At the root of recent debates over

Southern identity may be the fact not so much that identification is replacing division as the ruling order of the South but rather that Southerners are finally acknowledging that identification should be not only the private, back porch order of the South but also its public, front porch order.[4]

The four debates analyzed in this volume reflect the shift from division to identification as the more influential order in Southern public culture. The order of division ruled the South through slavery (the division of labor, master and slave, according to race), secession (the division of the nation as a consequence of different perspectives on states' rights), and segregation (the division of groups of people by race, gender, and other characteristics, both by law and social custom). So many instances of conflict have arisen since the late 1990s because this era may be a crucial turning point in this shift from the old order to the new order. By the turn of the millennium, legally mandated forms of division such as segregated public institutions had largely become things of the past, replaced by legally mandated ways of achieving identification such as integration and affirmative action. As a result, Southerners and others who continued to embrace the old order of division—through their reverence for and defense of Old South symbols, traditions, and institutions—found themselves in conflict with those who advocated more identification not only through legislation and the Constitution but also in what symbolism and traditions would be allowed to hold sway in the public sphere, especially in the former states of the Confederacy, with their many remaining memorials of the South's divided past.

At the Virginia Military Institute (VMI), the old order of division was evidenced in its identity as an all-white college until 1968 and as an all-male college until the 1996 Supreme Court ruling. Symbols of VMI's ruling order of division included the walls of its imposing, seemingly impassible Gothic-style barracks, its distinctive uniforms, and its unspoken promise of graduation into the ranks of the South's good-ol'-boy network. But with the integration first of racial and ethnic minorities and then of women into VMI's social mysteries, identification largely displaced division as the school's ruling order. Men and women, blacks and whites, can now identify with one another as fellow cadets, with identification brought before our eyes as women donned the VMI uniform, bunked inside the fortress-like barracks, and joined the ranks of privileged institute graduates. People formerly divided now can identify with one another within the institution of VMI as they together put on the vestments of its particular symbols and traditions.

Today, cadets of both sexes and of various races and ethnicities identify with one another within VMI, yet as a collective they can still claim a distinctive identity from other colleges and universities through their symbols and traditions (uniforms, rings, and class system), though perhaps not quite as distinct an identity as had previously been the case. A wider spectrum of people now have the possibility of being admitted (literally) into the social mystery that is VMI, but that does not mean that VMI's social mystery, the source of its distinctiveness, can no longer exist on any level. Rather than emphasize some of the former aspects of its distinctiveness—the fact that all students were white men—today's VMI should emphasize those aspects of its distinctiveness (such as its martial and Southern traditions) that have remained constant through such changes as racial and gender integration as well as potentially new aspects of its distinctiveness that have emerged as a result of such changes.

Elsewhere in Virginia, the old order of division was evidenced by Richmond's identity as the capital of the Confederate States of America—the capital of states that separated themselves from the Union—as well as in the deeply ensconced institution of racial segregation, which ruled the city both through law and social custom. The city's division into a hierarchy of white and black was seen vividly on the city's most famous street, Monument Avenue. By including only memorials to Confederates on Monument Avenue, those with the power and authority to order the city sent the message that only "dead white Confederate males" deserved this place of honor in Richmond's public commemoration of its history. When Arthur Ashe grew up there during the 1950s, not only did the imposing statues of Monument Avenue symbolize the ruling order of racial division, but Richmonders experienced this division in their daily lives. Whites and blacks not only attended "separate but equal" schools but also had to play tennis on separate courts in separate neighborhoods. However, in the years since *Brown v. Board of Education* and the Civil Rights Acts of 1964 and 1965, legally mandated segregation has been replaced gradually by legally mandated integration in Richmond and elsewhere. Though "white flight" has now given Richmond proper a majority African American population, legally mandated segregation no longer exists (though de facto segregation continues to exist in people's associations with one another, as evidenced in the city's racially distinct neighborhoods, churches, civic groups, and the like).

Nonetheless, as the legal barriers between people were removed, people of different backgrounds, ethnicities, races, and genders attained more influence in Richmond's public life. With this greater diversity of voices in the public forum came the recognition that others beyond Confederate white males have had important roles in Richmond's history and development and should have their contributions honored. Including Ashe in Monument Avenue's pantheon of heroes and representing a diversity of Richmonders in the floodwall murals depicting the city's history—and the community debates that led to these developments—created a symbolic identification among formerly divided segments of Richmond's populace. Perhaps such symbolic identification will eventually result in increased opportunities for identification in the daily lives of Richmonders.

In South Carolina, the philosophical cradle of the Confederacy, the old order of division was evidenced in the state's role as a hotbed of secession prior to the Civil War and more recently as home to segregationist presidential candidate

Strom Thurmond and by continuing to fly the Confederate battle flag atop the State Capitol. Whether one believes flag advocates' story that the flag was placed there to commemorate the centennial of the Civil War or flag opponents' narrative that the flag was hoisted to protest federally mandated integration, the flag was raised to honor and defend the old order of division, which accounted for both secession and segregation. Though the Civil War, Reconstruction, and federally enforced integration all seemed to mean the end for legally mandated division, de facto division lingered, as evidenced by the divergent narratives explaining the reasons behind secession and the Civil War, the flag's placement atop the Statehouse, and advocates' efforts to keep the flag flying high over the Capitol dome and in its legislative chambers.

However, the fact that multiple explanatory narratives now exist provides evidence that people of various backgrounds have gained a more influential voice in South Carolina's public life. The debate forced defenders of the old order to recognize that some South Carolinians were offended by the Confederate battle flag and its place of prominence at the State Capitol. By 2000, the presence of a diversity of voices in American and South Carolinian public life had opened up the possibility of a public debate about the flag; many of those offended by the flag had not previously believed that their voices would be heard, let alone have influence, in state politics. Relocating the flag to the Confederate memorial on the Capitol grounds demonstrates the increased influence of those formerly silenced by the order of slavery and segregation that the flag symbolized for many people involved in this debate. But those who debated the propriety of flying the Confederate flag atop the South Carolina Statehouse remained divided. Some flag opponents—most notably, the National Association for the Advancement of Colored People (NAACP)—wanted it removed from the Capitol grounds altogether. The placement of an African American history memorial along with the one to South Carolina's Confederate soldiers and its accompanying Confederate battle flag has increased identification. As K. Michael Prince observes, the juxtaposition of memorials to Confederate general Wade Hampton and Confederate soldiers alongside the collection of reliefs depicting the trials and triumphs of African American history reminds visitors "of our still-segregated sensibilities"; Prince argues that these "three belong together" as "a kind of triptych to the state's past."[5] In addition, promoting South Carolina tourism (the NAACP's boycott of which served as the opening salvo in this debate), with an emphasis on the state's historical significance both to the descendants of slaves and to the descendants of Confederates, could be another way to achieve increased identification between a diversity of Southerners, African American and white alike.

In December 2002, Trent Lott's comments about Strom Thurmond served as evidence of the lingering influence of the old order of division. Many observers interpreted Lott's comments as sympathetic to Thurmond's segregationist 1948 presidential bid, and the resulting debate concerned the propriety

The African American History Monument located by one of the side entrances to the Statehouse. Courtesy South Carolina Department of Archives and History.

The "Emancipation" panel of the African American History Monument at the Statehouse. Photograph by the author.

of allowing someone even seemingly sympathetic to the old order to serve as Senate majority leader at a time when politicians in general and Republicans in particular want to be seen as embracing the new order of identification. It is no longer politically correct to espouse publicly the order of division because people of diverse backgrounds and perspectives now have a more influential voice in public life. Even Thurmond seemed gradually to adopt a more unifying stance in the latter decades of his life.

Lott thus realized that to survive politically—to retain at least his Senate seat from heavily African American Mississippi—he had to show that he had had a change of heart, not just recently but over the course of his life. As Lott developed his apologia, he emphasized that he had come increasingly to embrace identification by offering examples of what he, as a Southern leader, had done and hoped to do to promote the new order of identification rather than the old order of division. Whether Lott's embrace of identification rather than division was pure political expedience, a true epiphany, or some combination of the two remains to be seen. But the result of this debate—Lott stepped down as majority leader—can be interpreted as evidence for the increased influence of those advocating identification and the decreased influence of those implicated in promoting division. Yet Lott's return to party leadership in November 2006 shows that whatever the motivations, redemption and reconciliation are possible.

The potential solution to this conflict between division and identification is not forcing acceptance of only division or only identification but rather coming to a compromise that combines the best aspects of both of these orders. Yes, Southerners should attempt to identify points of common ground they share as Southerners, but they should also attempt to appreciate and respect the diversity of people, backgrounds, experiences, and perspectives that exists among those who label themselves Southerners. In fact, precisely this diversity balanced with identification among the people of the South, especially in the area of race, is (or could be) what makes the South distinctive in the nation. In the South, African Americans, whites, and increasingly Latinos have long been living and working together in proportions heretofore unseen elsewhere in the United States. Together, these diverse Southerners retain their distinct regional heritage—for example, the shared Southern love of food, football, and faith—while agreeing to disagree in public debates such as those examined throughout this book.

Further, rather than trying to prove either that the South is really the same as the rest of the nation and that distinctiveness just a wishful figment of its collective imagination or that the South is so markedly different from the rest of the nation that its interests are not joined with it or that it has nothing to learn from or teach the rest of America, Southerners and Americans as a whole need to recognize that the South has played an influential role in American history and has lessons both to offer and learn from the rest of the nation. In this vein, C. Vann Woodward notes that the South's distinctive experience of loss and tragedy is "a dimension of historical experience that America very much needs, a heritage that is far more closely in line with the common lot of mankind than the national legends of opulence and success and innocence." Similarly, Richard Weaver observes, "Intercommunication and cross fertilization are necessary. I covet a chance to talk someday to a Southern audience on what they need to learn from the North. But these express two-way relationships."[6] The South is a distinctive part of the United States but remains a crucial piece of the whole. Perhaps John C. Calhoun's idea of the concurrent majority may continue to be useful to us today if we consider that the basic principle he hoped to achieve through this idea parallels the solution offered here. While the identification that results in collectives or majorities should be valued, it should not be valued at the cost of disrespecting the rights and value of minority or distinctive communities within the whole. Just as people within the South should learn to respect the value of the diversity of its people, so too should Southerners be respected as an element of the diverse people of the United States.

"Distinctiveness" may be the key to identifying Southerners with one another while recognizing the value to be found in the diversity that has kept them divided both from one another and the rest of the nation. As Kenneth Burke observes, it is possible to be consubstantial with one another in some respects while maintaining distinctiveness in other respects. This observation may be the key to fetching good out of the evil of the South's long history of being ordered according to the principle of division. The division that has been for so long the defining characteristic of the South's history may be the key to achieving identification in the South's present and future. Weaver concludes *The Southern Tradition at Bay* by observing, "The Old South may indeed be a hall hung with splendid tapestries in which no one could care to live; but from them we can learn something of how to live."[7] Contemporary Southerners should not try to recapture the division of the Old South by clinging stubbornly to its more divisive symbols and traditions or by using it as a model for reordering the New South. Instead, today's Southerners should look to debates and discussions about their divided history as the source of their identification with one another, the source of their distinctiveness from the rest of the United States, and the source of valuable lessons not only for the New South but for the rest of the nation.

Southerners' ongoing debate functions as a purifying, unifying fire. What ultimately joins or has the potential to join Southerners is the shared belief that continuing to discuss these issues has value. One of Southerners' defining characteristics has been their love for oratory, both as speakers and as listeners. Scholars such as Frank Owsley, Waldo W. Braden, and Cal M. Logue have traced the origins of this Southern "loquaciousness" (to echo Logue's term) to the frontier folklife of the antebellum South. Through their experiences of family storytelling, religious gatherings, small-town courtrooms, political campaigns, and literary societies, Braden argues, Southerners "developed an oral tradition" in which they were "more attuned to the spoken word than to the printed page." As a result, they "preferred having problems talked out, enjoyed face-to-face encounters, and took pleasure in hearing lawyers, preachers, and politicians let loose their oratorical devices." Braden implies that Southern orality is based not only in Southerners' experiences as speakers but also in their many experiences as listeners.[8]

Conversely, Allen Tate argues that the "traditional southern mode of discourse presupposes somebody at the other end *silently* listening: it is the rhetorical mode. Its historical rival is the dialectical mode, or the give and take between two minds, even if one mind, like the mind of Socrates, prevail[s] at the end. The southerner has never been a dialectician." Similarly, writing in 1941 of the "inseparable" Southern loves of rhetoric and politics, W. J. Cash does not think it possible for Southerners' rhetoric to fulfill "one of the proper functions of politics . . . the resolution of essential conflict in interest among groups and classes." Braden disagrees with such characterizations of Southern discourse as one-way communication that merely rouses the emotions without stimulating the mind. Instead, Braden encourages us "to consider the influence of those whom Tate refers to as being 'at the other end silently listening.' The question that I wish to pose is, What influences did the southern listeners of the antebellum South have on 'the traditional mode of discourse'? Sometimes observers give too much attention to southern orators as causative forces . . . instead of looking at the grass roots."[9] Those "grass roots" of the Southern oral tradition—the everyday experiences of all sorts of Southerners participating as speakers and listeners in debates of community issues—reveal a category of communication Tate and Cash ignore with their clear-cut depictions of an emotional, rhetorical mode and a more cerebral, dialectical mode.

"Dialectical rhetoric," however, allows interlocutors to engage in a persuasive exchange of ideas. Wayne Booth terms this concept "listening rhetoric" and describes it as encompassing the "whole range of communicative arts for reducing misunderstanding by paying full attention to opposing views." Such a dialectical rhetoric is, as I have shown here, a hallmark of contemporary Southern identity. In the closing decades of the twentieth century, with all that the civil rights movement accomplished, Logue wrote that the "most dramatic change in southern oratory" was the emergence of a "pluralistic public speaking . . . with a variety of views being stated on questions of race, economy, political parties, crime, national defense, ecology, industry, and education. Blacks were able publicly to communicate feelings, convictions, and aspirations previously kept private." After considering segregated Mississippi's closed society, Braden wrote (perhaps in a spirit of hope for the future) that we, including Southerners, can learn by negative example "the principle that humane government works best when the citizenry can express opposition through vigorous public debate."[10] Just such vigorous debates over Southern identity occurred with great frequency at the turn of the millennium as a consequence of a constellation of three factors: (1) the South's oral tradition; (2) the grievance-based, defensive identity of Southerners, especially white Southerners; and (3) the opening of the Southern public forum to all Southerners, including African Americans, in the late twentieth century. In the South of the early twenty-first century, advocates for the social order of identification can argue in tandem with advocates for the social order of division as part of this new dialectical rhetoric of Southern identity.

Notes

Introduction

1. Jonsson, "Battle over the Past."
2. Killian, *White Southerners*, xii, 3, 10, 11.
3. Reed, *Southerners*, 11, 15, 41, 83–84.
4. Ibid., 90; Reed, *One South*, 118; Potter, *South in the Sectional Conflict*, 15–16; Smiley, "Quest for the Central Theme," 325.
5. Cash, *Mind of the South*, xlviii; Weaver, *Southern Tradition*, 394–95.
6. Woodward, "Search for Southern Identity," 12.
7. Jonsson, "Battle over the Past."
8. Cash, *Mind of the South*, xlvii; Potter, *South in the Sectional Conflict*, 4; Smiley, "Quest for the Central Theme," 307; Cobb, *Away Down South*, 336–37.
9. Phillips, "Central Theme," 43 ("Until an issue shall arise predominant over the lingering one of race, political solidarity at the price of provincial status is maintained to keep assurance doubly, trebly sure that the South shall remain 'a white man's country'"); Twelve Southerners, *I'll Take My Stand*, xix.
10. Potter, *South in the Sectional Conflict*, 15–16 ("An explanation of the South in terms of a folk culture would not have the ideological implications which have made the explanation in terms of agrarianism so tempting and at the same time so treacherous. But on the other hand, it would not be inconsistent with some of the realities of Southern society, such as biracialism and hierarchy, whereas agrarianism is inconsistent with these realities").
11. Weaver, *Southern Tradition*, 391; Weaver, *Southern Essays*, 208 ("Belief in tragedy is essentially un-American. . . . If we are in for a time of darkness and trouble, the Southern philosophy, because it is not based upon optimism, will have better power to console than the national dogmas").
12. Woodward, "Search for Southern Identity," 17–25.
13. Degler, *Place over Time*, 127, 104–5, 125.
14. Rubin, "The Boll Weevil, the Iron Horse, and the End of the Line: Thoughts on the South," in *American South*, 366–67.
15. Weaver, *Southern Tradition*, 36.
16. Peterson, *Great Triumvirate*, 449–76.
17. Cooper and Terrill, *American South*, 294, 523, 527.
18. Foster, "Lost Cause," 1134.
19. Burke, *On Symbols and Society*, 70, 69 ("King and peasant are 'mysteries' to one another. Those 'Up' are guilty of not being 'Down,' those 'Down' are certainly guilty of not being 'Up.'"); Burke, *Language as Symbolic Action*, 18.
20. Burke, *On Symbols and Society*, 190, 181–82, 180.
21. Burke, *Permanence and Change*, 74, 94, 112–13, 163; Burke, *On Symbols and Society*, 70.
22. Burke, *On Symbols and Society*, 180.

23. Perelman and Olbrechts-Tyteca, *New Rhetoric*, 141; Burke, *On Symbols and Society*, 248, 247; Burke, *Rhetoric of Motives*, 53.

24. Gregory Clark, *Dialogue, Dialectic, and Conversation*, 19–20, 21. Clark provides a helpful distinction between dialogue and dialectic: "the term dialogue can be used to describe any exchange of assertions and responses, whereas the term dialectic is used to describe a particular kind of dialogue, one sustained exclusively for the purpose of *constructing and revising knowledge that its participants can share*. Whether the discourse that contributes to dialogue is dialectical or eristic depends upon the purposes that propel it" (19–20; italics added). Clark also clarifies the difference between eristic rhetoric, which "trains us in the art of authoritative statement," and dialectical rhetoric, which "guides us in the *process* of coming to agreement" (21; emphasis added).

25. Ibid., 71 (emphasis added).

Chapter 1

1. Weaver, *Southern Tradition*, 394.

2. Hamel, Smith, and Sullivan, "Partisan Conversation," 42; Norman, "Crashing VMI's Line," 39, 38, 40.

3. Hetter, "End of an All-Male Era," 50–51; Karen Johnson, "Statement of NOW National Secretary"; Gandy, "NOW Leaders."

4. Burke, *Rhetoric of Motives*, 122. *Class* as used here and in similar references in this chapter does not refer to class in the economic sense but rather to "a set, collection, group, or configuration containing members having or thought to have at least one attribute in common . . . [s]ocial rank or caste" ("Class," in Morris, *American Heritage Dictionary*, 278).

5. Carlyle asks, "Is it not to Clothes that most men do reverence?" (Burke, *Rhetoric of Motives*, 118). Burke later quotes Carlyle as stating, "Clothes gave us *individuality, distinctions, social polity*" and as noting "the moral, political, and even Religious influences of Clothes" as well as that people are "clothed with Authority" (119).

6. Ibid., 121; *United States v. Virginia et al.*

7. As Burke explains, "mystery is equated with class distinctions" because there is a "mystifying condition in social inequality," "a relation between mystification and class relationships" (*Rhetoric of Motives*, 122–23).

8. Statement of mission and basic philosophy from the *Regulations of the Virginia Military Institute*, quoted in Wise, *Drawing Out the Man*, 366. This is not the current VMI mission statement; the text of the present version appears at http://www.vmi.edu/Show.asp?durki=1793 (accessed March 22, 2007).

9. Wise, *Drawing Out the Man*, 489, 390.

10. Ibid., 395–99.

11. This account of the VMI controversy as it played out in the courts is general information confirmed through a number of my sources, but I gleaned this particular version from Norman, "Crashing VMI's Line," 37–40. For the Supreme Court decision itself, including Ruth Bader Ginsburg's majority decision, William Rehnquist's concurring opinion, and Antonin Scalia's dissenting opinion, see *United States v. Virginia et al.* (available online at http://www.law.cornell.edu/supct/html/94-1941.ZO.htm, http://www.law.cornell.edu/supct/html/94-1941.ZC.htm, and http://www.law.cornell.edu/supct/html/94-1941.ZD.htm (accessed March 22, 2007). For in-depth analysis of the various court cases leading to the gender integration of VMI, see Strum, *Women in the Barracks*. For summaries of Shannon Faulkner's quest to enter the Citadel, see McCandless, *Past in the Present*, 110–16; Strum, *Women in the Barracks*, 221. See also *Shannon Richey Faulkner v. James E. Jones*.

12. For more on Claunch, see White, "Loudoun Woman Attains Top Cadet Post," B01.

See also Virginia Military Institute Public Relations Office, "Claunch Named Battalion Commander." For a firsthand account of the gender integration of VMI written by an English professor at the school and based on interviews with various stakeholders, including administrators, alumni, and students, see Brodie, *Breaking Out*.

13. Turner, "Kappa Alpha Order," 290; Andrew, "Soldiers, Christians, and Patriots," 682. *United States v. Virginia et al.*; Edmonds, "How to Be a Southern Gentleman"; McCandless, "'Separate but Equal' Case Law," 131. See also Andrew, *Long Gray Lines*.

14. Anne Goodwyn Jones, "Belles and Ladies," 1527–28; Schwartz, *Southern Belle Primer*, x. Other sources on Southern women include Reed, *Southern Folk*; Wolfe, *Daughters of Canaan*; Roberts, *Confederate*.

15. McCandless, "'Separate but Equal' Case Law," 131; Cocke, "Tell All the Truth," 2.

16. Andrew, "Soldiers, Christians, and Patriots," 681–62. See also Andrew, *Long Gray Lines*.

17. Alvarez, "Letter to the Editor," 2–3; American Civil Liberties Union, "VMI Balks."

18. Stephenson, "Future of Single-Sex Education"; Norman, "Crashing VMI's Line," 34, 36.

19. Allison, "VMI Mystique Resists Change," A16; Karen Johnson, "Statement of NOW National Secretary."

20. Mitchell, "Thin Gray Gender Line," 66; Epstein, "Sex Segregation," 12–13.

21. Bunting, "Making Room for Sister Rat," 54; Rosen, "Boys and Girls," 16; McClay, "Of 'Rats' and Women."

22. Joynes, "Message to the Corps," 2; "Cadet's Voice," 2.

23. Chaisson, "Editorial," 2–3.

24. Kelleher, "Point Your Finger at Yourself," 2.

25. Seligman, "Keeping Up," 104; Stephenson, "Future of Single-Sex Education," 80–82; McClay, "Of 'Rats' and Women."

26. Genovese and Podles, "Two Views."

27. *United States v. Virginia et al.*; McClay, "Of 'Rats' and Women."

28. Burdon, "BOV Votes to Admit Women," 1; Bunting, "Making Room for Sister Rat," 54.

29. Duncan, "Here We Go Again," 2; "Letter to the Editor," 3.

30. Rosellini and Marcus, "Leader among Men."

31. Karen Johnson, "Statement of NOW National Secretary."

32. Rosen, "Like Race, Like Gender?"

33. Ibid.

34. Allison, "VMI Mystique Resists Change," A16; Ritchie, "Barracks Living Conditions," *VMI Cadet*, 2; Coupland, "Letter to the Editor," 2–3; Graham, "Letter to the Editor," 3; Prall, "Letter to the Editor," 3; "Top Ten Reasons," 8.

35. Karen Johnson, "Statement of NOW National Secretary"; Burke, *Rhetoric of Motives*, 121.

36. Taylor, "Corps Should Act 'Naturally,'" 3.

37. Margaret Carlson, "Crying Game," 34; Karen Johnson, "Statement of NOW National Secretary"; Gandy, "NOW Leaders"; Hetter, "End of an All-Male Era."

38. Bissell, "Assimilation Report #5," 1, 3.

39. Rosellini and Marcus, "Leader among Men," 46–47; "VMI Sets Rules," 11; Breaux, "Women Appear to be Adjusting Fine."

40. Chittum, "Female 'Rat' Cheerleaders," A1; Means, "Rah-Rah-Rah," B9.

41. Chittum, "VMI Delays Decision," B1; www.vmi.edu/media/registrar/Marriage%20&%20Parenthood%20Policy.pdf (accessed March 24, 2007).

42. Kahn, "Integration Lawsuit Dropped"; "VMI Should Revisit Its Pregnancy Policy," A14; Chittum, "Women's Rights Group Asks VMI to Rescind Family Status Policy," B5.

43. Trice, "VMI Still Working on Pregnancy Policy," B4.

44. Dick, "Sweet Briar Soiree," 7; Chris Wyatt, "Social Forecast," 7; Draper and Jacobs, "Baldwin Daze," 6; Lough and Thoma, "Sweet Briar and Macon Zeros," 6; Case, "Gurls, Gurls, Gurls," 9; Sweetwaters, "From Binky's Desk," 8; "If You Could Marry Anybody," 8; Dave Williams and Schanke, "Nobody Asked the Neanderthals, but . . . ," 7; Golden, "Hey Old Corps," 5; "Institute under 'Gentle' Gerald Baliles"; Felderstein, "Macho Woman," 5.

45. Obenchain and Stump, "Female Cadet," 1; "Brother Rat Speaks Out," 2; "Brother Rat Perspective," 2; Jolin, "Rat Perspective," 2; Jolin, "A Rat's Eye View—Shannon Faulkner," 2; Jolin, "Rat's Eye View: The Corps Speaks," 2.

46. Burke, *Rhetoric of Motives*, 123.

Chapter 2

1. Driggs, Wilson, and Winthrop, *Richmond's Monument Avenue*, 1. This book gives a thorough history of all the monuments and buildings located on Monument Avenue, including details of the selection and construction processes for all six monuments.

2. Burke, *Permanence and Change*, xxi; Burke, *Attitudes toward History*, 171.

3. Burke, *Permanence and Change*, xiii.

4. The bringing together of such previously disparate entities allows each to be seen from a perspective heretofore unknown; it allows these previously alienated entities to be seen in terms of one another. For further explanations of perspective by incongruity, see especially Rosteck and Leff, "Piety, Propriety, and Perspective"; Aune, "Perspective by Incongruity." Burke draws a number of physics analogies to convey his sense of perspective by incongruity. In *Attitudes toward History*, he describes perspective by incongruity as a "method for gauging situations by verbal 'atom cracking.' That is, a word belongs by custom to a certain category—and by rational planning you wrench it loose and metaphorically apply it to a different category" (308). Or, as he portrays the concept in *Permanence and Change*, it is "the methodic merger of particles that had been considered mutually exclusive . . . fusion" (xxi). However, this merging, cracking, and fusing together of particles or atoms is but one way of illustrating the juxtaposition at the core of perspective by incongruity. Burke uses another physics analogy to elaborate how perspective by incongruity can be understood as the synthesis of opposing forces: "A planet does not continually strike some kind of bargain between pulling away and falling back; *it moves in a path*—and this path is conceptualized, made available to astronomical calculations, if we compute it as a synthesis of tangential and centripetal forces. The actual motion is the synthesis, and it is never anything else. . . . [A] man solves a pseudo-problem who takes, not the *motion*, but the two *concepts* of centripetal and centrifugal forces, as the reality, thereupon devoting his energies to a scheme for uniting them into a synthesis." On one level, these forces act in opposite ways on the situation. On another level, however, the simultaneous working of these opposing forces results in the development of the community through the dialogue or juxtaposition of the two views brought together by their opposition to one another. The social forces of tradition-upholding/change-questioning and tradition-questioning/change-promoting indeed move in opposite directions, as do centrifugal and centripetal motion. But at the same time, these forces are juxtaposed or combined within the same community, and they thus work together, perhaps in spite of themselves, to create something greater than either force in itself: the exchange of ideas, which enhances the community through the conflict of its various factions (Burke, *Permanence and Change*, 93).

5. Burke, *Permanence and Change*, 74, 90; Burton, "Forgotten Constraint," A10.

6. Burke, *Permanence and Change*, 87.

7. Borja, "Coalition Ostracizes 2 Council Members," B1; McKelway, "Irreconcilable?" A1; Michael Paul Williams, "Pondering Rebels and Rockfish," B1. Burke, well known for his interest in motives, used medieval gargoyles to illustrate the idea of "planned incongruity": "The maker of gargoyles who put man's-head on bird-body was offering combinations which were completely rational as judged by his logic of essences. In violating one order of classification, he was stressing another." In other words, while most people would see a human head and an avian body as incongruous on a physical level, the artist who creates gargoyles melding these two parts into a whole is doing so because they seem congruous on a symbolic or spiritual level. What may widely be considered as incongruous from one perspective may just as well be considered congruous from another perspective (*Permanence and Change*, 112). Likewise, Burke perceived a "gargoyle element in Marx's formula of class-consciousness. . . . It is a new perspective that realigns something so profoundly ethical as our categories of allegiance. . . . [M]embers of the same race or nation who had formerly thought of themselves as allies become enemies, and members of different races or nations who had formerly thought of themselves as enemies become allies" (*Permanence and Change*, 112–13). In the spirit of understanding and unification through juxtaposition, Burke maintained, the "discordant 'sub-personalities' of the world's conflicting cultures and heterogeneous kinds of effort can be reintegrated only by means of a unifying 'master-purpose.' . . . The segregational, or dissociative state cannot endure—and must make way for an associative, or congregational state" (*Permanence and Change*, 163). One way of integrating formerly segregated terms or entities is to bring them together, no matter how much in conflict with established pieties that juxtaposition may be. When these previously incongruous entities can be seen side by side, in light of one another, the "comic frame . . . might mitigate somewhat the difficulties in engineering a shift to new symbols of authority, as required by the new social relationships that the revolutions of historic empowerment have made necessary" (Burke, *Attitudes toward History*, 173). In sum, Burke advocates that "we deliberately cultivate the use of contradictory concepts. . . . In cases where the synthetic word does not happen to be already given, [Henri Bergson] suggests we should get it by combining the antithetical ones (a proposal which seems to be accepted in such contemporary uses as space-time and mind-body)" (*Permanence and Change*, 94, 119).

8. Dabney, *Richmond*, 336; Pratt, *Color of Their Skin*, 13.
9. Dabney, *Richmond*, 336; Pratt, *Color of Their Skin*, 29.
10. Dabney, *Richmond*, 367, 389; Pratt, *Color of Their Skin*, 108.
11. Edds, "Ashe Is a Gentle Memory," D1. For more details on Ashe's life and views, see Ashe with Deford, *Arthur Ashe*; Ashe and Rampersad, *Days of Grace*.
12. "Timeline for a Monument."
13. Ibid; Edds, "Ashe Is a Gentle Memory," D1.
14. Edds, "Ashe Is a Gentle Memory," D1
15. Ibid.
16. Hickey, "Ashe Contest Proposal Doused," A1.
17. Allen, "Mayor Offers a Compromise," A1; Edds and Little, "Ashe Gets Place on Monument Ave.," A1.
18. King, "Letter from Birmingham City Jail"; Hickey, "Compromise Accommodates All," A1; "Ashe's Widow Objects," C4; Hickey, "Ashe Statue Delayed Again," A1.
19. Edds, "Ashe Site Was a 'Symbolic' Decision," A1; Edds, "Honoring Heroes' Strengths," J5.
20. Edds, "Honoring Heroes' Strengths," J5; Young, "Richmond Can Be Proud," F7; Edds and Little, "Ashe Gets Place on Monument Ave.," A1; Little, "Quiet Crowd," B7.
21. "Monument to Ashe," C1; Allen, "Mayor Offers a Compromise," A1; Edds, "Ashe Site Was a 'Symbolic' Decision," A1; Hickey, "Monumental Change," A1.

22. Edds, "Honoring Heroes' Strengths," J5; "Ashe Monument Unveiled," A1; Michael Paul Williams, "'An Avenue for All,'" A1.

23. Little, "Quiet Crowd," B7; "Monument to Ashe," C1.

24. Allen, "Mayor Offers a Compromise," A1; Little, "Quiet Crowd," B7; Edds and Little, "Ashe Gets Place on Monument Ave.," A1; Holmberg, "Statue Visitors Complain of Size," A8; Moutoussamy-Ashe, "New Year's Wish for Richmond," A7.

25. Edds and Little, "Ashe Gets Place on Monument Ave.," A1; McCallister, "Time to Accept the Statue," B1; "Ashe Monument Unveiled," A1; Michael Paul Williams, "'An Avenue for All,'" A1; O'Dell, "Duke Says Lee Flap Symbolic."

26. Hickey, "Council Again Gives OK," B1; Hickey, "Ashe Statue Fight Moves to Court," B3; Holmberg, "Statue Visitors Complain of Size," A8; Edward Smith, "Richmond Has Erected a Third-Rate Monument," A9.

27. Edds, "Ashe Statue Runs Afoul," C5; McCallister, "Time to Accept the Statue," B1; McCallister, "Point-Counterpoint on Richmond Issues," B1.

28. Giorello, "World-Class Statue Sought," A1; Hickey and Mason, "Ashe Statue a Monument to Controversy," B4; "Monument to Ashe," C1; McCallister, "Point-Counterpoint on Richmond Issues," B1.

29. Reynolds, "Arthur Ashe Deserves Best Available Monument," A11.

30. Hickey and Mason, "Ashe Statue a Monument to Controversy," B4; Edds, "Ashe Statue Again Object of Controversy," A1; Hickey, "Sculptor Makes Changes," A1.

31. Hickey and Mason, "Ashe Statue a Monument to Controversy," B4; Steve Clark, "Good Art or Bad Art?" B1.

32. Woody, "Towering Figure," D4; Edds, "Ashe Statue Again Object of Controversy," A1; Hickey, "Sculptor Makes Changes," A1; Moutoussamy-Ashe, "New Year's Wish for Richmond," A7.

33. Hickey, "Artist's Statue of Ashe Approved," A1; Edds, "Ashe Statue Again Object of Controversy," A1; Hickey and Mason, "Ashe Statue a Monument to Controversy," B4; Holmberg, "Statue Visitors Complain of Size," A8.

34. Hickey, "Lee Absent for Canal Walk's Opening," A1.

35. Ibid.

36. Shaffrey, "Ex-Council Member Had Contentious Career."

37. Applewhite, "Dominion Lands Announces Agreement"; Hinkle, "Long in the Planning," A9; Hickey, "Riverfront Project Director Leaves Post," B5; Hickey, "Plans for Riverfront's Future," B3; Richmond Riverfront Corporation Web site, "Visit the Beautiful and Historic Richmond Riverfront" (2006), available at http://www.venturerichmond.com/index.html (accessed March 22, 2007).

38. Hickey and Johnson, "R. E. Lee Portrait Removed from Wall," A1.

39. Hickey, "Mayor: 'Congratulations to Us,'" A1; Hickey, "Mural Will Be Restored," B1.

40. Hickey and Johnson, "Council Supports Mural of Lee," A1; Hickey, "Coalition's Shunning Is Risky Move," B1; Hickey and Johnson, "David Duke Brings Campaign," B1; Hickey, "Murals to Go Up Monday," B1.

41. Hickey, "Lee Likeness Returns to Wall," B3; Hickey, "Mural Will Be Restored," B1.

42. Fellman, *Making of Robert E. Lee*, 307, 308. For more on Lee's life, see also Thomas, *Robert E. Lee*. Perhaps the best-known account of Lee's life is Freeman, *Robert E. Lee*.

43. "Return Robert E. Lee to His Place in History," A10; McCallister, "Robert E. Lee and Sa'ad El-Amin," B1; Wayne D. Carlson, "White People Have Had Enough," A19.

44. Wayne D. Carlson, "White People Have Had Enough," A19; Hickey and Johnson, "R. E. Lee Portrait Removed from Wall," A1; Will Jones, "About 250 Protest Removal of Lee," B1; "Reaction," A6.

45. McCallister, "Here's What You'd Do on the Canal Walk," B1; Hickey and Johnson,

"R. E. Lee Portrait Removed from Wall," A1; Hickey, "Lee Absent for Canal Walk's Opening," A1; Previs, "Mural Lights Discussion," E5; "Robert E. Lee's Opinion Regarding Slavery," letter dated December 27, 1856, available at http://www.civilwarhome.com/leepierce.com (accessed March 22, 2007).

46. "Return Robert E. Lee to His Place in History," A10; "Protests Prompt Removal of Confederate General's Portrait"; "Reaction," A6; McCallister, "Robert E. Lee and Sa'ad El-Amin," B1.

47. Previs, "Mural Lights Discussion," E5; Hickey and Johnson, "R. E. Lee Portrait Removed from Wall," A1; Michael Paul Williams, "Pondering Rebels and Rockfish," B1.

48. "Protests Prompt Removal of Confederate General's Portrait"; Hickey, "Five Council Members Back Lee," B1; Hickey and Johnson, "Council Supports Mural of Lee," A1; Eric G. Williams, "To the Lion, Hunters Aren't Heroes," A10; Carrie Johnson and Hickey, "Many Say Put the Portrait Back," A1.

49. "Reaction," A6; Farmer, "Heritage, Hatred Still Burning Issues," B1.

50. "NAACP: Leave Lee Mural Down"; Hickey and Johnson, "Council Supports Mural of Lee," A1; Hickey, "Five Council Members Back Lee," B1; "City Council Approves Lee Portrait."

51. "Reaction," A6; Hickey and Johnson, "Council Supports Mural of Lee," A1.

52. Driggs, Wilson, and Winthrop, *Richmond's Monument Avenue*, 1; Burke, *Rhetoric of Motives*, 187–88; "Timocracy," in Morris, *American Heritage Dictionary*, 1271; McCallister, "Here's What You'd Do on the Canal Walk," B1.

53. "Return Robert E. Lee to His Place in History," A10; Hickey, "Mayor: 'Congratulations to Us,'" A1; Eric G. Williams, "To the Lion, Hunters Aren't Heroes," A10; Borja, "Put Mural Debate Behind," B3; Carrie Johnson and Hickey, "Many Say Put the Portrait Back," A1; "Reaction," A6; Hickey and Johnson, "Talking about the Walk," A1.

54. Burke, *Permanence and Change*, xxi; Burke, *Attitudes toward History*, 171; Hickey, "Monumental Change," A1.

55. Another such controversy arose in Richmond in April 2003, when a statue of President Abraham Lincoln was unveiled in the former Confederate capital. The monument depicted Lincoln and his son, Tad, on their visit to Richmond in April 1865, shortly after the close of the Civil War and just ten days before Lincoln's assassination. Richmonders who sympathized with the South in the War between the States found the statue incongruous. For more on this controversy, see Redmon and Kastner, "Lincoln Statue Unveiled," B1.

Chapter 3

1. James Forman Jr., "Driving Dixie Down: Removing the Confederate Flag from Southern State Capitols," in *Confederate Symbols in the Contemporary South*, ed. Martinez, Richardson, and McNinch-Su, 206.

2. Stephen A. Smith, *Myth, Media, and the Southern Mind*, 41; Wilhoit, *Politics of Massive Resistance*, 123–24, cited in Stephen A. Smith, *Myth, Media, and the Southern Mind*, 41; Weaver, *Southern Tradition*, 379; Killian, *White Southerners*, 38.

3. Prince, *Rally 'Round the Flag, Boys!* 29–30, 47; McDowell, "35 Years Ago," B1. Prince offers an in-depth consideration of the history of the Confederate flag in South Carolina, with the later chapters devoted to recounting the same recent debates analyzed here.

4. Levinson, *Written in Stone*, 24, 55, 103.

5. Pettys, "State Flag Fight Flies Again"; Galloway, "Perdue Pushes a Vote on Flag"; Kristen Wyatt, "Flag Deal Struck." For more detailed considerations of the Georgia flag debate, see two excellent chapters, "Traditionalists versus Reconstructionists: The Case of the Georgia State Flag, Part One" and "Confederate Symbols, Southern Identity, and Racial

Attitudes: The Case of the Georgia State Flag, Part Two," in *Confederate Symbols in the Contemporary South*, ed. Martinez, Richardson, and McNinch-Su.

6. Eisner, "Mississippi Vote Shows Power"; Branson, "Mississippi Rallies"; Manuel, "Mississippians Sticking with Flag." For an insightful scholarly analysis of the Mississippi flag debate as well as similar debates in Alabama, Georgia, and South Carolina, see Coski, *Confederate Battle Flag*.

7. "Key Dates"; "Lawsuit Seeks Removal."

8. Heilprin, "Race Relations Meeting Thursday," B1; Beasley, "Remarks."

9. National Association for the Advancement of Colored People, "Emergency Sanctions."

10. Bruce Smith, "Bush Avoids Confederate Flag Flap"; Strope, "Bush Says"; "Williams Booed"; Glen Johnson, "Bush, McCain Struggle to Avoid Problems over Confederate Flag"; "Laura Bush Says Confederate Flag Not Racist Symbol"; Strope, "GOP Candidates Try to Avoid Confederate Flag Issue"; "Bush Playing to 'Hateful' Attitude," A5; Davenport, "McCain Says Flag Should Come Down"; Swindell, "GOP Candidate Keyes Campaigns," B3; "Keyes Says Confederate Flag Is South Carolina Issue"; Bruce Smith, "Forbes Also Distances Himself from Flag Issue"; Kropf, "Forbes Warns," B3; Bruce Smith, "Dole Encourages Workers"; Swindell, "Buchanan Speaks," B3; Stensland, "Democratic Presidential Candidate."

11. Iacobelli, "Coaches March."

12. Haffner and Kirschbaum, *Unfinished Civil War*.

13. J. Michael Martinez and William D. Richardson, "Introduction: Understanding the Debate over Confederate Symbols," in *Confederate Symbols in the Contemporary South*, ed. Martinez, Richardson, and McNinch-Su, 6–7.

14. Ibid., 7.

15. Coski, *Confederate Battle Flag*, 302.

16. Bormann, "Fantasy and Rhetorical Vision"; Fisher, "Narration as a Human Communication Paradigm," 271.

17. Fisher, "Narration as a Human Communication Paradigm," 276–77, 270, 273.

18. Ibid., 279.

19. Burke, *Rhetoric of Motives*, 52–53.

20. Wells, "Talk at South Carolina State House." For further insight into the mind-set of Confederate enthusiasts, including members of the UDC and the SCV and especially reenactors, see Horwitz, *Confederates in the Attic*.

21. Wells, "Talk at South Carolina State House."

22. Ibid.

23. Chase, "Former NAACP Official."

24. National Association for the Advancement of Colored People, "Emergency Sanctions."

25. Jesse L. Jackson Sr., "Pandering to Racism."

26. Bryant, "Those with Close Ties to Confederacy"; Munday, "Churches Cancel S.C. Meeting," B8.

27. Heritage Roundtable, "Senators Unite."

28. Barker, "Clemson History," 2.

29. Beasley, "Remarks."

30. Hodges, "Full Text."

31. Bryant, "Those with Close Ties to Confederacy"; "More than 1,000 Honor Confederate Ancestors."

32. Wells, "Talk at South Carolina State House"; Chase, "Former NAACP Official."

33. National Association for the Advancement of Colored People, "Emergency Sanctions"; Mfume, "Speech"; Bryant, "Those with Close Ties to Confederacy."

34. Jesse L. Jackson Sr., "Pandering to Racism"; Filler, "S.C. NAACP Leader."
35. Heritage Roundtable, "Senators Unite."
36. Wells, "Talk at South Carolina State House."
37. Jesse L. Jackson Sr., "Pandering to Racism"; National Association for the Advancement of Colored People, "Emergency Sanctions."
38. Filler, "S.C. NAACP Leader"; Wilson, "South Carolina Senate."
39. Beasley, "Remarks."
40. Barker, "Clemson History," 2.
41. Wells, "Talk at South Carolina State House."
42. Verdin, "To: All Compatriots and Supporters of Southern Heritage"; Chase, "Former NAACP Official."
43. Sons of Confederate Veterans, "How to Handle a Heritage Violation"; Sons of Confederate Veterans, "Sons of Confederate Veterans: Heritage Issues."
44. Mfume, "Speech."
45. Jesse L. Jackson Sr., "On Super Sunday."
46. Filler, "S.C. NAACP Leader"; Moreton, "Granddaughter Revives Legacy"; Bryant, "Those with Close Ties to Confederacy."
47. Beasley, "Remarks."
48. Heritage Roundtable, "Senators Unite"; Strope, "Hodges in State of State Speech."
49. Barker, "Clemson History," 2.
50. Hodges, "Full Text."
51. Fisher, "Narration as a Human Communication Paradigm," 280.
52. Coski, *Confederate Battle Flag*, x, 306-7.

Chapter 4

1. Lott, *Herding Cats*, 245.
2. Ibid., 244-47; Lott, "U.S. Senator Trent Lott (R-MS) Delivers Remarks."
3. Edsall, "Lott Decried." Edsall, though the first print journalist to cover the story, was not the first in the media to cover it. Gwen Ifill of PBS's *Washington Week* had briefly asked viewers for their interpretation of Lott's remarks at the close her broadcast on December 6, 2002, the day after Lott's remarks. Timothy Noah, a writer for slate.com, had posted a column about Lott's comments in the wee hours of December 6, linking readers to C-SPAN video of Lott's remarks as well as audio of Thurmond's 1948 Dixiecrat nomination acceptance speech. Lott's account of the controversy recalls this "small fire" set "in the lower reaches of journalism" (Lott, *Herding Cats*, 247-49).
4. Edsall, "Lott Decried," A06; Jesse L. Jackson Sr., "Rev. Jackson Calls"; Gore, interview by Judy Woodruff; Edsall, "'Poor Choice of Words,'" A13; National Association for the Advancement of Colored People, "NAACP Calls for Senator Lott to Resign"; Family Research Council, "FRC Says Sen. Lott's Remarks Have Caused Considerable Damage."
5. Hulse, "Lott's Praise," A24; Lott, interview by Sean Hannity; Lott, interview by Larry King; Anti-Defamation League, "Deplores Comments."
6. Bush, "President Bush Implements Key Elements"; Congressional Black Caucus, "Congressman Elijah E. Cummings Supports Call"; Tumulty, "Trent Lott's Segregationist College Days"; Solomon, "Over 30 Years"; Frist, "Frist's Comments on Lott Statement."
7. Lott, "Remarks."
8. Nickles, "Statement."
9. Lott, interview by Ed Gordon.
10. Frist, "Frist Comments on Discussion"; Chafee, "Transcript"; Colin Powell et al., "Joint News Conference." The term *Dixiecrat* is often used interchangeably with the term

States' Rights Democrat by those critical of that party and its members. The term *Dixiecrat* was not created or embraced by the members of the States' Rights Democratic Party but was said to have been created by "William Weismer, telegraph editor of *The Charlotte* (N.C.) *News*, who couldn't squeeze 'States' Rights Democrats' into a headline" (Cohodas, *Strom Thurmond*, 142, 191). In 1948, *Atlanta Constitution* editor Ralph McGill argued that "the Dixiecrat type of mind, and the Dixiecrat type of politics . . . will set the South back thirty years or more" (8).

11. Frist, "Statement"; Lott, "Raw Data"; Byrd, "Lott Says He Fell into a 'Trap.'"

12. Riley, *Presidency and the Politics*, 159–60.

13. Thurmond, "Motion."

14. Riley, *Presidency and the Politics*, 163; Cooper and Terrill, *American South*, 680; Cohodas, *Strom Thurmond*, 185.

15. Thurmond, "Address"; Cohodas, *Strom Thurmond*, 189; Cooper and Terrill, *American South*, 681.

16. Cohodas, *Strom Thurmond*, 497–98; Lott, "U.S. Senator Trent Lott (R-MS) Delivers Remarks."

17. "Biography of U.S. Senator Trent Lott."

18. Tumulty, "Trent Lott's Segregationist College Days." The Confederate flag and singing of "Dixie" have since been banned at Ole Miss, though the school's teams continue to be known as the Rebels. Founded in 1868 at Virginia Military Institute, many of Sigma Nu's first chapters were located in the South, though Ole Miss's chapter was not established until 1927. The fraternity's official history describes the brotherhood as founded "in a period of civil strife known as the Reconstruction . . . when a Confederate veteran from Arkansas enrolled at the Virginia Military Institute in Lexington Virginia." At the time, the South "was in a state of turmoil and just beginning to recover from the devastating military defeat it had suffered" (Sigma Nu Fraternity, "Chapter Listing"; Sigma Nu Fraternity, "Our History").

19. "Biography of Senator Trent Lott."

20. Solomon, "Over 30 Years"; Fairness and Accuracy in Reporting, "Media Play Catch-Up"; Council of Conservative Citizens, "Frequently Asked Questions." In March 1999, prior to this controversy, FAIR issued a report on Lott's racist associations. See Rendall, "Sex-Free Scandal."

21. Ryan argues that "by identifying and assessing the issues in the accusation, the critic will gain insights into the accuser's motivation to accuse, his selection of the issues, and the nature of the supporting materials for his accusation. As a response to the accusation, the apology should be discussed in terms of the apologist's motivation to respond to the accusation, his selection of the issues—for they might differ from the accuser's issues—and the nature of the supporting materials for the apology." Further, he argues that accusations and defenses involve either character or policy, a shift from the traditional view that they concern only questions of character; he does, however, leave open the possibility that an accusation against policy could be answered with an apology for character, and vice versa. In addition, he does not "exclude the possibility that the critic may find in accusations and apologies elements of both policy and character in a speech. [He] merely contend[s] . . . that one motive/response will tend to dominate. . . . Moreover, a comparison of the accusation/apology speeches as analog will help the critic decide whether policy or character dominates the given instance of discourse." Further, Ryan espouses a broad concept of policy that includes "a wide range of actions or practices: vice, theft, sexual misconduct, libel, treason, illegal activities, etc." (Ryan, "*Kategoria* and *Apologia*," 254, 255, 257, 256).

Ryan advocates a three-pronged approach to analyzing accusation-defense speech sets: "(1) the accuser's and apologist's respective motives must be explicated; (2) what classical stases [fact, definition, quality, and, for apologia only, jurisdiction] the accuser and apologist argued in their speeches must be demonstrated; and (3) the rhetorical situations must be analyzed in terms of their exigencies and mediating audiences." Overall, Ryan's main contributions are his expansion of the concepts of *kategoria* and apologia to include more than just questions of character and his advice that critics enrich their analyses of rhetorical conflict by considering accusations and defenses together (Ryan, "Baldwin vs. Edward VIII," 126).

Ware and Linkugel draw on the "the theory developed by Robert P. Abelson pertaining to the resolution of belief dilemmas." They designate Abelson's "four 'modes of resolution': (1) denial, (2) bolstering, (3) differentiation, and (4) transcendence" as "factors" or choices available to someone engaging in self-defense ("They Spoke in Defense of Themselves," 275). These four "factors of verbal self-defense" have become commonplaces in the study of apologia, as the work of William Benoit and other contemporary scholars analyzing defensive communication attests. See, for example, Benoit, *Accounts, Excuses, and Apologies.*

Kruse came up with three categories of apologia: "(1) Replies demonstrating that the speaker feels some aspects of his security or safety ha[ve] been threatened, or *Survival Responses*; (2) Replies in which the primary need is to restore or regain affection, status, mastery, prestige, or esteem, or *Social Responses*; and (3) Replies produced when the speaker attempts to maintain, primarily for himself, an image consistent only with his idiosyncratic values and his personal sense of right and wrong, or *Self-Actualized Responses*" ("Motivational Factors," 14).

Burke's rhetorical theory centered on considering "the basic forms of thought which, in accordance with the nature of this world as all men necessarily experience it, are exemplified in the attributing of motives. These forms of thought can be embodied profoundly or trivially, truthfully or falsely. They are equally present in systematically elaborated metaphysical structures, in legal judgments, in poetry and fiction, in political and scientific works, in news and in bits of gossip offered at random" (*Grammar of Motives*, xv).

22. The first two ways in which a scapegoat is made apply to Lott: "(1) He may be made worthy legalistically (i.e., by making him an offender against legal or moral justice, so that he 'deserves' what he gets). (2) We may make him worthy by leading toward sacrifice fatalistically (as when we so point the arrows of the plot that the audience comes to think of him as a marked man, and so prepares itself to relinquish him) . . . while the transition into the sacrifice may often employ an intermingling of this second kind of worthiness with the first, as when the Greek dramatists reinforced the fatalistic operations with a personal flaw, hubris, punishable pride, the pride that goes before a fall" (Burke, *On Symbols and Society*, 294–95).

23. Burke, *Grammar of Motives*, 408.

24. Jesse L. Jackson Sr., "Rev. Jackson Calls"; Colin Powell et al., "Joint News Conference."

25. Jesse L. Jackson Jr., "Trent Lott."

26. Noonan, "Counsel for Trent"; Lott, *Herding Cats*, 249. The latter interpretations may have been true in light of Lott's statement in the epilogue of his autobiography, "The best government is the government closest to the people. Individual responsibility. Fiscal discipline. A strong national defense" (*Herding Cats*, 297).

27. "Lott's Disgrace"; "Lott Should Resign."

28. Daschle, "Statement"; Frum, "Moments of Truth."

29. Jesse L. Jackson Sr., "Casting the Lott's"; Fairness and Accuracy in Reporting, "Media Play Catch-Up."

30. National Association for the Advancement of Colored People, "NAACP Stands by Call"; Cottle, "Separate Ways," 14–15; National Association for the Advancement of Colored People, "NAACP Chairman Calls."

31. "Lott Should Resign."

32. Edsall, "Lott Decried," A06; Edsall, "'Poor Choice of Words,'" A13; National Association for the Advancement of Colored People, "NAACP Stands by Call"; "Lott's Disgrace";

Krauthammer, "Clear Choice"; Francis, "Lott May Have Unintentionally Said Something True"; Cottle, "Separate Ways," 14; NBC News, *Meet the Press*, December 8, 2002; Fairness and Accuracy in Reporting, "Media Play Catch-Up."

33. NAACP, "NAACP Calls"; Anti-Defamation League, "Deplores Comments"; "Lott's Disgrace"; Krauthammer, "Clear Choice," A45.

34. Jesse L. Jackson Sr., "Changing the Cover"; "Sorry Lott."

35. Noonan, "Counsel for Trent"; Noonan, "Rent by Trent."

36. Fairness and Accuracy in Reporting, "Media Play Catch-Up"; Edsall and Balz, "Lott Apologizes Anew," A01.

37. Bush, "President Bush Implements Key Elements"; Frum, "Whose Party?"; Noonan, "Counsel for Trent"; Frum, "Moments of Truth."

38. Edsall and Balz, "Lott Apologizes Anew," A01; Frum, "Diplomatic Approaches"; Frum, "Happy Birthday."

39. Nickles, "Statement."

40. Noonan, "Counsel for Trent"; Lott, *Herding Cats*, 257–59, 261, 271, 275; Hutcheson, "Bush Quietly Sealed Lott's Fate," A1, A10; "Frist Emerges as Lott's Leading Challenger," A1, A2.

41. Francis, "Lott May Have Unintentionally Said Something True"; Edsall, "Lott Decried"; Grissom, "What We Have Learned"; Kennedy, "Lotts to Consider."

42. Kay, "Lott's Lott"; Council of Conservative Citizens, "What Should Trent Do?"; Rockwell, "Trial of Lott"; Hill, "What's New on DixieNet."

43. Frum, "Whose Party?"; Grissom, "What We Have Learned"; Kay, "Lott's Lott."

44. Rockwell, "Trial of Lott"; Kay, "Lott's Lott"; Council of Conservative Citizens, "What Should Trent Do?"

45. Ware and Linkugel, "They Spoke in Defense of Themselves," 275. A more traditional example of the single accusation and defense speech set is Justice Hugo Black's 1937 radio address answering charges that he had been a member of the Ku Klux Klan (Carcasson and Aune, "Klansman on the Court"). While Black made but one apology, he did, however, address it to multiple audiences simultaneously.

46. Edsall, "Lott Decried," A06.

47. Edsall, "'Poor Choice of Words,'" A13;. Lott, interview by Sean Hannity.

48. Lott, interview by Sean Hannity; Lott, "Remarks of Senate Republican Leader Trent Lott." Lott's statement that he had made "a mistake of the head, not of the heart," echoed, to Jesse Jackson Jr.'s great dismay, the words of Jesse Jackson Sr. after he made controversial 1984 remarks about New York Jews. As Jesse Jackson Jr., complained in his December 14 PUSH Forum speech, "What has been Senator Lott's and the Republican Party's response? To attack my father and use my father's words at the 1984 Democratic Convention in San Francisco . . . as though there's some kind of 'moral equivalency' between my father's one-time New York 'mistake' (never to be repeated), and a 25-year pattern of racially insensitive statements and actions. No, Senator Lott and Republicans, it won't fly. There's no 'moral equivalency' between my father's personal mistake and your long- standing public record" (Jesse L. Jackson Jr., "Trent Lott is the Republican Party's Monica Lewinsky"). Jesse Jackson Sr.'s exact words of apology were, in part, "Charge it to my head and not to my heart. My head is so limited in its finitude; my heart is boundless in its love for the human family" ("The Rainbow Coalition").

49. Lott, interview by Sean Hannity; Lott, interview by Ed Gordon.

50. Ware and Linkugel, "They Spoke in Defense of Themselves," 277.

51. Lott, interview by Sean Hannity; Lott, "Remarks of Senate Republican Leader Trent Lott." According to the 2000 U.S. Census, 36.3 percent of Mississippi's population is African

American, compared to 12.3 percent for the United States overall (U.S. Census Bureau, "State and County Quick Facts).

52. Lott, "Remarks of Senate Republican Leader Trent Lott."
53. Lott, interview by Ed Gordon.
54. Lott, interview by Sean Hannity; Lott, interview by Larry King; Lott, interview by Ed Gordon.
55. Lott, interview by Sean Hannity; Lott, interview by Larry King.
56. Lott, interview by Ed Gordon. Among the others offering tributes to Thurmond were Senators Daschle and Byrd. Lott's exact words were, "Senator Thurmond is a different case in many ways. He is, of course, of a different generation and he exemplifies its strengths just as he has worked to leave behind its shortcomings." See *Congressional Record*, November 20, 2002, for the full text of the various senators' tributes to Thurmond.
57. Lott, interview by Sean Hannity.
58. Ware and Linkugel, "They Spoke in Defense of Themselves," 278.
59. Edsall, "Lott Decried," A06; Lott, interview by Sean Hannity; Lott, "Remarks of Senate Republican Leader Trent Lott"; Lott, interview by Larry King."
60. Lott, interview by Larry King; Lott, interview by Ed Gordon.
61. Lott, interview by Larry King; Lott, "Remarks of Senate Republican Leader Trent Lott"; Lott, interview by Ed Gordon.
62. Ware and Linkugel, "They Spoke in Defense of Themselves," 280; Bormann, *Force of Fantasy*, 228; Hofstadter, *Paranoid Style*.
63. Bormann, *Force of Fantasy*, 228; Lott, interview by Sean Hannity; Lott, "Remarks of Senate Republican Leader Trent Lott"; Lott, interview by Ed Gordon; Byrd, "Lott Says He Fell into a 'Trap.'"
64. Byrd, "Lott Says He Fell into a 'Trap.'"
65. Buchanan, "What Stinks about Washington"; Buchanan, "Trent Lott"; Buchanan, "Neocons and Nixon's Southern Strategy."
66. Council of Conservative Citizens, "Sucker Punched"; Kennedy, "Lotts to Consider"; Kay, "Lott's Lot."
67. "Who Decides?"; Frum, "Enter Bush"; "Sorry Lott"; Jesse L. Jackson Sr., "Changing the Cover."
68. Hofstadter, *Paranoid Style*, 4, 39, 23–28.
69. Burke, *On Symbols and Society*, 289.
70. Cited in Fairness and Accuracy in Reporting, "Media Play Catch-Up."
71. Milbank, "'Redemption,'" A02.

Conclusion

1. Biden, "U.S. Senator Joseph Biden (D-DE) Delivers Remarks"; McWhorter, "Strom's Skeleton." See also Bass and Thompson, *Ol' Strom*. The most comprehensive and direct source on Thurmond's out-of-wedlock daughter is her book, Washington-Williams and Stadiem, *Dear Senator*.
2. McWhorter, "Strom's Skeleton."
3. Biden, ""U.S. Senator Joseph Biden (D-DE) Delivers Remarks"; McWhorter, "Strom's Skeleton."
4. Biden, ""U.S. Senator Joseph Biden (D-DE) Delivers Remarks"; McWhorter, "Strom's Skeleton." For an interesting discussion of porches as a site for building Southern community and identity, especially across racial lines, see Donlon, "Porches."
5. Prince, *Rally 'Round the Flag, Boys!* 251.

6. Woodward, "Search for Southern Identity," 17–25; Weaver, *Southern Essays*, 229.

7. Burke, *On Symbols and Society*, 180; Weaver, *Southern Tradition*, 396.

8. Braden, *Oral Tradition*, 26–38, ix, 43. See also Logue, "Oratory," 782; Owsley, *Plain Folk*.

9. Tate, "Southern Mode," 100–101 (emphasis added); Cash, *Mind of the South*, 52; Braden, *Oral Tradition*, 22.

10. Booth, *Rhetoric of Rhetoric*, 10; Logue, "Oratory," 782; Braden, *Oral Tradition*, 124.

References

Allen, Mike. "Mayor Offers a Compromise; Ashe at Byrd Park, Monument Memorial." *Richmond Times-Dispatch*, July 17, 1995, A1.

Allison, Wes. "VMI Mystique Resists Change." *Richmond Times-Dispatch*, January 14, 1996, A16.

Alvarez, Pedro. "Letter to the Editor." *VMI Cadet*, February 23, 1990, 2–3.

American Civil Liberties Union. "VMI Balks at Supreme Court Ruling," July 11, 1996. Available online at http://www.aclu.org/news/w071196c.html. Accessed April 15, 2000.

Andrew, Rod, Jr. *Long Gray Lines: The Southern Military School Tradition, 1839–1915.* Chapel Hill: University of North Carolina Press, 2001.

———. "Soldiers, Christians, and Patriots: The Lost Cause and Southern Military Schools, 1865–1915." *Journal of Southern History* 64 (November 1998): 677–710.

Anti-Defamation League. "Deplores Comments by Sen. Trent Lott." December 11, 2002. Available online at http://www.adl.org/PresRele/DiRaB_41/4208_41.asp. Accessed January 29, 2003.

Applewhite, Hunter. "Dominion Lands Announces Agreement to Sell Historic Riverfront Property," January 25, 1999. Available online at http://www.dominionresources.com/news/dom1999/pro12599.jsp. Accessed February 22, 2007.

Ashe, Arthur, and Arnold Rampersad. *Days of Grace: A Memoir*. New York: Knopf, 1993.

Ashe, Arthur, with Frank Deford. *Arthur Ashe: Portrait in Motion*. Boston: Houghton Mifflin, 1975.

"Ashe Monument Unveiled Despite Protests." *Roanoke Times and World News*, July 11, 1996, A1.

"Ashe's Widow Objects to Site Planned for Husband's Statue." *Roanoke Times and World News*, January 2, 1996, C4.

Aune, James Arnt. "Perspective by Incongruity." In *Encyclopedia of Rhetoric*, ed. Thomas O. Sloane, 572–75. Oxford: Oxford University Press, 2001.

Barker, James. "Clemson History Offers Perspective for Flag Debate." *Clemson World Magazine*, Winter 2000, 2. Reprint of letter to the editor, *Columbia State*, December 3, 1999.

Bass, Jack, and Marilyn W. Thompson. *Ol' Strom: An Unauthorized Biography of Strom Thurmond*. Atlanta: Longstreet, 1998.

Beasley, David M. "Remarks of Governor David M. Beasley: The Flag Controversy, Nov. 26, 1996." South Carolina Archives, Papers of Governor David M. Beasley (1995–1999) (RG 556000).

Benoit, William L. *Accounts, Excuses, and Apologies: A Theory of Image Restoration Strategies*. Albany: State University of New York Press, 1995.

Biden, Joseph. "U.S. Senator Joseph Biden (D-DE) Delivers Remarks at Memorial Service for Senator Strom Thurmond," July 1, 2003. Available online at eMediaMillWorks/FederalDocumentClearingHouse. Accessed July 5, 2003.

"Biography of U.S. Senator Trent Lott of Mississippi." N.d. Available online at http://lott.senate.gov/leader/bio.html. Accessed March 4, 2003.

Bissell, Mike. "Assimilation Report #5." *VMI Cadet*, April 4, 1997, 1, 3.

Booth, Wayne C. *The Rhetoric of Rhetoric: The Quest for Effective Communication.* Malden, Mass.: Blackwell, 2004.

Borja, Rhea R. "Coalition Ostracizes 2 Council Members; Hedgepeth, Johnson Shunned for Mural Vote." *Richmond Times-Dispatch*, August 3, 1999, B1.

———. "Put Mural Debate behind, Hedgepeth Tells Her Critics." *Richmond Times-Dispatch*, August 5, 1999, B3.

Bormann, Ernest G. "Fantasy and Rhetorical Vision: The Rhetorical Criticism of Social Reality." *Quarterly Journal of Speech* 58 (December 1972): 396–407.

———. *The Force of Fantasy: Restoring the American Dream.* Carbondale: Southern Illinois University Press, 2001.

Braden, Waldo W. *The Oral Tradition in the South.* Baton Rouge: Louisiana State University Press, 1983.

Branson, Reed. "Mississippi Rallies 'Round Old Flag; Votes 2-1 to Keep Rebel Emblem in State Banner." *Memphis Commercial Appeal*, April 18, 2001, A1.

"Brave New World or Conquered Civilization? A Roundtable on the Future of Southern Rhetoric." Rhetoric and Public Address Division Panel, Southern States Communication Association, April 3, 2003, Birmingham, Ala.

Breaux, Kia Shante. "Women Appear to Be Adjusting Fine at Virginia Military Institute." Associated Press State and Local Wire, April 17, 2000.

Brodie, Laura Fairchild. *Breaking Out: VMI and the Coming of Women.* New York: Pantheon, 2000.

"Brother Rat Perspective: 'Sir' Is Not a Universal Term." *VMI Cadet*, October 17, 1997, 2.

"Brother Rat Speaks Out." *VMI Cadet*, October 10, 1997, 2.

Bryant, Joseph. "Those with Close Ties to Confederacy Have Differing View on Flag." Associated Press State and Local Wire, January 16, 2000.

Buchanan, Patrick J. "The Neocons and Nixon's Southern Strategy." *WorldNet Daily*, December 30, 2002. Available online at http://www.wnd.com/news/article.asp?ARTICLE_ID=30233. Accessed March 6, 2003.

———. "Trent Lott: Victim of a Hate Crime." *WorldNet Daily*, December 18, 2002. Available online at http://www.wnd.com/news/article.asp?ARTICLE_ID=30051. Accessed March 6, 2003.

———. "What Stinks about Washington." *WorldNet Daily*, December 13, 2002. Available online at http://www.wnd.com/news/article.asp?ARTICLE_ID=29975. Accessed March 6, 2003.

Bunting, Josiah, III. "Making Room for Sister Rat." *Newsweek*, December 23, 1996, 54.

Burdon, Aaron. "BOV Votes to Admit Women." *VMI Cadet*, October 11, 1996: 1.

Burke, Kenneth. *Attitudes toward History.* 3rd ed. Berkeley: University of California Press, 1984.

———. *A Grammar of Motives.* Berkeley: University of California Press, 1969.

———. *Language as Symbolic Action: Essays on Life, Literature, and Method.* Berkeley: University of California Press, 1966.

———. *On Symbols and Society.* Ed. Joseph R. Gusfield. Chicago: University of Chicago Press, 1989.
———. *Permanence and Change: An Anatomy of Purpose.* Los Altos, Calif.: Hermes, 1954.
———. *A Rhetoric of Motives.* Berkeley: University of California Press, 1969.
Burton, Mary B. "The Forgotten Constraint." *Roanoke Times and World News,* July 28, 1995, A10.
Bush, George W. "President Bush Implements Key Elements of His Faith-Based Initiative." December 12, 2002. Available online at http://www.whitehouse.gov/news/releases/2002/12/20021212-3.html. Accessed February 13, 2003.
"Bush Playing to 'Hateful' Attitude over Flag, Says Gore." *Charleston Post and Courier,* January 16, 2000, A5.
Byrd, Sheila Hardwell. "Lott Says He Fell into a 'Trap' Set by His Political Enemies." Associated Press State and Local Wire, December 22, 2002.
"The Cadet's Voice." *VMI Cadet,* May 2, 1997, 2.
Carcasson, Martín, and James Arnt Aune. "Klansman on the Court: Justice Hugo Black's Radio Address to the Nation." *Quarterly Journal of Speech* 89 (May 2003): 154–70.
Carlson, Margaret. "The Crying Game." *Time,* January 29, 1996, 34.
Carlson, Wayne D. "White People Have Had Enough of Oversensitivity: Calling Someone 'Racist' Doesn't Make It So." *Roanoke Times and World News,* June 17, 1999, A19.
Case, Dean. "Gurls, Gurls, Gurls." *VMI Cadet,* October 20, 1989, 9.
Cash, W. J. *The Mind of the South.* 1941. New York: Vintage, 1991.
Chafee, Lincoln. "Transcript of Chafee's Interview with WPRO's Steve Kass." Associated Press State and Local Wire, December 18, 2002.
Chaisson, Gregory. "Editorial: A Few Thoguths [*sic*] on Cadets at VMI at a Time of Decision Making for You." *VMI Cadet,* February 16, 1990, 2–3.
Chase, Randall. "Former NAACP Official an Unlikely Defender of Confederate Flag." Associated Press State and Local Wire, February 12, 2000.
Chittum, Matt. "Female 'Rat' Cheerleaders Treated Like Vermin: 'They Look Like Men in Skirts,' Says One Cadet." *Roanoke Times,* November 20, 1998, A1.
———. "VMI Delays Decision on Policy That Would Expel Parents-to-Be: 'We Want to Do It Right,'" *Roanoke Times,* August 29, 2001, B1.
———. "Women's Rights Group Asks VMI to Rescind Family Status Policy; Cadets Who Leave Can Apply for Readmission Later." *Roanoke Times,* January 15, 2002, B5.
"City Council Approves Lee Portrait for Public Mural." Associated Press State and Local Wire, July 27, 1999.
Clark, Gregory. *Dialogue, Dialectic, and Conversation: A Social Perspective on the Function of Writing.* Carbondale: Southern Illinois University Press, 1990.
Clark, Steve. "Good Art or Bad Art? Don't Ask This Oaf." *Richmond Times-Dispatch,* December 21, 1995, B1.
———. "Lincoln Statue Here Backed; 'The War Would Finally Be Over.'" *Richmond Times-Dispatch,* April 29, 2001, B1.
Cobb, James C. *Away Down South: A History of Southern Identity.* London: Oxford University Press, 2005.
Cocke, John D., IV. "Tell All the Truth, but Tell It Slant." *VMI Cadet,* February 28, 1997, 2.
Cohodas, Nadine. *Strom Thurmond and the Politics of Southern Change.* New York: Simon and Schuster, 1993.

Congressional Black Caucus. "Congressman Elijah E. Cummings Supports Call for Censure of Senator Trent Lott." December 12, 2002. Available online at http://www.house.gov/cummings/press/02dec12a.htm. Accessed March 12, 2003.

Cooper, William J., and Thomas E. Terrill. *The American South: A History*. 2nd ed. New York: McGraw-Hill, 1996.

Coski, John M. *The Confederate Battle Flag: America's Most Embattled Emblem*. Cambridge: Harvard University Press, 2005.

Cottle, Michelle. "Separate Ways: There Trent Lott Goes Again." *New Republic*, December 23, 2002, 14–15.

Council of Conservative Citizens. "Frequently Asked Questions about the Council of Conservative Citizens." Available online at http://cofcc.org/page12.htm. Accessed January 27, 2003.

———. "Sucker Punched." Available online at http://www.cofcc.org. Accessed January 27, 2003.

———. "What Should Trent Do?" Available online at http://www.cofcc.org/news.htm. Accessed January 27, 2003.

Coupland, R. C., Jr. "Letter to the Editor." *VMI Cadet*, February 9, 1990. 2–3.

Dabney, Virginius. *Richmond: The Story of a City*. Rev. and exp. ed. Charlottesville: University Press of Virginia, 1990.

Daschle, Tom. "Statement of Senate Democratic Leader Tom Daschle." December 10, 2002. Available online at http://daschle.senate.gov/~daschle/pressroom/releases/02/12/2002C13903.html. Accessed March 12, 2003.

Davenport, Jim. "McCain Says Flag Should Come Down, Acknowledges Compromising Principles." Associated Press State and Local Wire, April 19, 2000.

Degler, Carl N. *Place over Time: The Continuity of Southern Distinctiveness*. Athens: University of Georgia Press, 1997.

Demo, Anne Teresa. "The Guerrilla Girls' Comic Politics of Subversion." *Women's Studies in Communication* 23 (Spring 2000): 133–56.

Dick, Mark. "Sweet Briar Soiree." *VMI Cadet*, September 15, 1989: 7.

Donlon, Jocelyn Hazelwood. "Porches: Stories: Power: Spatial and Racial Intersections in Faulkner and Hurston." *Journal of American Culture* 19 (Winter 1996): 95–110.

Dow, Bonnie J. "AIDS, Perspective by Incongruity, and Gay Identity in Larry Kramer's '1,112 and Counting.'" *Communication Studies* 45 (Fall 1994/Winter 1995): 225–40.

Draper, Ken, and Todd Jacobs. "Baldwin Daze." *VMI Cadet*, October 6, 1989, 6.

Driggs, Sarah Shields, Richard Guy Wilson, and Robert P. Winthrop for the Historic Monument Avenue and Fan District Foundation. *Richmond's Monument Avenue*. Chapel Hill: University of North Carolina Press, 2001.

Duncan, James E. "Here We Go Again." *VMI Cadet*, September 12, 1997, 2.

Edds, Margaret. "Ashe Is a Gentle Memory; Racial Stress Still Fully Present." *Roanoke Times and World News*, July 16, 1995, D1.

———. "Ashe Site Was a 'Symbolic' Decision." *Roanoke Times and World News*, July 19, 1995, A1.

———. "Ashe Statue Again Object of Controversy; Art Critics Say It Lacks Sufficient Grandeur." *Norfolk Virginian-Pilot*, December 21, 1995, A1.

———. "Ashe Statue Runs Afoul of Art Critics." *Roanoke Times and World News*, December 21, 1995, C5.

———. "Honoring Heroes' Strengths, Not Their Times." *Norfolk Virginian-Pilot*, July 7, 1996, J5.

Edds, Margaret, and Robert Little. "Ashe Gets Place on Monument Ave.; Richmond Council OKs Statue Site in 7–0 Vote; Compromise Denied." Norfolk *Virginian-Pilot*, July 18, 1995, A1.

Edmonds, Brad. "How to Be a Southern Gentleman in 10 Easy Steps." June 2, 2005. Available online at http://www.lewrockwell.com/edmonds/edmonds249.html. Accessed September 15, 2006.

Edsall, Thomas B. "Lott Decried for Part of Salute to Thurmond: GOP Senate Leader Hails Colleague's Run as Segregationist." *Washington Post*, December 7, 2002, A06.

———. "'Poor Choice of Words,' Lott Says; Senator Apologizes for Recent Remarks about Thurmond." *Washington Post*, December 10, 2002, A13.

Edsall, Thomas B., and Dan Balz. "Lott Apologizes Anew for 'Terrible' Remark; GOP Leader Rejects Calls to Step Down." *Washington Post*, December 12, 2002, A01.

Eisner, Alan. "Mississippi Vote Shows Power of Civil War Legacy." *Daytona Beach News-Journal*, April 18, 2001. Available online at http://www.news-journalonline.com.

Epstein, Cynthia Fuchs. "Sex Segregation and the War between the States." *Dissent*, Fall 1996, 12–13.

Fairness and Accuracy in Reporting. "Media Play Catch-Up on Lott's Latest Endorsement of Racism: Coverage Mostly Omits Senator's History of Support for Segregation." December 11, 2002. Available online at http://www.fair.org/press-releases/lott-advisory.html. Accessed March 15, 2003.

Family Research Council. "FRC Says Sen. Lott's Remarks Have Caused Considerable Damage." December 10, 2002. Available online at http://www.frc.org/get/po2lo3.cfm. Accessed March 12, 2003.

Farmer, Robin. "Heritage, Hatred Still Burning Issues." *Richmond Times-Dispatch*, January 24, 2000, B1.

Felderstein, Clement. "Macho Woman Takes the Rugby Pitch!" *VMI Cadet*, November 3, 1989, 5.

Fellman, Michael. *The Making of Robert E. Lee*. New York: Random House, 2000.

Filler, Lane. "S.C. NAACP Leader Lived under Confederate Flag's Shadow." *Aiken Standard*, February 28, 2000.

Fisher, Walter. "Narration as a Human Communication Paradigm: The Case for Public Moral Argument." In *Contemporary Rhetorical Theory: A Reader*, ed. John Louis Lucaites, Celeste Michelle Condit, and Sally Caudill, 265–87. New York: Guilford, 1999.

Foster, Gaines. "The Lost Cause." In *The Encyclopedia of Southern Culture*, ed. Charles Reagan Wilson and William Ferris, 1134. Chapel Hill: University of North Carolina Press, 1989.

Fox-Genovese, Elizabeth, and Leon Podles. "Two Views: Is There a Place for All-Male Schools?" *American Enterprise*, January–February 1995, 21–22.

Francis, Samuel. "Lott May Have Unintentionally Said Something True." December 13, 2002. Available online at http://www.cofcc.org/article.htm. Accessed January 27, 2003.

Freeman, Douglas Southall. *Robert E. Lee: A Biography*. 4 vols. New York: Scribner's, 1934–35.

Frist, Bill. "Frist Comments on Discussion of Leadership Elections." December 17, 2002. Available online at http://frist.senate.gov/press-item.cfm?id=189348. Accessed March 12, 2003.

———. "Frist's Comments on Lott Statement," December 12, 2002. Available online at http://frist.senate.gov/press-item.cfm?id=189049. Accessed March 12, 2003.

———. "Statement by Senator Bill Frist on Leadership Elections." December 19, 2002. Available online at http://frist.senate.gov/press-item.cfm?id=189453. Accessed March 12, 2003.

"Frist Emerges as Lott's Leading Challenger." *Gulfport-Biloxi Sun-Herald*, December 20, 2002, A1, A2.

Frum, David. "Diplomatic Approaches." *National Review Online*, December 12, 2002. Available online at http://www.nationalreview.com/frum/diary121202.asp. Accessed March 6, 2003.

———. "Enter Bush." *National Review Online*, December 13, 2002. Available online at http://www.nationalreview.com/frum/diary121302.asp. Accessed March 6, 2003.

———. "Happy Birthday." *National Review Online*, December 10, 2002. Available online at http://www.nationalreview.com/frum/diary121002.asp. Accessed March 6, 2003.

———. "Moments of Truth." *National Review Online*, December 9, 2002. Available online at http://www.nationalreview.com/frum/diary120902.asp. Accessed March 6, 2003.

———. "Whose Party?" *National Review Online*, December 19, 2002. Available online at http://www.nationalreview.com/frum/diary121902.asp. Accessed March 6, 2003.

Galloway, Jim. "Perdue Pushes a Vote on Flag." *Atlanta Journal-Constitution*, January 15, 2003, A1, A6.

Gandy, Karen. "NOW Leaders Call Supreme Court Decision on VMI a 'Mixed Bag' Victory" (press release prepared by Shelley Golden and Diane Minor). June 26, 1996. Available online at http://now.org/press/06-96/06-26-96.html. Accessed April 15, 2000.

Gaulden, Sid, and John Heilprin. "Beasley Says Moving Flag 'Right' Thing." *Charleston Post and Courier*, November 27, 1996, A1.

Giorello, Sibella C. "World-Class Statue Sought." *Richmond Times-Dispatch*, December 15, 1995, A1.

Golden, ———. "Hey Old Corps, Keep Abreast with the VMI Cadet" (cartoon advertisement). *VMI Cadet*, September 1, 1989, 5.

Gore, Al. Interview by Judy Woodruff, *Inside Politics*, CNN, December 9, 2002. Transcribed by eMediaMillWorks/Federal Document Clearing House (FDCH); transcript 120900CN.V15.

Graham, George. "Letter to the Editor." *VMI Cadet*, September 20, 1996, 3.

Grissom, Michael Andrew. "What We Have Learned from the Trent Lott Affair." January 2003. Available online at http://www.cofcc.org/Views/htm. Accessed January 27, 2003.

Haffner, Craig, and Glenn Kirschbaum. *The Unfinished Civil War*. New York: A & E Television Networks, 2000.

Hamel, Charles, Oran Smith, and Chris Sullivan. "Partisan Conversation: Elizabeth Fox Genovese." *Southern Partisan* 17 (First Quarter 1997): 42–47.

Heilprin, John. "Race Relations Meeting Thursday; Governor's Commission: Gov. David Beasley Says He Will Use the Information Collected at Public Forums to Improve Matters in the State." *Charleston Post and Courier*, July 22, 1996, B1.

Heritage Roundtable. "Senators Unite to Find Resolution to Flag Controversy." February 8, 2000. Available online at http://www.jamespurck.com/scv/Legislation.html. Accessed April 10, 2000.

Hetter, Katia. "End of an All-Male Era." *U.S. News and World Report*, July 8, 1996, 50–51.
Hickey, Gordon. "Artist's Statue of Ashe Approved; Vote Unanimous; Slight Changes Due." *Richmond Times-Dispatch*, December 21, 1995, A1.
———. "Ashe Contest Proposal Doused; Council Thwarts Art Group, Adopts Plan." *Richmond Times-Dispatch*, March 26, 1996, A1.
———. "Ashe Statue Delayed Again; Action Deferred; Competition Plan Sought." *Richmond Times-Dispatch*, January 3, 1996, A1.
———. "Ashe Statue Fight Moves to Court; Suit Contends Council Overstepped Its Role." *Richmond Times-Dispatch*, March 28, 1996, B3.
———. "Coalition's Shunning Is Risky Move; Action Taken against Two Council Members Supporting Lee Portrait," *Richmond Times-Dispatch*, August 8, 1999, B1.
———. "Compromise Accommodates All in Ashe Debate; Monument, Competition, Hall of Fame Included." *Richmond Times-Dispatch*, January 9, 1996, A1.
———. "Council Again Gives OK to Ashe Statue." *Richmond Times-Dispatch*, February 27, 1996, B1.
———. "Five Council Members Back Lee; But Group Has No Say in Canal Walk Murals." *Richmond Times-Dispatch*, June 11, 1999, B1.
———. "Lee Absent for Canal Walk's Opening; Mayor Says Controversy Won't Affect Ceremonies." *Richmond Times-Dispatch*, June 4, 1999, A1.
———. "Lee Likeness Returns to Wall without a Shot Fired." *Richmond Times-Dispatch*, November 20, 1999, B3.
———. "Mayor: 'Congratulations to Us'; Praise, Protest at Waterway Ribbon-Cutting." *Richmond Times-Dispatch*, June 5, 1999, A1.
———. "A Monumental Change for City." *Richmond Times-Dispatch*, July 9, 1996, A1.
———. "Mural Will Be Restored; Firebombed Lee Image Is Due Back in 2–3 Weeks." *Richmond Times-Dispatch*, January 25, 2000, B1.
———. "Murals to Go Up Monday; 'Founders' Scene Is First, Will Be Along 17th Street," *Richmond Times-Dispatch*, October 30, 1999, B1.
———. "Plans for Riverfront's Future Taking Shape in Canal Work." *Richmond Times-Dispatch*, August 20, 1996, B3.
———. "Riverfront Project Director Leaves Post amid High Praise." *Richmond Times-Dispatch*, September 6, 1996, B5.
———. "Sculptor Makes Changes; Ashe Statue Receives Subtle Adjustments." *Richmond Times-Dispatch*, December 28, 1995, A1.
Hickey, Gordon, and Carrie Johnson. "Council Supports Mural of Lee; El-Amin's Proposal Is Rejected." *Richmond Times-Dispatch*, July 27, 1999, A1.
———. "David Duke Brings Campaign to Area; Ex-Klan Chief Speaks at Motel in Hanover," *Richmond Times-Dispatch*, July 16, 1999, B1.
———. "R. E. Lee Portrait Removed from Wall; City Councilman Protested Display." *Richmond Times-Dispatch*, June 3, 1999, A1.
———. "Talking about the Walk; Most Agree Lee Deserves a Spot in the Gallery." *Richmond Times-Dispatch*, July 7, 1999, A1.
Hickey, Gordon, and Jim Mason. "Ashe Statue a Monument to Controversy." *Richmond Times-Dispatch*, December 17, 1995, B4.
Hill, Michael. "What's New on DixieNet: Some Observations on Senator Lott and the Cultural Marxists." N.d. Available online at http://www.dixienet.org/ls-homepg/whats-new.htm. Accessed January 29, 2003.

Hinkle, A. Barton. "Long in the Planning, Canal Project Is Moving Full-Speed Ahead." *Richmond Times-Dispatch*, November 20, 1996, A9.

Hinman, Al. "Confederate Flag Must Come Down, Says S.C. Governor." *CNN Interactive*. November 27, 1996. Available online at http://cnn.com/US/9611/27/rebel.flag/. Accessed April 10, 2000.

Hirsch, E. D., Jr., Joseph F. Kett, and James Trefil. "Aesthetics." In *The Dictionary of Cultural Literacy*, 82–83. Boston: Houghton Mifflin, 1988.

Hodges, Jim. "Full Text of Gov. Jim Hodges Speech on the Confederate Flag." Associated Press State and Local Wire, May 23, 2000.

Hofstadter, Richard. *The Paranoid Style in American Politics and Other Essays*. Cambridge: Harvard University Press, 1996.

Holmberg, Mark. "Statue Visitors Complain of Size; Passers-By, Neighbors Say Ashe Figure Is Too Small." *Richmond Times-Dispatch*, July 7, 1996, A8.

Horwitz, Tony. *Confederates in the Attic: Dispatches from the Unfinished Civil War*. New York: Pantheon, 1998.

Hulse, Carl. "Lott's Praise for Thurmond Echoed His Words of 1980." *New York Times*, December 11, 2002, A24.

Hutcheson, Ron. "Bush Quietly Sealed Lott's Fate." *Gulfport-Biloxi Sun-Herald*, December 21, 2002, A1, A10.

Iacobelli. Pete. "Coaches March to Get Confederate Flag Down." Associated Press State and Local Wire, April 4, 2000.

"If You Could Marry Anybody, Who Would It Be?" *VMI Cadet*, September 15, 1989, 8.

"The Institute under 'Gentle' Gerald Baliles" (cartoon). *VMI Cadet*, May 19, 1989, 12.

Jackson, Jesse L., Jr. "Trent Lott Is the Republican Party's Monica Lewinsky." Speech delivered at the PUSH Forum, December 14, 2002. Available online at http://www.rainbowpush.org. Accessed January 27, 2003.

Jackson, Jesse L., Sr. "Casting the Lott's" [*sic*]. Tribune Syndicate, December 15, 2002. Available online at http://www.rainbowpush.org. Accessed January 27, 2003.

———. "Changing the Cover Not the Book." Tribune Syndicate, December 24, 2002. Available online at http://www.rainbowpush.org. Accessed January 27, 2003.

———. "On Super Sunday, Let's Celebrate One Flag and One Nation." Los Angeles Times Syndicate, January 26, 2000. Available online at http://www.rainbowpush.org/commentary/012600.html. Accessed April 10, 2000.

———. "Pandering to Racism." Los Angeles Times Syndicate, January 19, 2000. Available online at http://www.rainbowpush.org/commentary/011900.html. Accessed April 10, 2000.

———. "The Rainbow Coalition" (speech at the Democratic National Convention, San Francisco, Calif., July 17, 1984). In Halford Ross Ryan, *Contemporary American Public Discourse: A Collection of Speeches and Critical Essays*, 3rd ed., 316–26. Prospect Heights, Ill.: Waveland, 1992.

———. "Rev. Jackson Calls for Senator Lott's Resignation." December 8, 2002. Available online at http://www.rainbowpush.org. Accessed January 27, 2003.

Johnson, Carrie, and Gordon Hickey. "Many Say Put the Portrait Back." *Richmond Times-Dispatch*, June 4, 1999, A1.

Johnson, Glen. "Bush, McCain Struggle to Avoid Problems over Confederate Flag." Associated Press State and Local Wire, January 12, 2000.

Johnson, Karen. "Statement of NOW National Secretary Karen Johnson: Supreme Court

Should Halt VMI's Discrimination against Women" (press release prepared by Melinda Shelton and Susannah Schwartz). January 17, 1996. Available online at http://now.org/press/01-96/01-17b96.html. Accessed April 15, 2000.

Jolin, Jen. "A Rat's Eye View—Shannon Faulkner." *VMI Cadet*, November 7, 1997, 2.

———. "Rat's Eye View: The Corps Speaks." *VMI Cadet*, November 21, 1997, 2.

———. "The Rat Perspective: Who's *Your* Role Model?" *VMI Cadet*, October 24, 1997, 2.

Jones, Anne Goodwyn. "Belles and Ladies." In *The Encyclopedia of Southern Culture*, ed. Charles Reagan Wilson and William Ferris, 1527-28. Chapel Hill: University of North Carolina Press, 1989.

Jones, Will. "About 250 Protest Removal of Lee; Citizens' Committee to Meet This Week." *Richmond Times-Dispatch*, June 14, 1999, B1.

Jonsson, Patrick. "Battle over the Past Rages on in an Evolving South." *Christian Science Monitor*, February 24, 2005. Available online at http://www.csmonitor.com/2005/. Accessed September 21, 2006.

Joynes, Tom. "Message to the Corps." *VMI Cadet*, April 28, 1989, 2.

Kahn, Chris. "Integration Lawsuit Dropped against VMI, Pregnancy Policy Criticized by ACLU." Associated Press State and Local Wire, December 7, 2001.

Kay, Greg. "Lott's Lott." Council of Conservative Citizens Forum, as strand "'Lott's Lott' by Greg Kay" (posted December 19, 2002, by jimbob_rebel). Available online at http://www.cofcc.info/cofcc/viewthread.php?tid=24. Accessed January 27, 2003.

Kelleher, Mike. "Point Your Finger at Yourself." *VMI Cadet*, February 2, 1997, 2.

Kennedy, Walter D. "Lotts to Consider: Should Bush and the Republican Party Be Allowed a Free Ride over Dixie?" N.d. Available online at http://southerncaucus.org/222.htm. Accessed January 29, 2003.

"Key Dates in the Confederate Flag's Flying atop the South Carolina Statehouse." Associated Press State and Local Wire, April 13, 2000.

"Keyes Says Confederate Flag Is South Carolina Issue." Associated Press State and Local Wire, September 22, 1999.

Killian, Lewis M. *White Southerners*. Amherst: University of Massachusetts Press, 1985.

King, Martin Luther, Jr. "Letter from Birmingham City Jail." In *The Book of Virtues: A Treasury of Great Moral Stories*, ed. William J. Bennett, 258-62. New York: Simon and Schuster, 1993.

Krauthammer, Charles. "A Clear Choice of Words." *Washington Post*, December 12, 2002, A45. Available online at http://www.washingtonpost.com/ac2/wp-dyn/A429872002Dec11?language=printer. Accessed March 6, 2003.

Kropf, Schuyler. "Forbes Warns against Lottery, Gambling." *Charleston Post and Courier*, September 4, 1999, B3.

Kruse, Noreen W. "Motivational Factors in Non-Denial Apologia." *Central States Speech Journal* 28 (Spring 1977): 13-23.

"Laura Bush Says Confederate Flag Not Racist Symbol." Associated Press State and Local Wire, January 19, 2000.

"Lawsuit Seeks Removal of Confederate Flag." Associated Press State and Local Wire, April 2, 1999.

"Letter to the Editor." *VMI Cadet*, September 12, 1997, 3.

Levinson, Sanford. *Written in Stone: Public Monuments in Changing Societies*. Durham: Duke University Press, 1998.

Little, Robert. "Quiet Crowd at Ceremony Pays Its Respects to Ashe." *Norfolk Virginian-Pilot*, August 16, 1995, B7.

Logue, Cal. "Oratory." In *The Encyclopedia of Southern Culture*, ed. Charles Reagan Wilson and William Ferris, 782. Chapel Hill: University of North Carolina Press, 1989.

Lorber, Judith. "Profile of the ASA President . . . Pushing Social Boundaries: Cynthia Fuchs Epstein." September–October 2005. Available online at http://www.asanet.org. Accessed September 5, 2006.

"Lott Should Resign." *The Nation*, December 30, 2002, 3–4.

"Lott's Disgrace." *Roll Call*, December 12, 2002.

Lott, Trent. *Herding Cats: A Life in Politics*. New York: HarperCollins/Regan Books, 2005.

———. Interview by Ed Gordon. Black Entertainment Television, December 16, 2002. Federal News Service.

———. Interview by Larry King, *Larry King Live*, CNN, December 11, 2002. Available from eMediaMillWorks/Federal Document Clearing House.

———. Interview by Sean Hannity. ABC Radio Syndication, December 11, 2002. Available online at http://www.drudgereport.com/flashb.htm. Accessed March 6, 2002.

———. "Raw Data: Text of Lott's [Resignation] Statement." December 20, 2002. Available online at http://www.foxnews.com. Accessed December 21, 2002.

———. "Remarks of Senate Republican Leader Trent Lott, Pascagoula, Miss." December 13, 2002. Available online at http://www.npr.org/display_pages/features/feature_877622.html. Accessed January 24, 2003.

———. "U.S. Senator Trent Lott (R-MS) Delivers Remarks at Senator Thurmond's Birthday Celebration." December 5, 2002. eMediaMillWorks/Federal Document Clearing House.

Lough, Ashton, and Steve Thoma. "Sweet Briar and Macon Zeros." *VMI Cadet*, October 13, 1989, 6.

Manuel, Marlon. "Mississippians Sticking with Flag." *Atlanta Journal-Constitution*, April 18, 2001, 1A.

Martinez, J. Michael, William D. Richardson, and Ron McNinch-Su, eds. *Confederate Symbols in the Contemporary South*. Gainesville: University Press of Florida, 2000.

McCallister, Ray. "Here's What You'd Do on the Canal Walk." *Richmond Times-Dispatch*, June 25, 1999, B1.

———. "Point-Counterpoint on Richmond Issues." *Richmond Times-Dispatch*, December 18, 1995, B1.

———. "Robert E. Lee and Sa'ad El-Amin." *Richmond Times-Dispatch*, June 4, 1999, B1.

———. "Time to Accept the Statue." *Richmond Times-Dispatch*, July 10, 1996, B1.

McCandless, Amy Thompson. *The Past in the Present: Women's Higher Education in the Twentieth-Century American South*. Tuscaloosa: University of Alabama Press, 1999.

———. "'Separate but Equal' Case Law and the Higher Education of Women in the Twentieth-Century." In *Southern Women at the Millennium: A Historical Perspective*, ed. Melissa Walker, Jeanette R. Dunn, and Joe P. Dunn. Columbia: University of Missouri Press, 2003.

McClay, Wilfred M. "Of 'Rats' and Women." *Commentary*, Summer 1996, 46–50.

McDowell, Elsa. "35 Years Ago, the Battle Flag Was Temporary." *Charleston Post and Courier*, December 22, 1996, B1.

McGill, Ralph. "The Dixiecrat Mind." *Atlanta Constitution*, July 30, 1948, 8.
McKelway, Bill. "Irreconcilable? Past Crashes into Present; Flap over Lee Mural Underscores City's Daily Life in Shadow of Civil War." *Richmond Times-Dispatch*, June 6, 1999, A1.
McWhorter, Diane. "Strom's Skeleton: The Late Segregationist's Black Daughter." *Slate*, July 1, 2003. Available online at http://slate.msn.com/id/2085087. Accessed July 10, 2003.
Means, Marianne. "Rah-Rah-Rah: Male Cadets at VMI Should Grow Up." *Norfolk Virginian-Pilot*, December 24, 1998, B9.
Mfume, Kweisi. "Speech at NAACP Annual/Board Meeting." February 19, 2000. Available online at http://www.naacp.org. Accessed April 10, 2000.
Milbank, Dana. "'Redemption' for the Pariah from Pascagoula." *Washington Post*, November 16, 2006, A02.
Mitchell, Emily. "The Thin Gray Gender Line." *Time*, July 1, 1991, 66.
"Monument to Ashe Divides Hometown." *Roanoke Times and World News*, July 18, 1995, C1.
"More Than 1,000 Honor Confederate Ancestors in Ceremony." Associated Press State and Local Wire, May 7, 2000.
Moreton, Brandi. "Granddaughter Revives Legacy of Reconstruction Legislator." *Rock Hill Herald*, August 9, 1999, 4A.
Morris, William, ed. *The American Heritage Dictionary*, 2nd college ed. Boston: Houghton Mifflin, 1985.
Moutoussamy-Ashe, Jeanne. "A New Year's Wish for Richmond: Accept Gift of Arthur's Vision." *Richmond Times-Dispatch*, January 1, 1996, A7.
Munday, Dave. "Churches Cancel S.C. Meeting to Back Boycott." *Charleston Post and Courier*, September 23, 1999, B8.
"NAACP: Leave Lee Mural Down." Associated Press State and Local Wire, June 29, 1999.
National Association for the Advancement of Colored People. "Emergency Sanctions for South Carolina." July 12, 1999. Available online at http://www.naacp.org/em-resolution.html. Accessed April 10, 2000.
———. "NAACP Calls for Senator Lott to Resign from Majority Leader–Elect Post." December 10, 2002. Available online at http://www.naacp.org/news/releases/lott121002.shtml. Accessed January 27, 2003.
———. "NAACP Chairman Calls Latest Senator Lott Apology Insufficient: BET Interview Only Compounded Lott's Mistakes." December 17, 2002. Available online at http://www.naacp.org/news/releases/lottapology121702.shtml. Accessed January 17, 2003.
———. "NAACP Stands by Call for Senator Trent Lott to Resign from Majority Leader–Elect Post: Cites Latest Apology as 22 Years Too Late." December 13, 2002. Available online at http://www.naacp.org/news/releases/lottresign121302.shtml. Accessed January 27, 2003.
Nichols, Bill. *Ideology and Image*. Bloomington: Indiana University Press, 1981.
Nickles, Don. "Statement: Future of Senate Republican Leadership." December 15, 2002. Available online at http://nickles.senate.gov/legislative/templates/record.cfm?id=189190. Accessed March 12, 2003.

Noonan, Peggy. "Counsel for Trent: What Lott Told Us Last Week, and What He Should Do Now." December 13, 2002. Available online at http://opinionjournal.com/columnists/pnoonan/?id=110002761. Accessed March 6, 2003.

———. "Rent by Trent: Why We Mustn't Cast Our Lot with Lott." December 20, 2002. Available online at http://www.opinionjournal.com/columnists/pnoonan/?id=110002795. Accessed March 6, 2003.

Norman, Geoffrey. "Crashing VMI's Line." *American Spectator*, December 1996, 37–40.

Obenchain, Jeremy, and Tabitha Stump. "Female Cadet Looks to Tackle VMI Rugby Team." *VMI Cadet*, October 24, 1997, 1.

O'Dell, Larry. "Duke Says Lee Flap Symbolic of Broader Assault on White Rights." Associated Press State and Local Wire, July 16, 1999.

Owsley, Frank Lawrence. *Plain Folk of the Old South*. Baton Rouge: Louisiana State University Press, 1949.

Perelman, Chaim, and Lucie Olbrechts-Tyteca. *The New Rhetoric: A Treatise on Argumentation*. Trans. John Wilkinson and Purcell Weaver. Notre Dame, Ind.: University of Notre Dame Press, 1969.

Peterson, Merrill D. *The Great Triumvirate: Webster, Clay, and Calhoun*. New York: Oxford University Press, 1987.

Pettys, Dick. "State Flag Fight Flies Again." *Albany Herald*, January 8, 2001, 1A, 4A.

Phillips, Ulrich B. "The Central Theme of Southern History." *American Historical Review* 34 (October 1928): 30–43.

Potter, David M. *The South in the Sectional Conflict*. Baton Rouge: Louisiana State University Press, 1968.

Powell, Colin, Per Stig Moller, Chris Patten, and Javier Solana. "Joint News Conference Following U.S.-EU Ministerial." State Department Briefing. Franklin Room, State Department, Washington, D.C., December 18, 2002. Federal News Service.

Powell, Kimberly. "The Association of Southern Women for the Prevention of Lynching: Strategies of a Movement in the Comic Frame." *Communication Quarterly* 43 (Winter 1995): 86–99.

Prall, Josef D. "Letter to the Editor: Alumni Commends Assimilation." *VMI Cadet*, November 14, 1997, 3.

Pratt, Robert A. *The Color of Their Skin: Education and Race in Richmond, Virginia, 1954–89*. Charlottesville: University Press of Virginia, 1992.

Previs, Rebecca. "Mural Lights Discussion." *Richmond Times-Dispatch*, February 4, 2000, E5.

Prince, K. Michael. *Rally 'Round the Flag, Boys! South Carolina and the Confederate Flag*. Columbia: University of South Carolina Press, 2004.

"Protests Prompt Removal of Confederate General's Portrait." Associated Press State and Local Wire, June 4, 1999.

"Reaction." *Richmond Times-Dispatch*, June 5, 1999, A6.

Redmon, Jeremy, and Lindsay Kastner. "Lincoln Statue Unveiled: Reaction Mixed among Residents, Visitors to Area." *Richmond Times-Dispatch*, April 6, 2003, B1.

Reed, John Shelton. *One South: An Ethnic Approach to Regional Culture*. Baton Rouge: Louisiana State University Press, 1982.

———. *Southern Folk, Plain and Fancy: Native White Social Types*. Athens: University of Georgia Press, 1986.

———. *Southerners: The Social Psychology of Sectionalism.* Chapel Hill: University of North Carolina Press, 1983.
Rendall, Steve. "A Sex-Free Scandal: When Racism Is the Issue, Media Are Slow to Dig." *Extra!* March–April 1999. Available online at http://www.fair.org/extra/9903/lott.html. Accessed March 15, 2003.
"Return Robert E. Lee to His Place in History." *Roanoke Times and World News*, June 7, 1999, A10.
Reynolds, Beverly. "Arthur Ashe Deserves Best Available Monument." *Richmond Times-Dispatch*, May 28, 1996, A11.
Riley, Russell L. *The Presidency and the Politics of Racial Inequality: Nation-Keeping from 1831 to 1965.* New York: Columbia University Press, 1999.
Ritchie, Rob. "Barracks Living Conditions Seen as Cause for Concern." *VMI Cadet*, March 26, 1993, 2.
Roberts, Giselle. *The Confederate Belle.* Columbia: University of Missouri Press, 2003.
Rockwell, Llewellyn H. "The Trial of Lott." Council of Conservative Citizens Forum, as strand "lott and states rights" (posted December 14, 2002, by jimbob_rebel). Available online at http://www.cofcc.info/cofcc/viewthread.php?tid=31 (linked from lewrockwell.com). Accessed January 27, 2003.
Rosellini, Lynn, and David Marcus, "A Leader among Men." *U.S. News and World Report*, April 10, 2000, 46–47.
Rosen, Jeffrey. "Boys and Girls." *New Republic*, February 14, 1994, 16.
———. "Like Race, Like Gender?" *New Republic*, February 19, 1996, 21.
Rosteck, Thomas, and Michael Leff. "Piety, Propriety, and Perspective: An Interpretation and Application of Key Terms in Kenneth Burke's Permanence and Change." *Western Journal of Speech Communication* 53 (Fall 1989): 327–41.
Rubin, Louis D., Jr. *The American South: Portrait of a Culture.* Baton Rouge: Louisiana State University Press, 1980.
Ryan, Halford Ross. "Baldwin vs. Edward VIII: A Case Study in *Kategoria* and *Apologia*." *Southern Speech Communication Journal* 49 (1984): 125–34.
———. "*Kategoria* and *Apologia*: On Their Rhetorical Criticism as a Speech Set." *Quarterly Journal of Speech* 68 (August 1982): 256–61.
Schwartz, Maryln. *A Southern Belle Primer; or, Why Princess Margaret Will Never Be a Kappa Kappa Gamma.* New York: Doubleday, 1991.
Seligman, Daniel. "Keeping Up: Women on the Rat Line." *Fortune*, May 3, 1993, 104.
Shaffrey, Mary. "Ex-Council Member Had Contentious Career." *Washington Times*, July 26, 2003. Available online at http://www.washtimes.com/metro/20030726-104457-2924r.htm. Accessed September 5, 2006.
Shannon Richey Faulkner, Petitioner, v. James E. Jones, Jr., et al. No. 95-31, October 1995, Sup. Ct. Available at http://www.usdoj.gov/osg/briefs/1995/w9531w.txt. Accessed March 24, 2007.
Sigma Nu Fraternity. "Chapter Listing." N.d. http://www.sigmanu.org/collegians/chapterlisting/. Accessed March 31, 2003.
———. "Our History." N.d. http://www.sigmanu.org/fraternity/ourhistory/. Accessed March 31, 2003.
Smiley, David L. "The Quest for the Central Theme in Southern History." *South Atlantic Quarterly* 71 (Summer 1972): 307–25.

Smith, Bruce. "Bush Avoids Confederate Flag Flap." Associated Press State and Local Wire, August 25, 1999.
———. "Dole Encourages Workers, Refuses Comment on Flag." Associated Press State and Local Wire, July 28, 1999.
———. "Forbes Also Distances Himself from Flag Issue." Associated Press State and Local Wire, September 3, 1999.
———. "NuSouth Sees Black, Red, and Especially, Green in Flag Logo." Associated Press State and Local Wire, April 2, 1999.
Smith, Edward. "Richmond Has Erected a Third-Rate Monument ot [sic] a First-Rate Man." *Richmond Times-Dispatch*, January 18, 1997, A9.
Smith, Stephen A. *Myth, Media, and the Southern Mind*. Fayetteville: University of Arkansas Press, 1986.
Solomon, John. "Over 30 Years, Lott Brushed with Race, Confederacy Issues Several Times." Associated Press, December 12, 2002.
Sons of Confederate Veterans. "How to Handle a Heritage Violation." November 2, 1999. Available online at http://www.scv.org/scvhero2.html. Accessed April 10, 2000.
———. "Sons of Confederate Veterans: Heritage Issues." February 10, 2000. Available online at http://www.scv.org/scvhero0.html. Accessed April 10, 2000.
"A Sorry Lott." *The Nation*, January 13–20, 2003, 3.
Stensland, Jeff. "Democratic Presidential Candidate Calls for Confederate Flag's Lowering." *Columbia State*, February 9, 2000.
Stephenson, D. Grier, Jr. "The Future of Single-Sex Education." *USA Today Magazine*, January 1, 1997, 80–82.
Strope, Leigh. "Bush Says NAACP's National Boycott Is an Issue South Carolinians Should Settle." Associated Press State and Local Wire, September 6, 1999.
———. "GOP Candidates Try to Avoid Confederate Flag Issue in S.C." Associated Press State and Local Wire, January 7, 2000.
———. "Hodges in State of State Speech: Flag Issue Should Be Resolved 'Now.'" Associated Press State and Local Wire, January 19, 2000.
Strum, Philippa. *Women in the Barracks: The VMI Case and Equal Rights*. Lawrence: University Press of Kansas, 2002.
Sweetwaters, Binky J. [pseud.]. "From Binky's Desk: New Trends to Follow." *VMI Cadet*, September 15, 1989, 8.
Swindell, Bill. "Buchanan Speaks with S.C. Supporters." *Charleston Post and Courier*, October 28, 1999, B3.
———. "GOP Candidate Keyes Campaigns in Columbia." *Charleston Post and Courier*, September 23, 1999, B3.
Tate, Allen. "A Southern Mode of the Imagination." In *Studies in American Culture: Dominant Ideas and Images*, ed. Joseph J. Kwiat and Mary C. Turpie. Minneapolis: University of Minnesota Press, 1960.
Taylor, Jane R. "Corps Should Act 'Naturally.'" *VMI Cadet*, October 11, 1996, 3.
Thomas, Emory M. *Robert E. Lee*. New York: Norton, 1995.
Thurmond, J. Strom. "Address of J. Strom Thurmond, Governor of South Carolina, and States' Rights Democratic Candidate for President of the United States, in Radio Broadcast, over ABC Network Covering 14 Southern States, from Governor's Mansion, Columbia, South Carolina, at 8:45 p.m., November 1, 1948." Typescript.

J. Strom Thurmond Papers, Special Collections, Robert Muldrow Cooper Library, Clemson University, Clemson, S.C.

———. "Motion of J. Strom Thurmond, Governor of South Carolina, at Southern Governors' Conference, Wakulla Springs, Florida, Saturday, February 7, 1948." Typescript. J. Strom Thurmond Papers, Special Collections, Robert Muldrow Cooper Library, Clemson University, Clemson, S.C.

"The Timeline for a Monument." *Roanoke Times and World News*, July 10, 1996, Extra 1.

"Top Ten Reasons Why Shades on the Windows Are Great." *VMI Cadet*, September 12, 1997, 8.

Trice, Calvin. "VMI Still Working on Pregnancy Policy," *Richmond Times-Dispatch*, August 26, 2001, B4.

Tumulty, Karen. "Trent Lott's Segregationist College Days: At Ole Miss, the Senator Helped Lead a Fight to Keep Blacks Out of His National Fraternity." *Time*, December 12, 2002. Available online at http://www.time.com/time/nation/article/0,8599,399310,00.html. Accessed January 27, 2003.

Turner, Newell. "Kappa Alpha Order." In *The Encyclopedia of Southern Culture*, ed. Charles Reagan Wilson and William Ferris, 290. Chapel Hill: University of North Carolina Press, 1989.

Twelve Southerners. *I'll Take My Stand: The South and the Agrarian Tradition*. Gloucester, Mass.: Smith, 1976.

United States, Petitioner 94-1941 v. Virginia et al., Petitioners 94-2107, 518 U.S. 515 (1996).

U.S. Census Bureau. "State and County Quick Facts: Mississippi." Available online at http://quickfacts.census.gov/qfd/states/28000.html. Accessed April 22, 2003.

Verdin, Danny. "To: All Compatriots and Supporters of Southern Heritage, From: Danny Verdin, South Carolina Division Commander." March 1, 2000. Available online at http://www.jamespurck.com/scv/URGENT.html. Accessed April 10, 2000.

Virginia Military Institute Public Relations Office. "Claunch Named Battalion Commander." April 17, 2000. Available online at http://www.vmi.edu/pr/ir/apr00/claunch.html. Accessed April 25, 2000.

"VMI Sets Rules for First Female Class." *Black Issues in Higher Education*, June 12, 1997, 11.

"VMI Should Revisit Its Pregnancy Policy." *Roanoke Times*, July 6, 2001, A14.

Ware, B. L., and Wil A. Linkugel. "They Spoke in Defense of Themselves: On the Generic Criticism of Apologia." *Quarterly Journal of Speech* 59 (October 1973): 273–83.

Washington-Williams, Essie Mae, and William Stadiem. *Dear Senator: A Memoir by the Daughter of Strom Thurmond*. New York: HarperCollins/Regan Books, 2005.

Weaver, Richard M. *The Southern Essays of Richard M. Weaver*. Ed. George M. Curtis III and James J. Thompson Jr. Indianapolis: Liberty Press, 1987.

———. *The Southern Tradition at Bay: A History of Postbellum Thought*. Ed. George Core and M. E. Bradford. Washington, D.C.: Regnery Gateway, 1989.

Wells, June Murray. "Talk at South Carolina State House, Columbia, South Carolina, January 8, 2000." Available online at http://www.hqudc.org. Accessed April 10, 2000.

White, Josh. "Loudoun Woman Attains Top Cadet Post at VMI." *Washington Post*, March 23, 2000, B01.

"Who Decides?" *Roll Call*, December 19, 2002.

Wilhoit, Francis M. *The Politics of Massive Resistance*. New York: Braziller, 1973.

"Williams Booed When He Asks Bush about Confederate Flag." Associated Press State and Local Wire, January 7, 2000.

Williams, Dave, and Jon Schanke. "Nobody Asked the Neanderthals, but . . ." *VMI Cadet*, April 13, 1990, 7.

Williams, Eric G. "To the Lion, Hunters Aren't Heroes." *Richmond Times-Dispatch*, July 23, 1999, A10.

Williams, Michael Paul. "'An Avenue for All': At Least Some Ghosts Are Exorcised at Ceremony." *Richmond Times-Dispatch*, July 11, 1996, A1.

———. "Pondering Rebels and Rockfish." *Richmond Times-Dispatch*, June 4, 2001, B1.

Wilson, Zane. "South Carolina Senate to Debate Removing Confederate Flag from Capitol." *Myrtle Beach Sun News*, March 9, 2000.

Wise, Henry A. *Drawing Out the Man: The VMI Story*. Charlottesville: University Press of Virginia for the VMI Alumni Association, 1978.

Wolfe, Margaret Ripley. *Daughters of Canaan: A Saga of Southern Women*. Lexington: University Press of Kentucky, 1995.

Woodward, C. Vann. "The Search for Southern Identity." In *The Burden of Southern History*, rev. ed., 3–25. Baton Rouge: Louisiana State University Press, 1968.

Woody, Paul. "Towering Figure Deserves More Than a 12-Foot Statue." *Richmond Times-Dispatch*, December 31, 1995, D4.

Wyatt, Chris. "The Social Forecast." *VMI Cadet*, September 8, 1989, 7.

Wyatt, Kristen. "Flag Deal Struck." *Albany Herald*, April 5, 2003, 1A, 7A.

Young, Leonidas. "Richmond Can Be Proud of Its Plan to Honor Arthur Ashe's Vision." *Richmond Times-Dispatch*, January 14, 1996, F7.

Index

Abelson, Robert P., 175n21
accommodations, to women, 24, 36, 37
accusation and defense speech sets, 126, 139, 174n21, 176n43
accusations, 116, 119, 126–28, 130, 132, 139–40, 142, 145, 148, 152, 174–75n21
accusers, 127–28, 131, 138, 141–42, 150–51
Ad Hoc Committee on Justice, 81
ad hominem, 14
affirmative action, 121, 133, 135–36, 143, 150, 152, 156
African American History Monument, 104, 158
African American sports hall of fame, 54, 55, 63–64, 71
African Americans, 18, 87, 95, 101, 112, 127–28, 143, 176–77n51; as accusers, 141–42; civil rights activists, 115, 127; civil rights forebears, 73; civil rights leaders, 49, 78; civil rights movement, 11, 107–8, 119, 133, 162; as communicators, 162; as constituents, 142, 144, 151, 160; denied equal rights, 66; as elected officials, 147; equality for, 130; heroes, 57, 72; identity, 98; leaders, 144; Robert E. Lee's feelings toward, 79; oppression of, 104, 106; paternalistic view of, 96; in public forum, 163; and Republicans, 122, 127–28, 136, 143, 152; in Richmond, Virginia, 82–85, 87, 157; in servant role, 110; in South, 160; symbols of, 85; sympathetic with Confederacy, 100, 105
agonistic stress, 98, 115
Agrarian vs. industrial lifestyle, 7
Agrarianism, 96, 165n10
agriculture, 7, 8, 9
Aiken, South Carolina, 108
Air Force, 38
Air Force One, 136
Alabama: Birmingham, 123; Confederate flag, 113, 172n6; support for Thurmond in 1948, 123–24
all-seeing authority, 40
Alvarez, Pedro, 31
ambiguity, 129

American Civil Liberties Union (ACLU), 31; in Virginia, 45
American dream, 142
American flag, 89, 115
anachronicity, 68
anatomy, 20, 40, 41, 45
ancestors, 87, 98, 103–4, 106, 110, 113; sacrifices of, 99, 111
Anderson, State Senator Ralph, 106
Andrew, Rod, 28, 30
Annapolis, 41
Anti-Defamation League, 120, 133
anti-lynching legislation, 123, 129
anti-poll tax bill, 123
"anti-pool-mixin' platform," 154
anti-Semitism, 153
anti-taxation rallies, 129
apologetic discourse, four factors of, 140
apologia, 116, 119, 126–27, 132, 135, 137–41, 145–48, 150–51, 160, 174–75n21; Jesse Jackson, Sr., 120, 176n48
appearance, physical, 43
Appelbaum, Ralph, 73
aristocracy, 20; all-male, 33; Southern, 26, 28
arson, 76, 103
art critics, 68
Ashe, Arthur, Jr., 15, 49–73, 87, 157; achievements of, 67; activism regarding apartheid, 62; and AIDS, 70; athlete, 66, 70; with children, 69–72; as educator, 71; healer of racial rift, 64; humanitarian, 7; intellectual, 70, 72; intentions of, 71–72; statue of, 49–73; tennis player, 62, 69, 71–72. *See also* Ashe statue
Ashe, Johnnie, 63, 65
Ashe, Randy, 72
Ashe statue: aesthetic propriety of, 62, 68–70, 72; racial objections to, 62; scale and size of, 72
Assembly of African American Leaders, 96
assimilation, of women, 35, 42
Attitudes toward History, 168n4
Austin, Texas, 91
authorial intent, 132

Index

authority, 166n5
"avenue for all people," 65

back porch order, 156, 177n4
Bahen, Frank, 83
Balz, Dan, 134
Baptist General Convention of Virginia, 76
Barbour, Robert, 80
Barker, James, 102, 109, 114
Barnett, Governor Ross, 125
Barr, Representative Bob, 151, 152
barracks, 21, 24, 26, 31, 34, 39, 46, 156
barriers: gender, 42; racial, 62, 66
Baskerville, Councilwoman Viola, 63
battalion commanders, 25
Battle of New Market, 22, 30–32
Baum, Gordon, 137
Beasley, Governor David, 93, 102–3, 108, 113
Beauregard, General P. G. T., 137
belle, Southern, 28–30
"beltway liberals," 139
Benoit, William, 174–75n21
Bentham, Jeremy, 39
betrayal, 139
Bible, 114, 142–43
Biden, Senator Joseph, 154–55
bipartisan, 144
biracialism, 165n10
Birmingham, Alabama, 123
Bissell, Colonel Mike, 42
Black, Justice Hugo, 176n45
Black Entertainment Television (BET), 121, 131, 133, 141–44, 146–47
Black Mountain, North Carolina, 100
blaming, 140
Bobb, Robert, 65
Bogdon, Derek, 38
bolstering, 126, 140–43, 175n21
Bond, Julian, 131
Bonjean, Ron, 119, 121, 129, 139–40, 145
Boone, Ray, 57
Booth, Wayne, 162
Bormann, Ernest, 147–48
Bost, Andrew P., 79–80
Bowden, Tommy, 94
boycott, 93, 109–10, 112–13, 158
Braden, Waldo W., 161–62
Bradley, Senator Bill, 94
British Union Jack flag, 92
Brooks, Thelma, 63
Brother Rats, 18, 23, 29, 38

Brown, Nelson, 93
Brown v. Board of Education, 11, 53–54, 88, 92, 107, 157
Bryant, Joseph, 104
Buchanan, Pat, 94, 140, 148–49
Bumiller, Elisabeth, 137
Bunting, Commandant Josiah, III, 33, 37, 46
Burke, Kenneth: agonistic stress, 98, 115; *Attitudes toward History*, 168n4; class distinctions, 20, 69, 166n7; comic frame, 50, 169n7; congregational state, 169n7; consubstantiality, 13, 16, 161; definition of man, 12; dialectic, 16–17, 83, 127; differentiation, 16; dissociative state, 169n7; division, 6, 9, 11–13, 16, 18–19, 31, 48, 50, 57, 69, 85–87, 98, 103, 109, 113, 117, 153, 155–57, 160–61, 163; entelechy, 13; hierarchy, 12; identification, 6, 11–14, 16–18, 50, 57, 72–73, 85–87, 98, 103, 117, 127, 141–42, 144, 155, 156, 158, 160–61, 163; juxtaposition, 14, 49–52, 54, 60, 62, 64, 86, 168n4; "maximum consciousness," 85; mortification, 119; motives, 104, 124, 126, 135, 142, 174–75n21; order, 13; perfection, 13; *Permanence and Change*, 50, 168n4, 169n7; perspective by incongruity, 13, 15, 44, 48, 50–54, 65–66, 69–71, 73, 77–85, 168n4; "perspective of perspectives," 17; pieties, 13, 51–52, 63–64, 80, 84–85; planned incongruity, 52, 65, 67, 169n7; platonic dialogue, 17; pride, 12; propriety, 51, 72, 158; purification, 121, 126; purpose, 52; redemption, 126; rhetoric and dialectic, 17, 98; *Rhetoric of Motives*, 21; rhetorical theory, 174–75n21; rottenness, 13; scapegoating, 117, 119, 126–28, 151–53, 175n22; segregational state, 169n7; sense of order, 12; social mystery, 14, 18–21, 26–27, 33–35, 37–38, 42, 46, 48, 69, 156–57, 165n19, 166n7; terministic screens, 16, 133; ultimate term, 83–84, 86; victimage, 119, 149–51
Bush, President George W., 94, 120, 135–37, 142, 149–50, 152
Bush, Governor Jeb, 122, 137
Bush family, 149
Bush White House, 134, 136–37
business interests, 106, 110, 113–14
business leaders, 102
"butch," 44, 48
Byrd, Senator Robert, 133, 151, 177n56
Byrd, Sheila Hardwell, 122
Byrd, William, 73
Byrd Park, 55

Index

Cadet, The, 46-48
Cadre, 25
"Caesar knifed Brutus," 149
Calhoun, John C., 10, 118, 161
"called us out-our-names," 128-29
Campsen, George, Jr., 91
Canal Walk, 49, 52, 67, 73-86; dedication, 52, 76; symbol of evolving Richmond, 81
capitalistic compromisers, 115
careerism, 135, 138
Carlson, Margaret, 41-42
Carlyle, Thomas, 21, 27, 40, 43, 166n5
Carr, Mary Lou, 69
Cash, W. J., 5-6, 162
caste system, 129
centrifugal and centripetal motion, 51
Chafee, Senator Lincoln, 122
Chaisson, Gregory, 34
cheerleaders, 25, 40, 44-45; and uniforms, 40, 45
Chewning, Thomas, 55, 72
children, 69-72, 83, 103, 113
Chittum, Matt, 44
chivalry, 27, 39
Christianity, 122, 142; discrimination against, 148, 150; Robert E. Lee and, 79
church attendance, 142-43
church burnings, 103
Churchill, Prime Minister Winston, as admirer of Robert E. Lee, 79
"circling the wagons," 136
"circling vultures," 136
Citadel, The, 14, 19, 24, 29, 33, 42, 96, 166n11; cadets who lowered flag, 94
Citizens for Excellence in Public Art (CEPA), 62, 68-70
citizens' panel, 76
citizenship: and Jefferson Davis, 121, 131; and Robert E. Lee, 80-81
citizen-soldiers, 20, 37-38
civic leaders, 102
civil rights, 145; activists, 115, 127; forebears, 73; initiatives, 153; leaders, 49, 78; legislation, 123, 124, 126-27; movement, 11, 107-8, 119, 133, 162; pioneers, 86; program, 123-24; sites, tour of, 144
Civil Rights Act of 1990, 146
Civil Rights Acts of 1964 and 1965, 11, 131, 146, 157
Civil War, 11, 63, 87, 108, 157; African Americans' role in, 105; Battle of New Market, 22, 30-32; centennial, 89, 90, 107-8, 158; flag controversy reenacting, 110-11; interpretation of, 91, 104; Robert E. Lee and, 80; loss of, 7-8, 12; narratives of, 104-6, 109, 115; New Market cadets, 31; parallel with Revolutionary War, 98; reasons for fighting, 77, 80-81; reenactors, 104, 110-11, 172n20; Richmond in, 50, 84; Union forces, 31, 137; VMI's role in, 31. *See also* War Between the States; War of Northern Aggression
civility, 13, 146
Clark, Gregory, 17; rhetoric of democratic practice, 17
Clark, Steve, 70-71
class, 166n4; consciousness, 169n7; disparity, 33; distinctions, 20, 32, 69, 166n7; stratification, 31; system, 22, 156
classical stases, 174n21
Claunch, Erin, 25, 43-44
Clay, Henry, 10
Clemson University, 96, 102, 109, 114
Clinton, President Bill, 122
"clothed with authority," 166n5
clothing, 21-22, 31, 40, 43-45, 47, 166n5
Clough, Jason, 45
Coalition for Racial Justice (CRJ), 76, 84
Cobb, James, 6-7
Coble, Bob, 93
Cocke, John D., IV, 30
"Code for a Gentleman," 28
Cohodas, Nadine, 124
collective imagination, 160
college football, 89, 125, 160
Collins, R. Lee, 60
Colorado Springs, 41
Columbia, South Carolina, 16; Capitol, 87; Confederate Relic Room, 16; intersection of Main and Gervais, 16; mayor, 93
comic frame, 50, 169n7
Commission of Architectural Review, 68, 70-71
common ground, 84, 102, 106, 140, 143, 160
common identity, 65
Communism, 138
community renewal, 148
competitive stress, 98
compromise, 102, 109, 114
Compromise of 1850, 10
Conason, Joe, 151
concurrent majority, 10, 161
Confederacy, 7, 99, 100, 104-5, 111; celebration

of, 131; commemorations, 67; cradle of, 157; defense of constitutional principles, 80; defense of slavery, 79; descendants, 87, 99, 104, 115, 128, 137, 158; descendants, symbols of, 85; enthusiasts, 172n20; evacuation, 73; forebears, 73; heritage, 81, 106; heritage, defenders of, 67; heroes, 57, 64, 66–67, 72, 83; leaders, 57, 66, 70, 78, 84, 86; Lost Cause of, 9, 11–12, 32, 67, 99, 111; Lott as son of, 150; memorials and monuments, 49–73, 82, 84, 100, 111, 157; military, 91, 107; motivations, 104–5; purity, 65; reasons for fighting war, 77, 80–81; secession and, 77, 80; states' rights and, 80; symbols, 51, 87, 89, 95; as traitors, 83; uniforms, 76; victory at New Market, 31; white males, 157
Confederate Americans, 60, 62
Confederate Army, 78
Confederate battle flag, 12, 15, 86–89, 93–94, 97, 99, 100, 103, 107–9, 111–12, 116–17, 147, 149, 158; advocates, 96, 99, 104, 106–8, 158; compromisers, 96–98, 106, 108, 114; defenders, 98; displayed at football games, 125, 174n18; in Georgia, 15, 92, 100, 171–72n5; history of, in South Carolina, 171n3; neutralists, 102; opponents, 96, 98, 100, 104–5, 107, 108, 113, 158; raising, 107–8, 115; in Richmond controversies, 67, 76; supporters, 113
Confederate cause, 79–80
Confederate Memorial Association, 6
Confederate Relic Room, 16, 94
Confederate Soldier's Monument, 93–94, 115
Confederate States of America, 12, 49, 88, 91, 96, 99, 105, 107, 157
Confederate Veteran magazine, 91
congregational state, 169n7
Congress of Black National Churches, 96
Congressional Black Caucus, 120, 127, 142–43
Conrad, John, 64
Conroy, Pat, 94
conservatism and conservatives, 8, 122, 126–27, 129–30, 135–36, 138–39, 151; discrimination against, 148, 150; Southern, 150; true, 153
conspiracy theory, 140, 148–51
constitutional arguments, 123–24, 156
Constitutional Convention, 10
constitutional interpretation, 91, 95
constitutional principles, 80
consubstantiality, 13, 16
continuity, 8–9
Cooper, Rev. Roscoe, 81
Coski, John, 96–97, 116

cosmetics, 24, 43–44
Cottle, Michelle, 131–32
Council of Conservative Citizens (CCC), 96, 121, 125–27, 137–39, 141, 149, 152–53
Country Gentleman mascot, 109
Coupland, R. C., 39
Craig, Matthew, 66–67
"Cultural Marxism," 138
Cummings, Rep. Elijah, 120

Dabney, Virginius, 53
Daschle, Senator Tom, 130, 177n56
Daughters of the American Revolution (DAR), 68
Davis, Confederate President Jefferson, 49, 69, 82, 91, 121, 131, 134–35; efforts to restore citizenship of, 121, 131
"dead white Confederate males," 157
"Defender of the Defenseless," 28
defenders, 127; of Robert E. Lee, 78–79; of slavery, 51, 60, 66–77
defenses, 132, 139, 174–75n21
Degler, Carl, 8
demagoguing, 155
Democratic National Convention, 120, 176n48
Democratic Party, 118, 145, 154
denial, 126, 140–41, 175n21
Department of Justice, 24
descendants: of Confederates, 99, 104, 115, 137, 158; of slaves, 115, 158
desegregation, 53, 89, 108
Dewey, Thomas, 124
dialectic, 16–17, 83, 98, 127, 162, 166n24
dialectical rhetoric, 17, 162–63; purifying fire of, 17, 161
dialogue, 98, 166n21, 168n4; Platonic, 17; public, 116; reconciliation through, 65
differentiation, 16, 126, 135, 140, 145–46, 175n21
DiPasquale, Paul, 54–55, 62, 65, 68–72, 85
discipline, 20; adversative approach to, 20–21, 34, 36; rigorous system, 22; self-, 36
discourse, Southern mode of, 162
discrimination, 123, 131
dissociative state, 169n7
distinctions, 17, 19–20; class, 20
distinctiveness, 5–10, 16, 153, 157, 160–61
divergent narratives, 86, 115, 158
diversity, 16, 83, 103, 116, 143–44, 157–58, 160–61
division, 6, 9, 11–13, 16, 18–19, 31, 50, 57, 69,

85–87, 98, 103, 109, 113, 115, 117, 153, 155–57, 160–61, 163
"Dixie," 89, 109; sung at football games, 125, 174n18
Dixiecrats, 118, 122–24, 128, 132, 136, 154–55, 173–74n10
Dole, Senator Bob, 118, 125
Dole, Elizabeth, 94
Downs, Timothy, 101
Drake, Professor W. Avon, 82
Drummond, State Senator John, 108
Duke, David, 67, 76–77
Duncan, James E., 37

Eads, Randy, 44
Ecclesiastes, 142
economic development, 145–46
economic growth, 106, 114
economic opportunity, 113, 142, 146, 148
economic reputation, 114
economic sanctions, 105, 109, 112
Edds, Margaret, 64, 67–68, 72
Edgerton, H. K., 100, 105, 111
Edmonds, Brad, 28
Edsall, Thomas, 119, 129, 134, 148
education, 36, 102, 142, 146, 148, 162; of military leaders, 38; to initiate, 36; racial preferences in, 136
El-Amin, Sa'ad (Jeroyd W. Greene), 67, 73, 75–76, 81
Emancipation Proclamation, 11
entelechy, 13
Epstein, Cynthia Fuchs, 33
equal opportunity, 20, 112, 121, 129, 146, 148
Equal Protection Clause, 20
equal rights, 130, 135–36; denial of, 66; opposition to, 107
Erhardt, David, 72
eristic, 17, 166n24
European Americans, 125
evil, 147, 151
Executive Order 9008, 122

Fair Employment Practices Commission (FEPC), 124
Fairness and Accuracy in Reporting (FAIR), 125, 130–31, 133, 134, 174n20
faith, 142–43, 148, 150
Family Circle Cup, 94
family policy, 26, 45–46
Family Research Council, 120
fantasy themes, 97, 147–48

Farmer, Robin, 82
Faulkner, Shannon, 14, 24, 166n11
Faulkner, William, 8
Faulkner v. Jones, 24, 33
Fellman, Michael, 78
female anatomy, 40–41, 43; different from male, 42
femininity, 44, 47
"fetching good out of evil," 140, 147–48, 161
Filler, Lane, 108
First Amendment, 88
fiscal conservatism, 128
fiscal discipline, 175n26
Fisher, Walter, 97–98, 115
Fleischer, Ari, 136, 150
flogging, 138
floodwall murals, 73–86, 157
folk culture, 5, 7, 161, 165n10
football (college), 89, 125, 160
Forbes, Steve, 94
forgiveness, 121, 142–43, 148, 155
Forman, James, Jr., 88
Foster, Gaines, 12
Foucault, Michel, 39
"founding ideals," 135
Fourteenth Amendment, 20
Fourth Circuit Court, 24
Fox-Genovese, Elizabeth, 36
Foxman, Abraham H., 133
Francis, Samuel, 132, 137
Franklin, Florence, 82
fraternity, 120–21, 125, 130–31, 141, 174n18
fraternization, 25, 47
Freeman, Douglas Southall, 79
Freudian slip, 133
friendship, 142, 144–45
Frist, Senator Bill, 121–22, 137, 152
front porch order, 156, 177n4
Frum, David, 127, 130, 135–36, 138
Fulbright, Senator William, 151

Gallman, James, 106, 108, 113
Gandy, Kim, 42
gargoyles, 169n7
gender, 20, 157; differences, 21; division, 9, 156; norming, 37; role reversal, 44; stereotypes, 36; stratification, 48
genealogy, 111
gentleman, 27, 30, 34–35; code for, 28, 35; conduct, 34; cursing, 34; as "Defender of the Defenseless," 28; as knight, 27–29;

Robert E. Lee as, 79; Southern, 28, 30, 33, 111–12
Georgia: boycott, 113; Confederate flag, 15, 92, 100, 171–72n5; referendum, 92
"Get in Step March," 94
Gibson, William, 93
Ginsburg, Justice Ruth Bader, 21, 24, 36–37, 166n11
Goldwater, Barry, 154
good-ol'-boy network, 26, 32–33, 129, 156
Gordon, Ed, 121, 139, 142–44, 146–48
Gore, Vice President Al, 94, 119
Governor's Commission on Racial Relations, 93
Graham, George, 39
Grant, General Ulysses, 67
Great Triumvirate, 10
Green, Terone B., 63
Grenada, Mississippi, 124

haircuts, 19, 24, 36, 43–45, 47–48
Halsey, Brenton S., 75
Hampton, General Wade (statue), 158
Hannity, Sean, 120, 133, 139–44, 148
Hard Road to Glory Hall of Fame, 54–55, 63–64, 71
Harnesberger, Douglas, 70
hate, 87, 100, 105, 112, 151, 153; crimes, 76, 103, 149; heritage of, 100, 106
Hedgepeth, Gwen, 76, 84
Henry, Patrick, 73
heritage, 98–100, 105–6, 109, 112, 161; debunked, 67; groups, 110; preservationist traditionalists, 96; regional, 160; Southern, 102, 104
Heritage Park, 106
Heritage Preservation Association, 60
"Heritage Report," 91
Heritage Roundtable (HR), 96, 102, 106, 114
"Heritage Violations," 91, 111
heroes, 73, 85; African American, 57, 72–73, 85; Confederate, 57, 64, 66–67, 72–73, 81, 83, 85; pantheon for, 65; Virginia, 52, 55, 57, 65–66; worship of, 78
Hickey, Gordon, 79
hierarchy, 12, 38, 165n10; racial, 157; social, 13
Hill, Oliver, 52, 81
Hines, Richard, 67
Hinkle, A. Barton, 75
Hirth, Marc, 75
Historically Black Colleges and Universities (HBCUs), 143

history, 103, 106; of Confederate flag in South Carolina, 171n3; honoring, 72; piety of, 85; of race relations, 86, 153; rewriting, 106; of Richmond, 53, 65, 73–86; Richmond's valuing of, 83–86; role of South in American, 160; ultimate term, 83–84, 86
Hitler, Adolf, 81
Hodges, Governor Jim, 93, 94, 103–4, 114–15
Hofstadter, Richard, 147, 150–51
Hollins College, 29
Holtz, Lou, 94
honor, 28, 108, 111; Lee's deserving place of, 79; Richmond ruled by, 84; system, 22
Honor code, 22
Honor Court, 22, 25
Hulse, Carl, 120
Hunter, Ruth, 83
Hurley, John, 6
Hutcheson, Ron, 137

identification, 6, 11, 12, 14, 16–18, 50, 57, 72–73, 85–87, 98, 103, 115, 117, 127, 141–42, 144, 155–58, 160–61, 163
Ifill, Gwen, 173n3
I'll Take My Stand, 7
imagery, 137–38
incongruity, 48–50, 53–54, 62, 65–67, 69, 70–71, 73, 77–79, 81–82, 85, 169n7, 171n55
individual responsibility, 175n26
individualism, 8
initiation, 35–36, 42
Inside Politics, 119
Institute of Reconciliation, 147
integration, 12, 53, 62, 73, 87–88, 121, 125, 129, 131, 154, 156–58, 166n11, 167n12; through symbolism, 66
Intercollegiate Studies Institute, 36
interpretation: of Civil War, 91, 104; of Constitution, 91, 95; of flag, 86, 104; of Lott's comments, 140, 173n3, 175n26; of Thurmond's life, 155

Jackson, Representative Jesse, Jr., 128–29, 176n48
Jackson, Reverend Jesse, Sr., 92, 101, 105–7, 113, 119–20, 128, 130, 134, 150, 176n48
Jackson, General Thomas "Stonewall," 22–23, 26, 49; hero, 83; holiday, 76
Jefferson, Thomas, 73
"Jerusalem of political correctness," 138
Jesus Christ, 114
Jim Crow, 11, 57, 129, 134

Johnson, Bill, 76
Johnson, Representative Eddie Bernice, 120
Johnson, Karen, 38, 40–41
Jolin, Jen, 47–48
Jones, Anne Goodwyn, 28
Jones, Bob, III, 94
Joyner, Colonel James, 37
Joynes, Tom, 34
Justice Department, 24
juxtaposition, 14, 49–52, 54, 60, 62, 64, 86, 168n4

Kaine, Mayor Timothy, 65, 83
kategoria, 119, 126, 175n21
Kay, Greg, 138–39, 149
Kelleher, Mike, 35
Kemp, Rep. Jack, 134–35
Kennedy, President John F., as admirer of Robert E. Lee, 79
Kennedy, Walter D., 149
Keyes, Alan, 94
Khalfani, King Salim, 83
Khayat, Robert, 147
Kidd, Henry, 79–80
Killian, Lewis M., 4, 89
King, Larry, 120, 139, 143–44, 146
King, Martin Luther, Jr., 11, 63; as admirer of Robert E. Lee, 79; holiday honoring, 121, 131, 146
Kinsley, Michael, 132
Krauthammer, Charles, 132–33
Kruse, Noreen W., 126, 175n21
Ku Klux Klan, 11, 67, 87, 100, 108, 133, 141, 176n45

Lamb, Robert H., 66
Lambert, State Senator Benjamin, 57
Larry King Live, 120, 139, 143–44, 146
Latinos, in the South, 160
League of the South, 96, 127, 137, 153
Lee, General Robert E., 15, 49–51, 73–86, 87; anti-secessionist, 79; as anti-slavery, 78–80; character of, 77–79; as Christian, 79; citizenship, 80–81; as conciliator, 79; Confederate Army, 78, 81; conflicted about slavery, 82; critics of, 78–79, 81; defenders of, 78–80; enhancement of ethos, 79; faith of, 79; faithful to Confederate cause, 80; as gentleman, 79; "healing force," 81; as hero, 83, 85; holiday, 76; as honorable man, 77, 80; invited to lead Union Army, 79; Lost Cause, 78; as loyal American, 78, 81; as loyal Virginian, 77–78, 80; memorials to, 84; as noble, 82; as non-Richmonder, 83; as pariah, 81; as pro-slavery, 77, 81–83; racist attitudes of, 77, 79, 81; respected by leaders, 79; role in history, 84–85; as savior of Richmond, 79; as slave owner, 79; as stainless, 78; support for Confederate cause, 79, 82; as symbol of slavery, 81–82; as traitor, 78, 80–81, 83; as unheroic, 81; veritable sainthood of, 78; words about slavery, 79–80, 82
Lee mural, 51–52, 67, 73–86; arson, 76; symbol of slavery, 81–82
left (political), 149
"Letter from Birmingham Jail," 63
Levinson, Sanford, 91
Lewis, Frances, 71
Lewis, Senator John, 144
Liasson, Mara, 137
Library of Congress, 73
Lincoln, President Abraham, 10, 105, 135; adversaries of, 131; party of, 134–35; respect for Robert E. Lee, 79; statue in Richmond, 15, 171n55
Lincoln, Tad, 15, 171n55
Lincoln Memorial, 51
Linkugel, Wil A., 126, 140, 175n21
listening rhetoric, 162
Little, Robert, 64, 66–67
Logue, Cal M., 161–62
Long, John D., 89
Lord, Gussie, 44
Lost Cause, 9, 11–12, 32, 67, 99, 111; forebears, 16, 73; Robert E. Lee and, 78; myth of, 99; saints, 64; symbols, 12, 73, 84
Lott, Chester, 124
Lott, Iona, 124
Lott, Senator Trent, 16, 116–53; attitudes, 145; constituents of, 142, 144, 151; disloyalty to South, 149–50; pariah, 153; racist associations, 174n20; rags-to-riches story of, 124; religious faith, 142–43, 148; resignation of, 148; sharecropper's son, 124, 142; son of Confederacy, 150; target of conspiracy, 148–50; victim of hate crime, 149; working-class roots, 124, 142
Louisiana, 91; support for Thurmond in 1948, 124

male anatomy, 40–41; different from female, 42
man, definition of, 12
"manifesto on racism," 137

Maoist Communism, 138
Marshall, George, 22
Martin Luther King Jr. Commission, 131
Martin Luther King Jr. Day, 76, 121, 146, 154
Martinez, J. Michael, 95–96
Marxism, 138, 169n7
Mary Baldwin College, 24–25, 46
Maslow's hierarchy, 126
Maury, Matthew Fontaine, 49, 69
May, John "Mr. Confederate," 90–91
McCain, Senator John, 94, 101
McCallister, Ray, 67, 69, 78
McCandless, Amy Thompson, 28
McCarthy, James J., 75
McClay, Wilfred, 33, 35
McCollum, Rudolph C., Jr., 83
McConnell, Senator Mitch, 121
McDowell, Elsa, 90
McGill, Ralph, 174n10
McJunkin, James, 101, 105, 113
McWhorter, Diane, 154–55
Means, Marianne, 44
media: attention, 34, 130; mainstream, 130; scrutiny, 34, 151
Medlock, Travis, 93
men: as defenders of the defenseless, 28; as honorable, 28; as knights, 27–29; physical strength, 28; Southern, 27
Meredith, James, 125
Mfume, Kweisi, 105, 112, 131–33
middle-grounders, 96, 98, 102, 113–14
military, 20; attire, 48; Confederate, 91; force, 66; glory, 84; rituals, 26, 39; schools, 28, 30; service, 30; stereotypes, 29; tradition, 28, 35; training, 28; women's experiences in, 38
Miller, Emilie R., 32–33
Miller, Governor Zell, 92
Milsap, Helga, 104
Mind of the South, The, 5
Minor, Donald, 82
minority rights, 10, 161
minority students, 33–34
Mississippi: African Americans in, 142, 151, 160, 176–77n51; Confederate flag, 15, 92, 100, 172n6; constituents of Lott, 128, 139, 143; discrimination against people from, 148, 150; Grenada, 124; Pascagoula, 121–22, 125, 139, 141–42, 147–48, 153; Reagan 1980 campaign rally in, 118, 120, 146; referendum, 92; segregated, 162; support for Thurmond in 1948, 123–24; Supreme Court, 92; University of, 120, 125, 143, 147, 174n18

"mistake of the head, not of the heart," 141
Mitchell, Emily, 33
"modes of resolution," 174–75n21
Monument Avenue, 15, 49–73, 157, 168n1; "avenue for all people," 65; bastion of segregation, 66; Confederate purity, 66
Moore, Reverend Sam W., 113
Morris, Dick, 152
motives, 174–75n21; apologist's, 174n21; behind civil rights legislation, 124; behind scapegoating, 127; of South, 104
Moutoussamy-Ashe, Jeanne, 54, 63, 67, 71–72
Mr. Confederate, 90
murals, 67, 73–86, 157
Musgrove, Governor Ronnie, 92
myth, 30; of Lost Cause, 99

narrative paradigm, 97, 115
narratives, 15, 16, 97, 98, 104–8, 111–13, 158; alternative, 102, 105, 109; divergent, 86, 115, 158; explanatory, 158; hopeful, 115; personal, 107–8; of reconciliation, 114; redemption, 154
Nation of Islam, 73
National Association for the Advancement of Colored People (NAACP), 16, 76, 83, 87, 89, 93–94, 96, 100–1, 105–7, 110, 120, 126–27, 131, 133, 158; boycott, 93, 101, 110, 112, 158; in Virginia, 83
National Collegiate Athletic Association (NCAA), 94
national defense, 128–29, 162, 175n26
National Organization of Women (NOW), 33, 40–42
National Public Radio (NPR), 137
National Urban League, 96
National Women's Law Center, 46
neo-Confederates, 72, 87, 95, 127, 131, 139
neoconservatives, 127, 132, 135–39, 149, 153
New Market Ceremony, 18, 30–31
New Market parallel, 31
New South, 161; façade, 133; Richmond in, 52, 64, 78, 82; symbols, 49
New Testament, 114
New York Knicks, 94
"New York mistake," 176n48
New York Public Library, 73
Nickles, Senator Don, 121, 136
Noah, Timothy, 173n3
nondenial apologia, 126
Noonan, Peggy, 127, 129, 135–36
Norman, Geoffrey, 31–32
North, the, 104, 161

North Carolina, 100
Northern aggression, 77
Norwich University, 25, 47
Novak, Bob, 132-33

Old South, 5, 88; beliefs, 133; juxtaposition with New South, 64; symbols, 9, 49, 88, 156; wall hung with tapestries, 161
Ole Miss, 120, 125, 174n18. *See also* University of Mississippi
Operation Desert Storm, 38
oral tradition, 161-63
oratory, 161-62
order: changing, 154; concern with, 9; division, 6, 9, 11-13, 16, 18-19, 31, 48, 50, 57, 69, 72, 85-87, 98, 103, 109, 113, 115, 117, 153, 155-57, 160-61, 163; identification, 6, 11-12, 14, 16-18, 57, 73, 85-87, 98, 103, 115, 117, 127, 141-42, 144, 155-56, 158, 160-61, 163; new, 153; peace and good, 123; sense of, 12; social, 9
Orleans Parish School Board, 91
Owsley, Frank, 161

paideia, 36
paleoconservatives, 127, 132, 137-39, 149, 153
Palmetto Battalion, 104
Palmetto Business Forum, 96
palmetto flag, 115
palmetto tree, 102
panopticon, 39
paranoid disposition, 148, 151
"Paranoid Style in American Politics," 147, 150
pariah: Lee as, 81; Lott as, 153
Pascagoula, Mississippi, 121-22, 125, 137, 139, 141-42, 147-48, 153
paternalism, 96
paternity, 40, 46
pathos, 124
patriarchy, 33
penance, 138, 152
Pender, Willie, 82
Penn, Eric, 84-85
Perdue, Governor Sonny, 92
Perelman, Chaim, 16
Permanence and Change, 168n4, 169n7
Persian Gulf War, 38
perspective by incongruity, 13, 15, 44, 48, 50-52, 65, 168n4
"perspective of perspectives," 17
phallocracy, 40-41
Philadelphia, Pennsylvania, Bush speech in, 136
Phillips, Ulrich B., 7-8

physics analogies, 168n4
Pickering, Charles, 122, 141
pieties, 13, 51, 52, 63-64, 80, 84-85
planned incongruity, 52, 65, 67, 169n7
Platonic dialogue, 17
Pleasant, Arrelius D., 66
pluralistic public speaking, 162
Podles, Leon, 36
Poe, Edgar Allan, 73
political correctness, 138-39
political establishment, 151
political expediency, 155, 160
political solidarity, 165n9
political strategy, 152
poll taxes, 123
Potter, David, 5-7
Powell, Secretary of State Colin, 122, 127-28, 152
power, 22, 27, 32, 36, 48; symbolic, 100; whites', 107
Powhatan, Chief, 73
Prall, Josef D., 40
Pratt, Robert A., 53
pregnancy, 25-26, 40, 45-46
President's Committee on Civil Rights, 122
Previs, Rebecca, 79-80
Prince, K. Michael, 90, 158
privacy, 21, 24, 35-36, 39-40, 43
propriety, 51, 158; symbolic, 72
Prosser, Gabriel, 78, 84, 86; hero, 85
Protestant Christianity, 142
provincial status, 165n9
Psalms, 142
public art, 15
public moral argument, 97
public order, 155
public schools, 53-54, 88, 91, 104, 108, 129, 157
public speaking, 162
Pulley, Collin, 79
pundits, 130, 135-36, 149

"Quest for the Central Theme in Southern History," 5

race, 4, 9, 11, 33, 57, 65, 70, 107, 116, 127, 129, 145-46, 151, 154, 156, 162, 165n9; and agrarianism, 7; barriers, 62, 66; card, 134; caste system, 129; consciousness, 7-8; demagoguing, 155; desegregation, 53; integration, 12, 53, 62, 73, 87-88, 121, 125, 131, 157; integrity and purity, 123; oppression, 34, 81, 88, 96, 100, 104, 106; preferences, in education, 136;

reconciliation, 53, 67; relations, 50, 106, 113, 115, 153, 155; segregation, 11, 62–63, 117, 132–33, 140, 142, 145, 147, 157; struggle, 86; supremacy, 105; understanding, 104
racial attitudes, 132, 142
racism, 103, 108, 119, 127, 129, 132–33, 140; accusations of, 145; attitudes towards, 142; beliefs, 133; causes, 131; charges of, 152; in Congress, 151; institutional, 152; intent, 132, 140; Lee and, 81; lifetime of, 130–32; Lott's groups, 96, 174n20; manifesto on, 137; record, 131–32; rhetoric, 155; sins of, 153
racist behavior: allegations of, 141; pattern of, 130–32
racists, 66, 98, 112, 127–29, 131, 152; Confederates as, 77; Reconstruction-era, 129
Rainbow/PUSH Coalition, 96, 101, 119, 127
Randolph-Macon Women's College, 46
Rat Bible, 28, 39
Rat Line, 18–20, 22, 24–25, 29, 35–37
Rats, 18, 22, 35, 38, 44; as cheerleaders, 44; transition for females, 25
Reagan, Ronald, 118, 149; 1980 campaign rally in Mississippi, 118, 120, 146
reconciliation, 65, 67, 113–16, 144, 160; Robert E. Lee and, 79; "task force of," 144
Reconstruction, 8, 11, 63, 129, 174n18
Reconstructionists, 96, 106, 108
redemption, 121, 126–27, 142–43, 148, 152–54, 160; narrative, 154
Reed, John Shelton, 4
reenactors, 104, 110–11, 172n20
Rehnquist, Chief Justice William, 166n11
Reister, Ned, 44
religious faith, 142–43, 148, 150; of Robert E. Lee, 79
religious imagery, 137–38
religious gatherings, 161
Religious Right, 143
repentance, 138, 142–43, 148
Republicans and Republican Party, 101, 118, 120–22, 125, 127–28, 134–36, 138–39, 143, 145, 149–50, 152–54, 160; moderate, 136; minorities, recruitment by, 152
resolution, four modes of, 175n21
respect, 115, 142, 144–45
restoration of citizenship: for Jefferson Davis, 121, 131; for Robert E. Lee, 80–81
Revolutionary War, 98; battlefields, 102
Reynolds, Beverly, 62, 70

rhetoric: of democratic practice, 17; and dialectic, 17, 98, 162–63, 166n24; eristic, 166n24; listening, 162; paranoid, 151; and politics, 162; of race, 127; racist, 155; of sin, sacrifice, and redemption, 127
Rhetoric of Motives, 21
rhetorical situation, 119, 139, 155, 174n21
rhetorical strategy, 151
rhetorical theory, 175n21
Rice, Secretary of State Condoleezza, 152
Richardson, William D., 95–96
Richmond, Virginia, 15, 87, 157; African Americans in, 82–85, 87, 157; American city, 81; and Arthur Ashe, 67; burning of, 73; Byrd Park, 55; Canal Walk, 49, 52, 67, 73–86; as capital of Confederacy, 15, 49, 64–65, 81, 84, 157; as capital of Virginia, 81; Centre, 76; Circuit Court, 68; citizens' panel, 76; Civil War, 50, 84; Commission of Architectural Review, 68; Confederate evacuation, 73; Confederate-American population, 60; distinctiveness, 84; divisiveness, 81; floodwall murals, 15, 51–52, 73–86, 157; history, 53, 65, 73–86; Robert E. Lee and, 76, 79, 83–84; Lincoln statue, 15, 171n55; Lost Cause symbols, 84; Monument Avenue, 15, 49–73, 157, 168n1; in New South, 52, 64, 78, 82; public schools, 53–54; race relations, 50, 53, 57; racially reconciled, 67; rally at Statehouse in, 79; Riverfront redevelopment, 15, 75; Shockoe Slip, 75; symbol of evolving, 81; timocracy, 84; tourism, 64, 75; Tredegar Iron Works, 75; ultimate term of, 84; urban revitalization, 73; Valentine Museum, 73; valuing of history, 83–86; "white flight" from, 157
Richmond Historic Riverfront Foundation (RHRF), 50, 73, 76–77, 84; citizens' panel, 76
Richmond Renaissance, 54, 75
Richmond Riverfront Development Corporation (RRDC), 75
Ridge, Jim, 104
Riley, Joe, 94
rituals: military, 26, 39; and traditions, 35
Robinson, Bill "Bojangles," 73, 76
Rockwell, Lew, 138
Rogers, James E., 75, 77
Roosevelt, President Franklin, 90
Rosen, Jeffrey, 33, 38
ROTC classes, 24

Rove, Karl, 137, 149
Rubin, Louis D., Jr., 9
Ruth, Babe, 51
Ryan, Halford Ross, 126, 128, 174–75n21

sacrifice, 117, 126, 138–39, 151–53, 175n22; and Thurmond, 151
Samuels, Jocelyn, 46
Santorum, Senator Rick, 121
Scalia, Justice Antonin, 24, 28, 166n11
scapegoating, 117, 119, 126–28, 151–53, 175n22
Schomburg Center for Research in Black Culture, 73
Schwartz, Maryln, 29
Scripture, 142
"sea of forgetfulness," 101
secession, 7, 9, 31, 77, 80, 87, 104–5, 111, 156–57; contemporary pieties against, 80
secret society, 33, 41
sedition, 105
segregation, 9, 13, 62, 73, 88, 98, 100, 105, 108, 117, 119, 121, 124, 126–27, 130, 132–34, 140, 145, 147, 156–57; attitude towards, 142; bastion of, 66; defense of, 12, 123, 128, 154; repudiation of, 121; and states' rights, 154; of tennis courts, 157
segregational state, 169n7
segregationists, 129, 131, 152, 157; sins of, 151
self-actualized responses, 175n21
Seligman, Daniel, 35
Senate, 144; comments on floor of, 144–45
"separate but equal," 157
sexual harassment, 25, 47
Shedets, 34
Sigma Nu fraternity, 120–21, 125, 130–31, 141–42, 174n18
sin and sinfulness, 13, 117, 119, 126–27, 135, 138, 143, 145, 150–53
single-sex education, 19–20, 28, 32
Sister Rats, 26
slavery, 7–9, 57, 63, 88, 98, 101, 104–5, 112, 128, 156; cause of war, 81; contemporary pieties against, 80; defenders of, 51, 60, 66, 77, 80–81; defense of, 79, 96, 104–5; Lee and, 77, 79–82; opposition to, 78, 80; peculiar institution, 7, 32, 77, 82
slaves: descendants of, 115, 158; and Robert E. Lee, 79
Smiley, David, 5–6
Smith, Cotton Ed, 90
Smith, Professor Edward, 68, 79

Smith, Stephen A., 88–89
social knowledge, 27, 36, 48
social mystery, 14, 18–21, 26–27, 33–38, 42, 46, 48, 69, 156–57, 165n19, 166n7
social responses, 175n21
socioeconomic division, 9, 30
Socrates, 84, 162
Soldier's Monument, 93–94, 115
Solomon, John, 120, 125
Sons of Confederate Veterans, 60, 67, 75–77, 79–80, 87, 91, 95, 110–12, 121, 126, 172n20
Soren, Tabitha, 34
South, the: Agrarian lifestyle, 7; antebellum, 96, 161–62; collective imagination of, 160; as enigma, 6; porches in, 177n4; segregated, 101, 108; sins of, 153; slavery in, 81; white, 78
South Carolina: African American History Monument, 104, 158; Capitol, 15, 87, 89, 158; centennial Commission, 90; Chamber of Commerce, 96; changing, 155; the Citadel, 14, 19, 24, 29, 33, 42, 166n11; cradle of Confederacy, 157; Division of the Sons of Confederate Veterans, 110–11; economy, 106, 114; Edgefield, 154; Governor's Commission on Racial Relations, 93; history of Confederate flag in, 171n3; legislative chambers, 87, 89, 158; NAACP, 106; palmetto flag, 115; presidential primary, 94; race relations, 86, 106; racism, 103; reputation, 114; scenic beauty, 102; secession of, 11, 104, 157; state flag, 102, 115; Statehouse, 89, 93, 101, 103, 104, 107, 108, 112, 158; story of, 103; support for Thurmond in 1948, 124; symbols of, 102; Travel and Tourism Commission, 96; ultimate term of history, 86; Upstate, 96
South Carolina Exposition and Protest, 10
Southeast Conference of the United Church of Christ, 101
Southern belle, 28–30
Southern Belle Primer, 29
Southern Christian Leadership Conference (SCLC), 11, 96
Southern conservatives, 127, 129, 150
Southern culture: conservative nature of, 8; continuity of, 8; defensive nature of, 8, 163; distinctiveness, 5–9, 115–16, 160–61; folk, 5, 7, 161, 165n10; food, 160; gentility and civility, 13; heritage, 102, 104, 161; identity, 115–16, 177n4; military schools, 28, 30; military tradition, 28; myth of, 30; mode of discourse, 162; nationalistic nature of, 8; oral

tradition, 161–63; oratory, 161–62; rhetoric, 162; traditions, 85, 157; way of life, 12, 124
Southern Governors' Conference, 123
Southern Legal Resources Center, 100
Southern paleoconservatives, 138–39
Southern politicians, 151; old-school, 151
Southern studies, 6
Southern Women's Seminary, 46
Southerners: African American, 4–5, 100; aristocracy, 26; authors, 8; gentleman, 28, 30, 33, 79, 111–12; lady, 28–30; loquaciousness of, 161; man, 27, 30, 138; as minority group, 4; self-identifying, 4; unreconstructed, 12, 15–16, 127, 131, 137, 139, 153; white, 4, 12, 95, 99–100, 107, 127, 129, 139, 151, 163; women, 27–29, 30
sovereignty, 101, 123
Stafford, Virginia, 91
Statehouse dome, 89, 108, 112, 115
states' rights, 8–9, 12, 32, 77, 80–81, 87, 105, 111, 116, 123, 154; as contemporary argument, 80
States' Rights Democratic Party, 118, 122–24, 132, 136, 154, 173–74n10
"steel magnolias," 29
Stephenson, D. Grier, 31, 35
stereotypes, 29, 34, 36
stories, 87, 103, 108–10, 115, 158; rags-to-riches, 124
storytelling, 97, 161
Stovall, Reverend Sandi, 71
strategic ambiguity, 129
strategy, political, 152
stratification, 31–32, 41, 48
"strong national defense," 128–29, 145, 175n26
Stuart, General J. E. B., 49, 82
Supreme Court, 11, 14, 18, 21, 24, 31, 36, 88–89, 136, 156
Sweet Briar College, 29, 46
symbolic identification, 157
symbolic power, 100
symbolic propriety, 72
symbolism, 63, 87; positive, 65; powerful force of, 66
symbol(s), 87, 109; of African Americans, 85; anti-Semitic, 112; of belonging, 66; of bigotry, 112; Canal Walk as, 81; of change, 50; Clemson, 114; Confederate, 51, 86–87, 89, 95; of Confederate descendants, 85; contentious, 103; of dead man, 81; of division, 85, 117, 161; of hate, 105; of identification, 85; incongruous, 15, 62; of Lee, 81; Lee as, 81–82; of legal apartheid, 107; Lost Cause, 12, 73, 84; New South, 49; Old South, 9, 49, 88, 156; of race relations, 153; of racist oppression, 96, 100, 112; reconciliation through, 65; of resistance, 107; of slavery, 82; of social mystery, 21; of South Carolina, 102; Southern, 17, 110, 117; of struggle, 102; Thurmond as, 153; of tradition, 50

"task force of reconciliation," 144
Tate, Allen, 162
"tax and spend liberals," 129
Taylor, Allen J., 72
Taylor, Jane R., 41
tennis, 62, 69–72, 157
terministic screens, 16, 133, 148
Texas A & M University, 25
Texas State Capitol grounds, 91
"thinking mistake," 129
Thomas, Justice Clarence, 24, 124, 154
Thomas, State Senator David, 106
Thornton, Andy, 85
three-fifths compromise, 10
Thurmond, Senator J. Strom, 11, 16, 116–19, 121–24, 129, 131–32, 137, 140–42, 144–48, 151–55, 158, 160; death of, 153; evolution of, 154–55; integrationist, 155; presidential nomination acceptance speech, 173n3; racial demagoguing by, 155; racist rhetoric, 155; senators' tributes to, 144–45, 177n56; symbol for race relations in South, 153. *See also* Washington-Williams, Essie
"Tiger Rag," 109
Tillman, Benjamin "Pitchfork," 154
timocracy, 84
To Secure These Rights, 123
Tocqueville, Alexis de, 8
Todd, Sally, 69
Toppin, Professor Edgar, 84
tourism, 64, 75, 93, 96, 110, 158
traditions, 27, 35, 109; divisive, 85, 161; family, 103; martial, 157; Old South, 156; oral, 161, 162; Southern, 157
tragedy and loss, 7, 8, 160, 165n11
transcendence, 57, 126, 140, 147, 151, 175n21
transgressions, 138, 141, 146, 150
Tredegar Iron Works, 75
triptych, 158
Truman, President Harry, 122–24
Tumulty, Karen, 120
Turner, Sylvester "Tee," 64, 72
Twelve Southerners, 7, 8

"Uncle Tom," 100
uniform: cheerleading, 40, 44; Confederate, 76; Lee in, 76; VMI, 19, 21, 24, 26, 31, 39, 43, 47, 156
Union forces, 31, 137
Union Jack, 92
United Church of Christ, 101
United Confederate Veterans, 107
United Daughters of the Confederacy, 95, 99, 109, 172n20
United States, 88
United States v. Virginia, 36
University of Mississippi, 120, 125, 143, 147; and Chancellor Robert Khayat, 147; Institute of Reconciliation, 147; and Vietnamese students, 143. See also Ole Miss
University of South Carolina, 96
"unnatural practices," 41
unreconstructed, 127, 131, 137–39, 153
Urban Design Committee, 55
U.S. Air Force, 38
U.S. Air Force Academy, 41
U.S. District Court, 24
U.S. Military Academy, 41
U.S. Naval Academy, 41
U.S. Senate, 144; comments on floor of, 144–45, 177n56
U.S. Supreme Court, 11, 14, 18, 21, 24, 31, 36, 38, 88–89, 136, 156

Valentine Museum, 73
values, 142, 144, 151
verbal self-defense, four factors of, 126, 140
victimage, 119, 149–51
Virginia, 20, 24; daughters of, 42; history of, 84; Lee's loyalty to, 77–78, 80; SCV, 79–80; slavery in, 81; Stafford, 91
Virginia Heroes, 52, 55, 57, 65–66
Virginia Military Institute, 14, 18–48, 117, 156–57; accommodations to women, 24, 36–37; admission, 19–20; adversative discipline, 20–21, 34; African Americans, 18; all-male tradition, 19; alumni, 24, 31–32, 39–40; assimilation of women, 35, 42; bathrooms, 39, 42; barracks, 21, 24, 26, 31, 34, 39, 46, 156; battalion commanders, 25; Battle of New Market, 22, 30–32; Board of Visitors, 24–26, 37, 39; Brother Rats, 18, 23, 29, 38; *The Cadet*, 46–48; cadre, 25; cheerleaders, 25, 40, 44–45; citizen-soldiers, 20, 37–38; Civil War, 31–32; class system, 22, 156; Erin Claunch, 25; "Code for a Gentleman," 28; condom machine, 34; cosmetics, 24, 43–44; discipline, 20, 22; distinctiveness, 157; door locks, 39; "dykes," 23; endowment, 24; exchange cadets, 25, 40; family policy, 26, 45–46; fraternization, 25, 47; gender-norming, 37; gentleman's code, 18; good-ol'-boy network, 26, 156; guard tower, 39; haircuts, 24, 36, 43–45, 47; honor code, 22; Honor Court, 22, 25; honor system, 22; Institute men, 27, 29, 35; jewelry, 43–44; living arrangements, 36; makeup, 24, 43–44; male bonding, 19, 26; marriage, 36; George Marshall, 22; matriculation book, 47; media attention, 34; mental stress, 35; military rituals, 26; military service, 30; minority students, 33–34; mission statement, 22; mixers, 46; New Market cadets, 31; New Market Ceremony, 18, 30–31; out-of-state students, 20; parenthood, 46; physical fitness requirements, 24; pregnancy, 25–26, 40, 45–46; privacy, 21, 24, 35–36, 39–40, 43; racial integration, 20; rank system, 39; Rat Bible, 28, 39; Rat Line, 18–20, 22, 24–25, 29, 35–37; rats, 18, 22, 25, 35, 44; restrooms, 25; rings, 156; sexual harassment, 25, 47; shaved heads, 36; Shedets, 34; shower stalls, 39, 42; Sigma Nu founding at, 174n18; Sister Rats, 26; standards, 37; Stonewall Jackson, 22–23, 26; sweat parties, 23; toilets, 40, 42; traditions, 27; transfer students, 25; uniforms, 19, 21, 24, 26, 31, 43, 47, 156; walls, 27; window shades, 21, 24, 39–40; women's restrooms, 25, 42
Virginia Women's Institute for Leadership (VWIL), 20, 24–25, 32, 38–39
voting rights, 123, 129–30
Voting Rights Act, 121, 131; 1992 extension, 146, 154

Wakulla Springs, Florida, 123–24
Walker, Maggie, 73
Wallace, Governor George, 11, 124
War Between the States, 77, 87, 102, 106, 108, 111. See also Civil War
War of Northern Aggression, 87, 138. See also Civil War
Ware, B. L., 126, 140, 174–75n21
Washington, George, 73
Washington Week, 173n3
Washington-Williams, Essie Mae, 154, 177n1
Watts, Rep. J. C., 122, 144, 152
Weaver, Richard, 5, 7–9, 18, 88, 161
Webster, Daniel, 10, 118

Wednesday Morning Fellowship, 76
Weismer, William, 173–74n10
Wells, June Murray, 99, 104, 107, 109
Wellstone, Senator Paul, 145
Welty, Eudora, 8
West Point, 41
White Citizens' Councils, 11, 125
"White European Americans," 126
"white flight," 157
White House, 134, 136–37, 150; and conspiracy, 150
white Southern conservatives, 127, 151
white supremacists and white supremacy, 73, 100, 110, 131
Wilder, Governor L. Douglas, 52, 57, 65–66, 84
Wilder, Thornton, 8
Wilhoit, Frances, 88

Williams, Eric G., 81, 84
Williams, Serena, 94
Willis, Edward J., 68
Willis, R. Kent, 31, 45
Wilson, Zane, 108
women: accommodations to, 24, 36–37; admission of, 21; assimilation of, 35, 42; "butch," 44, 48; as delicate, 27; G.I. Janes, 47; honoring, 35; proper place for, 27; respect for, 34; restrooms for, 25, 42, 48; roles of, 43; Southern, 27–29; as "steel magnolias," 29
women's liberation movement, 35
Woodruff, Judy, 119
Woodward, C. Vann, 6–8, 160
Woody, Paul, 71
Wright, Governor Fielding, 123–24

Young, Mayor Leonidas, 57, 62–64

www.ingramcontent.com/pod-product-compliance
Lightning Source LLC
Chambersburg PA
CBHW030622230426
43661CB00053B/2110